HOW TO BURN A
RAINBOW

*My Gay Marriage Didn't Make Me
Whole, My Divorce Did*

by

KARL DUNN

DISCLAIMER:

This is the story of my divorce, from my perspective. All the dialogue and interactions are recounted to the best of my recollection and through the lens of my own experience. Several names and other identifying characteristics have been changed to protect the identity of those who were supporting characters in my story.

How To Burn A Rainbow

Copyright © 2024 by Karl Dunn. All rights reserved.

No part of this book may be reproduced in any form or by any electronic or mechanical means, including information storage and retrieval systems, without written permission from the author, except for the use of brief quotations in a book review.

ISBN 979-8-89316-004-8 (Paperback)
ISBN 979-8-89316-005-5 (Ebook)

DOWNLOAD THE FREE COPY OF THE PREQUEL

HOW TO CHASE A RAINBOW

Click here to tell me where to send it
https://bit.ly/HTCAR

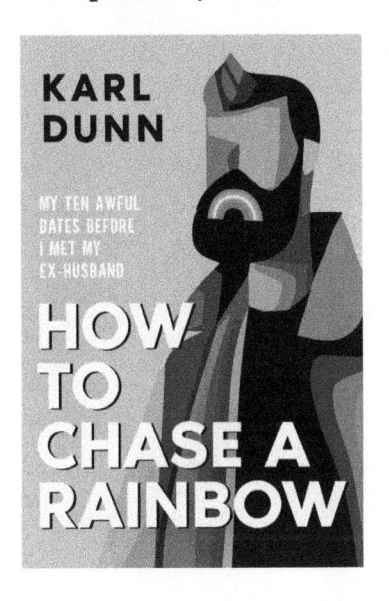

After returning to LA from his brother's wedding, Karl Dunn was determined–2008 was the year he would finally meet The One.

So Karl set out on "Operation Husbandhunt" ending up on ten sometimes tragic, sometimes hilarious dates in Tinseltown as he searched in vain to find the right guy…

Until date #11 when he met his future ex-husband.

And he ignored every red flag along the way, especially his own…

For Brian,
without you, this book would never have been started.

For Uli,
without you, this book would never have been finished.

A HUMBLE REQUEST FROM THE AUTHOR

Before I decided to publish *How To Burn A Rainbow* independently, I spent years writing into the abyss of publishing houses and agents. No Reply is the new No. Without that kind of industry backing, it's a long, slow, and expensive process to get a book out there in the world.

I can't tell you how happy I am that this book has found you. So if anything in it touches or helps you, I humbly ask that you do me a favor.

Please post about *How To Burn A Rainbow* on your social feeds. Put the cover and your review in posts or videos using the hashtags below.

Your posts and reviews matter. They teach the algorithms to push the book to more people who are looking for something like it. Which means that you can play a vital role in the ongoing success and reach of *How To Burn A Rainbow*.

I thank you in advance, and hope you see yourself somewhere in the pages here.

—KARL

#KarlDunn #HowToBurnARainbow
#MemoirWriting #OwnVoice
#LGBTQ #Divorce #GayDivorce
#GayMarriage #GayCulture #GayPride
#QueerLiterature #QueerBooks #NewBookAlert #GayAuthor
#SelfHealing #SelfLove #LoveIsLove
#LifeAfterDivorce #LifeLessons
#BookTok #Bookstagram

CONTENTS

Introduction xvii

Chapter 1
The Honeymoon 1
Myriam's Law 6
An Accidental Angel 9
Time Is The One Ingredient You Can't Fake 12

Chapter 2
The Beginning Of The End 15
Who Do I Tell? 18
Wait… Do I Need To Get A Divorce? 20
I'm Sorry, I Tried 21
Write Your Intention, And Don't Try For A Cookie 25
The Legals 28
The Offer 32
One Ring To Wreck Them All 35

Chapter 3
The Voice And The Chorus 38
This Is How Not To Hire Lawyers 39
You Leave When You Have Nothing Left To Learn ... 42
My Dreams Come In Waves 43
The Crisis Of Identity 46

Chapter 4
My Brother Gives Me The Gift Of Time 49
Everything You Post Can And Will Be Used Against You In A Court Of Law 52
The Friend Filter 53
The Financials And My Underwear Drawer 55
Let The Lying Begin 59
Welcome Home 62

Chapter 5
I've Chosen The Explorer's Life 66
You Got Engaged?! 68
Jesus, Are We Getting Divorced Now? 70
Here's Your Car, And Some Truth 71
This Is How It Feels To Be Karl Today 75
The Past Haunts Me. And Vice Versa 76
The Emotions Diary 80
The Head Is Faster Than The Heart 83
Look For The Signs 86
What Do I Do With The Rage? 87

Chapter 6
October 2017 92
Charles Darwin And The Theory Of Divorceolution 92
A Visit From The Husband And A Visit To The Lawyers 94
You're Already Free And You're Missing It 98
How Long Were You Happy For? 100
Every Dog Has Its Day In Court 102
Straight Divorced Guys Are Your New Best Friends 105
You Need To Shut The Divorce Up 107
Do A Fourth Step. Then A Fifth. Then Remember Your Golden Moment. 108

Chapter 7
Vegan Special And A Broken Leg 111
For You, Not Against Him 115

I Don't Care What Happens To Me 117
Do I Still Have A Pulse? 119
My Girlfriend Francine 120
Let The Real Divorce Begin 121
Road Trips And Regret 124

Chapter 8
Why Kevin Died 130
Bye Frannie, It's Been An Honor 132
Freedom Isn't Free 135
Expectations Will Kill You 137
I'm Dreaming Of A White Post-Xmas 140
Loneliness Vs Aloneness 140
I Get A Second Divorce 141
Jealousy, Xmas Dinners, And Land Mines 143

Chapter 9
Berlin 147
Money Makes The World Go Down 150
Write Your Manifesto 152
New Year, Old Me 155
Why Did I Get Married? 156
Top Five Reasons Why I Got Married 157
Money Can't Buy You Chocolate Cake 162
Your Flight Back To That Unholy Mess Is Now Boarding ... 165

Chapter 10
Primary And Secondary Emotions 167
My Husband Has A New Boyfriend 170
My Dick Doesn't Work 171
Happiness Isn't A Right Or A Recipe, It's A Habit 173
You Need To Do Something With All This Ugly 176

Chapter 11
Pack Your Boxes. All Your Boxes. 179
Why Am I Meeting You Now, Martin? 182
The Wind Down 186

The Three-Legged Dog 187
The Rest Of Your Life Is Now Boarding 188

Chapter 12
Berlin. Again. 191
Physically, Emotionally, And Legally Speaking, You're
Screwed 197
Hi Gunnar. It's Me. 202
Money, Money, Always The Stupid Money 204
This Is How You Hire A Lawyer 208
The Best Things In Life Aren't Things 210

Chapter 13
The Disappearance Of John Hare 213
The Crying Tree 216
Berlin Will Offer You More Than You Can Imagine 218
Stop Hiding, Start Building 221
Evolution Is A Messy Business 223
The Court Is Now In Session 225
Surrender At The Tv Tower 227
One Beer And An Apartment Please, Barman 229

Chapter 14
Would You Ever Get Married Again? 233
So What Is This Marriage Thing, Exactly? 235
Divorce Needs A Divorce 240
The Right To A Gay Divorce 244
I Don't Want A Prenuptial, I Want A Pre-Equitable 246
Get Your Hands Out Of My Pockets 248

Chapter 15
I Thought My Best Would Be Better Than This 250
Patience And Perfection 252
The Gay Way Back Machine 254
There Is A Warrant Out 258
I Get Out Of Jail 260
August 2018 262

Are We Friending?...262
We Are Beginning Our Descent..264
The Epiphany..265
Suddenly, It All Made Sense..270
The End?...273

Chapter 16
Leaving The Temple...275
Back To The Past..278
Let's Go To Court. Again. 282
The Last Word..285
Make Friends With Normal..287
Tear Down Old Statues...289
The End Of The Statue Era..295

Chapter 17
Learning To Live In Peacetime..297
December 2018...302
Where's Your Line?..302
A Life Without Grace..304
Back To The Puddle, Then To The Ocean......................306
You Don't Need Other People To Have Sex, It's Already In You..308

Chapter 18
Goodbye John...310
Cut The Head Off Buddha...312
The Rest Of The Year..313
Acknowledgments..321
Footnotes..323

INTRODUCTION

G'DAY. I'M KARL.
    This is the story of my divorce.

Actually the divorce was just the inciting incident. The bigger and more important story is that it sent me on a journey to figure out who I really was.

If this book has found you, maybe it's because you're about to embark on a divorce—if you're not already going through one. I'm not going to lie. It will be one of the worst things that's ever happened to you. If you're LGBTQ+, it's even more isolating since our community knows almost nothing about it.

However, my divorce was also the greatest thing that ever happened to me. Mostly because of what I decided to do with it. But we'll get to that.

Even if you're not getting divorced, or not even LGBTQ+, this book is also for you. It's the story of a human being, who went through a human experience. Someone who, in just a few months, went from a high-flying advertising career and a loft house in the LA Hills to sleeping on an air mattress in a former squat in Berlin—in a room with no electricity, with a busted leg, and a few hundred dollars left to their name. Someone who ended up wondering what the hell they had done with their entire life.

One thing people asked me a lot when I was writing this book was, "Isn't a gay divorce the same as a straight divorce?" In a word, no.

There are tons of books on divorce written by heterosexuals. But if the book was written by a man, it generally came down on his side, her side if it was written by a woman. Neither camp spoke to me.

For starters, I wasn't dealing with a battle of the sexes. My husband was from Mars and so was I.

Plus, none of these books spoke to the kinds of loss I felt either.

Like the loss of social standing. It wasn't just the recognition and kudos of being married; I'd also lost the new and powerful feeling of equality in the straight world that the ring on my left hand had magically conferred on me.

Gone too was my hiding place in the gay community. When my work life got on top of me, I could always go out, have a gay old time, and lose myself for a night. Now total strangers would walk up in bars and ask, "Are you the one getting a divorce?"

By far the biggest loss I dealt with was from my failure. Yes, I'd failed in my marriage, but I also felt that I'd spectacularly failed the cause. We fought so hard for the right to marry. It was a landmark moment in US civil rights. My husband and I were part of history. And my divorce seemed to me like a total mockery of that, like I'd taken a machete to the wedding cake of every other gay couple about to walk down the aisle—or worse, like we'd never deserved the right in the first place.

After a fruitless hunt for a gay divorce book, my online searches found only the odd unhelpful article and a lot of ads from lawyers eager to represent divorcing gays. There was next to nada on what to expect emotionally and mechanically. As subjects go, gay divorce was a desert. And I was a broken unicorn walking blindly through it.

So I decided to write a book about it myself. It started as a private video diary to chronicle what I was going through. It turned into advice I handed out to other divorcing gays on late-night calls after they were put in touch with me. Then finally I showed some entries to a friend of mine, Brian, who said, "Y'all need to put this in a book, queen." And so here we are.

Like everyone encountering divorce for the first time, I went through a massive learning curve on the law. Plus, I discovered a ton of practical stuff about how to handle yourself while going through a divorce—all things I wished I'd known at the start. I made a ton of expensive mistakes, embarrassed myself at work and with friends, and tried to choke answers out of completely the wrong people and places. Hopefully, if you're reading this book, you won't have to repeat my blunders.

I also had to figure out my attitudes to love, relationships, and marriage, something I didn't do enough of before I tied the knot. Now, having been through a divorce as well, I believe there are a lot of questions LGBTQ+ folks should be asking about the whole institution: why we raced to get married, what we expected it to be, and why it's such legal torture for anyone to get out of it.

Along the way, I was lucky enough to meet a lot of smart, empathetic, and generous people who shared their own stories and wisdom—gay, straight, bi, queer, trans, male, female, young and old. Their advice changed my life. Saved it sometimes. Some were friends I'd known for decades, some were there for a season, and some for just a conversation. For many reasons, I've changed the names of nearly everyone in this book. They're all real, but many wanted to remain ungoogleable. After all they did for me, it's the least I can do in return.

One thing I must say before we get into the story is that it is just that—a story. Told from my perspective, and from a time when I was under an enormous amount of pressure, stress, and upheaval. It's written to the best of my recollection. That said, some people and elements have been deliberately fictionalized for brevity and consistency.

The life-changing lessons I learned, however, are 100% true. And I hope they will be helpful to you too.

I don't really know what genre this book fits into. It's a memoir but also has a lot of self-help, travel, pop-culture analogies, references to authors I adore, anecdotes, spirituality, practical knowledge, analysis and essay, and is also a little cinematic at times.

I hope you find it to be a glorious buffet, because that's what life is like at its best—and even at its worst.

As for the title *How To Burn A Rainbow*, I'd followed every script the gay world and straight world gave me. I dutifully chased the rainbow. Yet I never found that elusive golden pot of happiness. Then, without realizing what I was starting, I set it all on fire. But I will never regret striking the match—because the further I went along this journey, the more I became the person I'd always wanted to be.

My marriage didn't make me whole, my divorce did.

CHAPTER 1

"Sounds to me like you might be suffering from premature enlightenment."

— JOHN

JUNE 2016

THE HONEYMOON

I WAS LYING IN BED IN the hotel where Gunnar and I were staying on our honeymoon.

We'd had to wait a whole year after the wedding for me to get a month off work and to save enough money for the European extravaganza that we'd dreamed of. It had kicked off in Vienna, and if I didn't know that by the mountain of pastries we'd inhaled over the last few days, or the ornate yellow-and-white corniced ceilings I was looking up at, the horse-drawn carriages clacking among the cars on the cobblestone streets outside were the dead giveaway.

The hotel's cotton sheets and duvet over the ridiculously comfy mattress literally begged you to stay in bed all day, and

I was seriously considering doing just that as I thumbed the wedding ring on my finger and wondered how life had led me here. Gay, married, and cocooned in five-star European opulence. Ten-year-old me, experiencing his first terrified suspicions that he was different, would never in his wildest dreams have imagined anything like this.

As I lay there, I replayed our entire relationship. Then I hit the pause button on one day with Gunnar in particular. It was the happiest I'd ever remembered us being together. Actually, it was the happiest I'd ever remembered being, period.

It was a wedding. Not ours, though. Like many people had warned me, our wedding day—which was wonderful—had sprinted by in an anxious blur of fuzzy moments. "Spend the money on a photographer," I was told. "It's the only way you'll ever remember it."

The day I was thinking of, this golden moment, was our friends' wedding in their lovely backyard garden in LA. Gunnar and I had a rule with events—dress up, show up. So we were among the first to arrive with presents in hand, turned out in summer suits, with beards combed and shoes shining. We loved getting parties started. It was a joyous little mitzvah of ours. Secretly we were both introverts, but together, we were the Wonder Twins; we just also liked to be in bed with the cat by 10:30 p.m.

Post-ceremony, meal, and speeches, the bride and groom had their first dance. At that awkward moment when it becomes obvious that others should be joining the couple on the floor, I looked over at Gunnar. My God, I thought, he's so beautiful. He was 6'3", like me, and built like a linebacker, unlike me. The only thing I loved more than him dressed up was him completely naked. The thickness of his legs, the girth of his trunk, the shoulders that could hug a whole planet happy. He was hairy in all the right places, had a smile that shone through his magnificent beard, and those blue-green Swedish eyes.

Those eyes...

It's such an icky cliché to say you could get lost in someone's eyes, but Gunnar's were the forest lakes I would fall into. No map, no compass.

On that day, he smiled back at me, extended a paw, and the next moment we were walking to the dance floor. His smell unfurled in my nostrils, a mix of man, linen, smoky florals from his cologne, and something warm I could never quite name.

Setting up shop next to the dancing newlyweds, we grooved with abandon. When the other was around, I don't think either of us cared who was watching. There was a look Gunnar always got on his face as he danced: eyes closed, half smile, neck forward like he was waiting to be kissed, lost in the music. Cutting a rug and beaming to himself, he looked so light and free and beautiful. I couldn't believe how lucky we were. Happy and whole. I tossed my head back and laughed as we clasped hands and moved together.

Back in Vienna I rolled over, my arm falling onto the empty side of the bed. I wondered if Gunnar was up yet. We were sleeping in different hotel rooms. And I was thinking very seriously about leaving him.

Gunnar and I had been together for seven years by this stage. We'd opened our relationship up a few years earlier. It's not uncommon in the gay world for committed couples to be open, sometimes after a few years, sometimes from the get-go. My hope was that it would bring back an intimacy with him that I desperately missed, that having sex with others would jump-start our routine, which had almost rusted into nonexistence. Instead, it had had the opposite effect. Our home life felt to me like we were really close friends who lived together, laughed a lot together, kissed and said we loved each other, slept in the same bed, and talked about the men we were shagging—or not, in my case, thanks to my long work hours and frequent business travel. Sex-wise, I felt like I was getting the worst of both worlds.

It felt like that should be different now, post-marriage, but I didn't know how. I didn't want the openness to stop and neither did he, but it was often a source of jealousy and competition. Especially from me. We'd talk about it two or three times a year, have a heart to heart, hug it out, and then nothing would change. Like we were both waiting for the other to make the first move. But this was our honeymoon! This was the trip that would reignite the passion! That's what I had been telling myself and hinting loudly at him before we left.

Instead, Gunnar had hooked up with a guy in Vienna unannounced the day before. He was then over an hour late to the café where he'd agreed to meet me, with no communication. When he finally turned up—after an initial wave of relief that he wasn't in the hospital—I'd proceeded to lose my mind.

I'd seen holidaying couples have very public fights before and thought, "Wow guys, take it home." But there I was in broad daylight, screaming accusations of disloyalty and utter disrespect. "I'm your husband! I come first!" I bellowed like a wounded beast, not believing my own behavior and yet completely unable to make myself stop.

Gunnar looked on, stunned, as I ran out of words and started to cry. I walked back to the hotel, only stopping once to yell, "Stop following me!" I went to reception, got another room for myself, and hadn't left it since.

The honeymoon was quite literally over.

What it took me a long time to realize was that it wasn't my perception of a lack of respect that had made me lose my mind that day. It was my own jealousy. It felt as though someone had once again gotten the one thing that I wanted from my husband, this time on the honeymoon I'd built up so much expectation around. It was the final explosive straw.

So as I lay in bed alone that morning, I did the only thing I could think of. I bought a ticket to Berlin for later that day.

Ten years earlier, when I was a screenwriter in LA waiting for my green card and still unable to work in America, a freelance job had taken me to Berlin five winters in a row. That job was my lifeline. Not only would I make what I'd live on for the rest of the year, but Berlin was like a magical harbor. Walking its streets in the snow, I'd put in context all the failed projects, unmaterialized script sales, and will-I-ever-make-it-in-Hollywood angst; figure out the next part of the journey; and return to LA ready for another year of hustling under the palm trees. I hoped it might do the same for my marriage now.

Gunnar and I met in the lobby. He eyed my packed bags.

"I'm off to Berlin for the rest of the trip," I said stiffly.

"OK. Yeah, that makes sense," he replied, quickly staring off. I got the feeling he'd been planning to offer a different suggestion.

"Since we're flying home from there, just come the night before, OK?" I told him. "Go wherever you want till then. Do whatever. Text if you're in trouble or something but… I just want to be alone."

"Yeah. OK. I need some time to think about what happened too."

We both looked down at the hotel carpet.

"Well, I gotta go," I said.

"Take care," Gunnar said, awkwardly stepping forward.

He hugged hard. I hugged cold. But I still smelled him as I pulled away.

Not long after, I was on a plane to Berlin feeling lighter. It was a relief to be on my own. I'd opened the exit door at the back of our relationship and walked through it. But I'd left it ajar. I just needed to step outside for a moment and breathe some different air.

I dumped my bags at the hotel, rented a bike, and pedaled the city. Berlin was beautiful. I'd never seen it without a blanket of snow, and it was a completely different town. So alive, so vibrant—the banks of the River Spree humming with people, the parks full of folks soaking up rays and drinking beers. The joy in the air was intoxicating.

Berlin was working its magic. I was already feeling happy to be free, to be quiet, to remember myself. I felt like an actor who'd stepped off the stage after a grueling performance, growing back into his own skin.

But I had this nagging sensation I couldn't shake. That something like Vienna was always going to happen, and that I'd already known that deep down.

MYRIAM'S LAW

Myriam was one of the owners of the advertising agency where I'd worked in Berlin those five winters. She has a kind face and is quietly spoken, but is one of the most determined and steadfast people I've ever met. She started that agency of hers two days after she'd given birth to her first child, nursing the kid in one arm and writing ideas with the other in a rented single-room office. Myriam's made of that stuff.

Our friendship was forged over late nights in the agency office that used to be a chocolate factory before the war. We'd make each other laugh with dumb ideas into the night, chugging endless cups of coffee and hunting inspiration as the snow danced on the giant industrial window ledges outside, uplit with a butter-yellow glow from the streetlights below. Techno quietly throbbed through the floorboards from an illegal party somewhere in the building.

Life had changed a lot for Myriam since we'd last worked together all those years ago. We'd arranged to meet for breakfast in a Berlin café and she was telling me about her new agency and another new baby. Though she was a little tired she felt vital to me, exuding that quiet determination of hers that I loved so much.

I was curious though. Why the new agency? Then Myriam told me a story.

She went away to have her baby but when she returned to work, she discovered that her two partners had basically made her redundant. It had been organized so that she didn't have a spot to fill when she came back. Instead, they'd offered to buy her out. Fresh off my own betrayals, I was incensed on her behalf.

"What were they thinking?!" I said, probably way too loudly. "How could they do that?!"

"Anger's not required, Karl," Myriam replied, calmly waving away my rage. "I know those boys better than they know themselves. I knew they would try something like this if I was ever away for a while. So, when I found out I was pregnant, I chose to have my child over my business."

I was shocked at her matter-of-factness about it all. Then she said the words that set my life on a new course.

"How can I get angry at them for doing exactly what I expected them to do?"

This was radical responsibility.

This was 100% owning your part.

And this was not at all how I'd lived.

After we said our goodbyes, I walked up the street ruminating on Myriam's words and came to a realization. What Gunnar had done was in keeping with a pattern of behavior that I'd left unchallenged because I was too tired from work, or couldn't be bothered having that same fight again, or any of a dozen other excuses. Then I got really honest—I'd not only been expecting Gunnar to do something like this, I'd been waiting for it. I'd been rehearsing the fight we would have about it for years. Half the things I'd yelled at him on the street were from that script.

Gunnar had done exactly what I'd expected him to do.

Which meant that I was at least fifty percent of the reason why Vienna had happened. Definitely no less. Maybe more.

This knowledge had the unmistakable flavor of the truth.

I cast my mind back even further. I had basically dated the same guy four times in a row: Gunnar, Jochen, Robert, Leonard. And each time, I would complain about the injustices of what they'd done to me. Occasionally to them, but mostly to my friends. And everyone would agree what bastards they all were.

I'd lap it up. And I'd stay in my relationships. Even though the events hurt, the script felt familiar, so it felt good. I'd typecast myself as the Oscar-worthy, hard-done-by victim. No one had held a gun to my head. I'd sought these men out because, clearly, this was what I thought I deserved.

This overwhelming string of realizations felt like a silent bomb going off every thirty feet, like a year's worth of therapy delivered over two city blocks. Pausing to balance myself, I glanced over at a shop window and saw something.

Me.

There have been these rare moments in my life, usually post-breakup crises, where I would suddenly find myself staring back at the real me in a nakedly honest mirror moment.

Shocked by this sudden intimacy, I'd stare into the depths of all the unresolved emotions and questions in my eyes. And then I'd panic and make myself busy, pretending the moment had never happened.

But not this time. I stared back at myself in that shop window as the final bomb went off: In order to hold on to this relationship with my husband, I'd buried myself down so far that I'd lost my way. I didn't know who I was anymore.

Instead of turning away, angry and ashamed of myself, I looked back with kind eyes and made a promise. I wanted my freedom, to be truly me. Whoever that was.

If I could do that with Gunnar, wonderful. But if not, then so be it.

AN ACCIDENTAL ANGEL

Little did I realize it at the time, but that moment was the start of the journey. My declaration in the shop window pricked up the universe's ears. When your case file lands on its desk, the universe starts sending guides in the oddest of times, places, and guises. As weirdly fairytale as your encounters may seem, your job is to recognize you're being helped and to step through the looking glass.

The next morning I was on Museum Island in the middle of Berlin, watching tourists take selfies on the bridge over the Spree with the domed buildings as their backdrop, when suddenly I felt a compelling urge to look over my shoulder. I slowly turned my head, and about a hundred feet away was a man glancing over his own shoulder. Our eyes met, and all I can say is that some kind of electricity passed between us. We tentatively waved hello.

As we walked toward each other, I started taking him in. Built like a footballer, black hair and beard, jersey and shorts. Handsome, no doubt. The odd part was that he wore an open kimono and an ornate 1930s-style women's necklace. Eccentric streetwear, I thought, but Berlin has a real don't-give-a-fuck attitude to life—do, wear, eat, kiss, and be whatever and whoever you want. This guy made sense here.

"Hi," I said.

"Hello," he replied.

"I think we're supposed to meet."

"Apparently so, since we just have."

We smiled and shook hands.

"I'm Karl," I said.

"I'm John. Karl, huh? Are you German?"

"Australian. My mum really liked the name. Judging by your accent, British?"

"Guilty as charged. Well, Karl, the non-German Australian, shall we get a coffee?" And that was how I met John Hare.

The rest of the afternoon involved me spilling my guts to John about why I was in Berlin on my own, what had happened with my husband—pretty much the entire history of our relationship, that I now thought at least half of it was my fault, that I didn't know what the next steps were…

"… and now I'm sitting here with you, and that just about brings us up to this moment."

"Well, you picked the right place," John said. "This is a town that rebuilds. If it hadn't been for Berlin, I would never have become myself."

John proceeded to tell me the wonderous tale of how he'd ended up here. A plane he was on had to make an urgent landing in Berlin in the middle of an airport strike. Stranded and knowing no one in the city, he found himself in a café that night, where he met some folks who offered to put him up. They all lived in an artists' collective in the north of the city, a former squat bought by the residents and now run like a commune. And that's where he'd been living for the last fifteen years.

What he'd found in Berlin was a community of queer artistic folks he'd been unsuccessfully searching for in the UK. An English teacher by trade, John soon found a job at a language school, and the longer he stayed, the more obvious it became that he was never going to leave. Turned out John was a writer, queer, wore women's clothes when the mood took him, but presented like a tradesman. It also turned out that he had been on the verge of entering an advertising career earlier in his life but had decided instead to pursue art.

To say I was mesmerized was an understatement.

In my early twenties, I'd given some serious thought to becoming an actor. I had been about to audition for some acting schools when I'd heard that 90% of actors were unemployed at any one time. The young man I was then wasn't brave enough to choose that life. So I started work at my first ad agency as a junior copywriter when I was twenty-three. I loved it. But I often looked over my shoulder at that other life. Especially when I was writing tray mats for McDonald's or the like.

John had stood at that same crossroads and chosen the other path, living what had seemed to me at the time an exciting, worthy, and noble life. He was self-realized and free in ways I didn't think I'd ever been. John was my alternate universe, my sliding door.

We eventually paid the bill for the coffee and I turned to him, preparing to say my goodbyes, go sit in a park, and think about how I'd wasted my life.

"So, fancy a cuddle?" John inquired.

TIME IS THE ONE INGREDIENT YOU CAN'T FAKE

It was like we'd known each other for years. John and I spent the week lying together and talking in his bedroom, in the rambling, ancient building of the collective—a labyrinthine, stoic, crumbling holdout against the creep of gentrification. Held together with gaffer tape and rescued timbers, the thirty or so apartments were arranged around a massive courtyard that filled with the sounds of the next-door playground every morning.

We ventured outdoors for gallery visits, breezy summer walks in the city, and a long, winding conversation about life, the universe, and everything. What was happening between me and John was intimate, but not really sexual. I just wanted someone to hug me and listen. And since John was happy to do both so deeply, I felt like I was cheating. Especially since I was in the no-man's-land beyond the exit door.

Then I'd go all Californian: John is a gift from the universe to help you figure things out, so say "Namaste" already.

I told John the worst, ugliest, hardest stuff about me, some of which I was only just starting to realize after my chat with Myriam. And that I wanted to change, to just be happy.

"Sounds to me like you might be suffering from premature enlightenment," John said one day as we walked along the river.

"Well, how do I get there then?" I asked, hoping to be let in on the secret.

"Good question. It's the one everyone's been asking since the time we could first think. The most important thing is to keep asking it."

"So where are you at with it?" I asked.

"It's not a competition, Karl."

John stopped us, looked at me, and cocked his head. He'd clocked my impatient and competitive nature. That I was hurt and wanted to feel better as fast as possible. Then, as I soon discovered was *his* nature, John asked what seemed like a random yet also rehearsed question.

"When do stews and curries taste best?"

I smiled again. "After a night on the stove."

"Exactly. Time is the one ingredient you can't fake."

And so, the conversation and the walk went on.

I spent my last night in Berlin having dinner with John in a darkly lit German restaurant eating pork hocks the size of our heads, that strange final meal sadness tinting our conversation and laughter. Then on the street outside I hugged him, thanking him for everything he'd done for me while I was there.

"Accidental Angel is kind of my thing," he replied.

My phone pinged. It was Gunnar.

Hi babe. I'm at my hotel. I'll see you in the morning. I missed you.

"That him?" John inquired.

I nodded.

"How do you feel?"

I smiled back. "Ready."

"Then be on your way, sir."

We hugged under the streetlights, listening to the moths mosh pit against the lamp covers.

"Have fun, Karl Dunn."

"Take care, John Hare."

He did a little jig, a curtsey, then John Hare disappeared around the corner. I watched for a moment, waiting for him to stick his head back round the ornately patterned tiled wall. He didn't. I wondered if I'd ever see John again. Or if maybe I'd conjured him out of thin air.

I slept deeply and, in the morning, went to Gunnar's hotel. We had a long hug in the lobby. It felt good to be in each other's orbit again.

Over breakfast, Gunnar shared his take on what had happened in Vienna. He knew he'd hurt me many times by doing things like this. I also confessed my part in indulging behavior I hated in order to keep the peace, then attacking him for it later in a million small ways. So I told him about what I had started to call "Myriam's Law." Gunnar got it straight away. He loved it.

We agreed we were now both 100% responsible for our half of the relationship. Anything that either one of us did, we'd both share responsibility for. No more playing victim, no more blaming, no more throwing side-eye on the couch as we watched another episode of *Game of Thrones*.

Myriam's Law also gave us a way to talk about our relationship that was nonthreatening—there was him, there was me, and our relationship was a separate object in between us. Like we were architects looking at a 3D plan of a building. And it worked really well.

For a while.

CHAPTER 2

"If you really want to see who you're married to, divorce them."

— Lily

AUGUST 2017

THE BEGINNING OF THE END

IF YOU WOKE UP AT 3 a.m. with a dead hookup in your bed, who would you call?

I'd call Brian Meiler. Brian would arrive five minutes early after swinging by the hardware store for supplies, picking up snacks, and finding the best coordinates in the desert to bury bodies, and he would still find time to put together a themed outfit with a "Digging In The Desert" playlist blasting from the car speakers.

Brian was an LA-resident Oklahoma boy who blew into my life a decade earlier. A bear of a man who knew everything there is to know about pop culture, Japanese collectibles, and music from obscure SoundCloud pop acts to 80s metal bands. Loyal as fuck to his friends, we'd played in two bands together in LA—Brian on drums and me on bass. One band was good. The other was loud.

Brian and I were sitting in a booth in a diner in LA. Not a fancy diner. None of the wait staff were aspiring actors. Just an average, back-of-the-parking-lot-in-a-strip-mall, one-of-the-neon-letters-on-the-sign-isn't-working kind of diner. He listened patiently, occasionally straightening his manga T-shirt as I regaled him with the latest round of Gunnar stuff while we drank thin coffee and ate pie from plates dulled by a thousand dishwasher cycles.

It had been a full year since the honeymoon in Europe. With Myriam's Law, Gunnar and I had progressed in leaps and bounds for six months. We'd looked at every disagreement as a chance to make us better. But bit by bit we were returning to our old ways. Myriam's Law had been on life support, but now it was flatlining.

My absences weren't helping. I had been struggling to find work in San Francisco and so had been away for weeks at a time, freelancing in LA. Of my life in America, I'd spent nine years as an Angeleno. My network, best friends, our house, and my heart were in LA. I'd missed her. Now a full-time gig had come up there, working with an old friend of mine. Since an internal transfer from SF to LA was looking good for Gunnar, we'd made the decision to move back down. I'd headed there a couple of months early.

"But then," I said to Brian, "the job they eventually offered him was a step down. I think he's going to resign over it. And apparently this is all my fault, because I started the move."

"That sucks," Brian said quietly in his Southern drawl.

"Right?! It's going to be just like it was before he got this job. Unemployed for years. By choice. I swear, it's like I'm a single parent, not a husband. Did I tell you he bought a car? I said to him, go look. And he bought one! Blew our entire car budget on one vehicle! How the hell am I supposed to get to work?"

Brian put his fork down loudly on his plate, silencing me. It was then I noticed he hadn't been eating his pie, just picking the cherry filling apart.

"OK," he said. "I need to say something to you, and you need to hear this."

I waited, weirdly afraid as he composed himself.

"I've known you for over ten years," Brian went on. "I've known you from before you were with Gunnar and the whole time you've been with him. I've been watching a long time and I've been thinking this for a while." He took a deep breath. "He's just not that into you. Gunnar is into Gunnar. You are the stage manager and financier for the one-man show called 'The Life of Gunnar.' And you deserve way better than that."

I blinked back at Brian.

Then I stared off into space, processing what he'd said.

It was just a couple of sentences. But it was everything that I'd been struggling for years to put into words about our relationship.

There, in a dodgy diner in LA, my entire universe changed forever. All those years, all that work, all those times.

Done.

Over.

Finished.

"Sorry, man," Brian continued, "I just can't sit by and watch this anymore. I had to say something."

All of my insides were rewiring themselves. For a second, I was standing in front of that shop window again in Berlin, looking at my reflection, remembering the promise I'd made to myself.

"You're right," I said. "Oh Jesus, Brian. I have to get a divorce. How do I even do that?"

"I don't know, man."

"Me either."

WHO DO I TELL?

When I woke the next morning, I had that wonderful moment when you open your eyes but your brain hasn't fired yet. Then the night before uploaded, and I sat bolt upright up in bed. I thought maybe if I just had a shower, I could forget about it all. But as I got dressed and then drove to work, everything Brian had said made even more sense.

I really had to do this. I had to get a divorce.

Face to face. That was the only way to tell Gunnar. And now that I knew I had to, I wanted to do it as soon as possible. I needed some time off work. So the first person I decided to tell was Joshua, one of my oldest friends and my boss at this gig. I walked straight into his office.

"You busy?" I asked, closing the door behind me.

"No, surprisingly. What's up?" Joshua replied.

I had a sudden flashback to when I was sixteen years old, and a bunch of school friends and I sat in my friend Justin's bedroom. They were the first people I told I was gay. But it took several tries; I had to force the words out.

Sixteen again in Joshua's office, it took a few moments to get these awful-tasting words to come out of my mouth.

"I have to tell Gunnar that I want a divorce."

"Oh, dude! OK. Are you sure?" a shocked Joshua asked.

"Yeah. We're done. I need to go to San Francisco tomorrow."

"What happened?"

I had to think for a moment. How could I say it simply?

"There are things about him that are never going to change. Not for me anyway."

"Man, I'm so sorry. Take your time. Work from there if you need to. Ah, mate!" Joshua got up and we hugged. I'd told someone. It was real now.

Looking back on that moment, all I can say is that I was very fortunate. I worked for a supportive and caring friend, was out in my company in an industry where being gay isn't a problem, working in a state where I couldn't be fired for being homosexual. It was a lot and I didn't take it for granted. There were still twenty-eight states in America where I could have been dismissed in 2017 for having that same conversation.

Back at my desk, I started googling "gay divorce." To my amazement, there wasn't much to be found. Just a lot of lawyers saying they handle cases for gay couples. Did I need a lawyer?

My phone buzzed. It was a text from Gunnar.

Morning babe. How you doing?

I stared at the phone. I felt like the person in a movie who'd accidentally killed someone and was covering their tracks.

Good. Busy. In a meeting. Crazy day. Call you tonight? I clumsily texted back.

I kept looking at the text. Did I sound normal?

Chat then! he responded.

XO, I shot back, and felt like a liar.

The day crawled as I went through the motions with presentations and meetings, my dark secret stalking me from room to room. I spent my lunch break staring out over the parking lot, watching the cars zoom past on the freeway. All these people, living their normal lives.

WAIT... DO I NEED TO GET A DIVORCE?

The next morning, after another night of half-sleep, I sat on the edge of the bed looking at the thick pile of the carpet coming up between the toes of my cold feet. I had no idea how long I'd been sitting that way. The air-con unit hummed. There was a bird somewhere. I had a flight to catch.

Brian.

Joshua.

Only two people knew.

It still wasn't too late to wind it back, I thought, as I mentally stood on the edge of the diving board.

Then I remembered something I'd read.

Mark Manson is a *New York Times* bestselling author and also wrote regularly for the newsfeed *Quartz*, who published his article "Every Successful Relationship Is Successful For The Same Exact Reasons."[1]

Mark was getting married, and like most about-to-be-weds was soliciting advice from people he thought had successful relationships. Then he had a brainwave. He wrote for a newsfeed read by hundreds of thousands of people. Why not ask them? So, he laid out the criteria—if you had been in a relationship for 10+ years and were still happy, what advice would you want to pass down to people? If you were divorced, what hadn't worked?

To their surprise, *Quartz* received over 1,500 responses. Often pages in length. The good news was that it was repetitious, meaning the same things worked for everyone regardless of age, race, religion, culture, or sexual orientation.

Everyone less than fifteen years into a relationship said that communication was the most important thing. But readers with relationships in the fifteen-year-plus range had a different idea of what was most crucial.

Respect.

To quote a *Quartz* reader who wrote in: "What I can tell you is the #1 thing, most important above all else, is respect. It's not sexual attraction, looks, shared goals, religion or lack of, nor is it love. There are times when you won't feel love for your partner. That is the truth. But you never want to lose respect for your partner. Once you lose respect you will never get it back."

I would love to say that I flew to San Francisco and told Gunnar that I had thought about ending it, but the one thing keeping me here was that I hadn't lost respect for him. And that he had said the same thing to me. That we'd then embraced, cried, and made it work.

But as I sat on the edge of the bed looking at the carpet, I sadly admitted to myself that I had lost all respect for him. Years ago.

Worse than that, I'd lost all respect for myself. This relationship had revealed a terrible truth: I was prepared to give up everything I liked about me to be with someone who treated me with as much respect as I had for myself.

If I was on my own again though, maybe I could create a life where I'd never lose respect for myself ever again.

I looked up from the floor.

Decision made.

I'M SORRY, I TRIED

San Francisco seemed like a foreign country from the taxi window, like a half-remembered movie I'd watched late one night.

I turned the key to our front door and the dogs, Penny and Ginger, came bounding down from the top of the stairs. Then Francine, the cat, came over to yell at us for making so much noise. Gunnar had all the animals when we met, so I guessed they'd all go with him. I lay down on the carpet and let my pack mob me, their hot scratchy tongues flipping over my face and clothes. Then we settled into one big, quietly breathing shape. Maybe for the last time.

I don't know how long we'd been lying there when I heard his key in the door. My stomach dropped. The lock turned. And then his footsteps were coming up the stairs.

"Hi!" I called out.

"Hello!" he bellowed back.

I was trying to act normal as we hugged. Then we sat on the couch and I listened to my husband talk about office politics, current projects, restructuring. His words bounced off the hot roar in my ears.

"Are you OK? You seem off," he observed, stopping mid-story.

Everything went very quiet.

"There's something I need to tell you," I began. From the flicker across his face, I sensed he already knew what I was about to say. My mouth was sandpaper.

"I'm not happy with us," I continued, telling him my take on recent events. About being blamed for his job. About him buying a car and not telling me. About us having reached such highs with Myriam's Law, but that it had all gone backward in the last six months and we were worse than ever. I owned my part of how we'd gotten there, that I'd let a kind of behavior foster in him again that I hated, that I was also slipping backward as well, and that I'd exhausted every possible thing I could think of to make it work between us. "So… I've decided I want a divorce," I concluded.

Gunnar stared back at me with a blank yet hard look on his face.

"I'm sorry. I tried," I said.

"Tell me what I did wrong, so I don't make the same mistake with the next person I'm with," he said flatly.

Of all the responses I'd prepared for, that wasn't one of them. I parked it to one side. We talked it over for another twenty minutes or so, him defending everything he'd done. No responsibility taken. I realized then that some part of me was holding out for him to meet me in the middle. Maybe to save it? But the longer he spoke, the further the sun set on us. Gunnar had his side and wasn't moving. And I had mine.

Then we were all talked out. A few moments of silence passed.

"Are you hungry?" Gunnar asked.

"God, yes!" I replied. "Dong's Chopsticks?" And like that, we were weirdly all smiles, out the door, and chatting as we headed down the hill.

We had this running joke that there's good Chinese food and there's bad Chinese food. But really good, bad Chinese food is a rare art form. Our local, Dong's Chopsticks, excelled at glow-in-the-dark sweet and sour pork and stain-your-shirt-forever mapo tofu. They didn't bother giving us menus; we always ordered the same thing.

Gunnar and I made small talk about friends in LA, the tech takeover of San Francisco, a play he'd seen. To anyone watching, we would have looked like a regular couple on a regular night out. He even made a joke about me leaving him and threw a comedy slow-motion punch that I dodged, playing along. We both laughed hard.

Then we stopped laughing. We stared at each other in the red neon light that blinked from the window. Leaving behind plates of barely touched food, we walked back to the house in silence.

I put on the kettle. We stood in the kitchen with our arms folded, facing each other over the island table. We stood here every morning, eating a breakfast of scrambled eggs, toast, and coffee that I'd make. "Industry breakfast" we'd called it, a nod to both our hospitality days. The adrenaline was wearing off. I was exhausted.

"Are you heading back tonight?" Gunnar asked.

"Up to you. Do you want to talk tomorrow, in person?" I asked back. "Yes. Yes. That would be good…" He trailed off.

"I can sleep on the couch," I offered. "Wait, is that weird?"

"Yeah."

"Weirder if we shared the bed, right?"

"Uh, yeah, definitely," Gunnar said, thinking out loud. "Couldn't you stay with one of our friends?"

"What am I going to tell them, Gunnar?"

"Right… Yeah."

The kettle started whistling. I remembered when we'd bought it. We'd giggled and kissed in the store because we'd both reached for the same blue one. I turned the burner off and poured water into the mugs with the big K and big G on them. Something about the mugs did it.

"I think I'll go now," I said. Gunnar nodded.

We hugged for a long time in the kitchen. Then we pulled each other in even tighter for another while.

"OK," I said, breaking away first. "Tomorrow."

"Tomorrow," Gunnar replied.

I went down the stairs with my bag, not looking back when I closed our front door.

That was the last time I saw the dogs.

WRITE YOUR INTENTION, AND DON'T TRY FOR A COOKIE

Swimming my way out of a coma sleep, I slowly sat up the next morning, got out of bed, and went to the hotel room window. The sun was tickling the horizon, orange tinting the city. I was free of all the stress, strain, and drama of trying to make our failed relationship work. I felt good, then immediately guilty that I felt good.

Picking up my phone, I could see Gunnar had texted just after 6 a.m.

I don't want to meet this morning. I need a couple of days.

Sorry, just woke up. Are you sure? I texted back.

Three dots on the screen rippled.

Yes, I'm sure.

OK. I'll head back to LA this morning.

I wished Gunnar had wanted to talk. I'd wanted to see how he was. I may not have been in love with him anymore, but I still loved him. Or what we'd been. But I had to respect his decision. I'd dropped a bomb on him.

From San Francisco airport, I called Gideon.

Gideon blew into my life in a bar a decade earlier, with an impish smile. "I know you don't live here in New York. Because if you did, I'd know who you were. Grab your drink. You're joining me and my friends on the balcony. I'm Gideon, by the way." Gideon turned, I—of course—followed, and a friendship was born.

Of the many things I admire about Gideon, one is his incredibly tactical mind. It seems like there is no negotiation he can't win, no workable angle he can't find, no situation he can't read like a book then have everyone eating out of his hand. I doubt Gideon's ever paid retail. Even before the internet.

Gideon had also been in a ten-year relationship with a man that had ended a few years before. While it hadn't been a marriage, cohabiting for that long made it the same in the eyes of the law. Gideon's experience was the closest to what I imagined Gunnar and I were about to go through.

"Hey, doll. What's up?" Gideon asked.

"I'm on my way back to LA. Just visited Gunnar."

"How's the move going?"

"Well, I told Gunnar I want a divorce."

"Oh… OK." I could hear Gideon's brain ticking. "You're sure?"

"Yeah. It's time."

Between old friends, sometimes all you need to hear is the tone of their voice, and volumes are conveyed.

"I'm sorry to hear that," Gideon said.

"Thanks, mate. Listen, I need some advice. You and Jaden seemed to end your relationship well. From the outside looking in anyway. How do I start?"

"All right," Gideon said, getting down to business. "First question: How do you want this to go?"

"I don't know," I said. "I guess we figure out how to divide up the assets. I was thinking…"

"I'm not talking about the spoils," Gideon interrupted. "*Emotionally*. How did you want this to go, emotionally?"

Since I was the one leaving, I'd presumed that I should accommodate how Gunnar wanted to do it. And if it was hard and it hurt, then that would be my punishment.

"Amicably, I hope," was the best I could come up with.

"You know there's no brownie points for ending your marriage amicably, right? There's no special place in heaven. You don't get a cookie for being amicable. Being amicable usually means that later on you regret the things you gave away because you wanted to be nice. Divorces aren't nice. That's why there aren't Hallmark cards for them.

"Uh, yeah. I guess so," I fumbled back.

"Here, I'll give you some examples. Do you want to write a check and never speak to him again from this moment forth? Do you want to try to negotiate with him to a point, and what is that point? Do you want to mediate or fight it out?"

I was catching up to this idea.

"Take your time, doll," Gideon counselled. "You won't know the answer right now. But when you do, write it down. That is your 'intention.' And that's how you carry yourself all the way through it, because that's how you need it to go."

"That makes sense. Thank you."

"Something else," Gideon continued. "Gunnar's going to write an intention too, consciously or not. And it may not match up with yours at all. He may want to get back together, he may want revenge, he may want to drag it out as long as possible to keep it alive. Be ready for that. When you know his intention, you may want to change yours."

That night, back in the serviced apartment in LA, I wrote it down: *I want this divorce to go as cheaply and quickly as possible.*

In retrospect, I got it totally wrong. I wrote down a result about costs and speed, not an emotional intention. And it was a result that I didn't realize at the time was way, way out of my control. Committing to this was the first big mistake I made in our divorce.

What I wish I'd written, and what I actually meant, was: *I want my husband and I to build the end of this marriage and the start of a friendship together.* I wish I'd stuck that up on my bathroom mirror and read it every day. It's action-oriented, it's progress, and it's partnership. But I thought that was only possible if we had a fast divorce at minimal cost to us both.

Later that night in bed, the one thought I couldn't shake was Gunnar's response.

"Tell me what I did wrong, so I don't make the same mistake with the next person I'm with." It was reflex. I knew that some true part of him had been revealed. I wanted to believe that it was vulnerability or shock. But there was something about the way that he'd said it… It felt like a gauntlet being thrown down.

THE LEGALS

Gunnar and I texted over the next couple of days. I asked how he was doing, but he wasn't giving much away. However, the first agreement we made was to not talk about this on social media at all. The last thing we wanted was for our divorce to be consumed like a piece of entertainment.

And also, no lawyers. We wanted to see what other options were out there. Turns out there were a lot.

Shopping around, the first big lesson I learned was that divorce law changed dramatically state by state. California was renowned for having some of the toughest in the country. Thank God we weren't going to court, I thought.

There were summary and collaborative divorces, where the two of us could basically come to an agreement ourselves. Or mediation if we couldn't do it on our own. Whatever the method, a lawyer would have to be involved at some point to ratify any agreement. Some legal firms offered both services. So, I thought, first step, find us a lawyer.

Pride Legal in California is an independent service where you are matched up within a network of LGBTQ+ or LGBTQ+-friendly law firms. Brilliant, I thought, and punched their number into my phone.

Then I couldn't press the dial button.

Brian knew, Joshua knew, Gideon knew. Maybe Gunnar had told a friend by now. This would be the first stranger though, the first person who didn't care about us that would be invited in. My thumb hovered, shaking, over the dial pad. I couldn't do it yet.

It took another day and a half of building up the courage before I finally took the plunge. Never had I been so happy to hear a queen's voice on the other end of a phone line. The guy was sweet as could be and shot a list of law firms with mediation services over to me by email.

I picked the first one off the list and called them. Part of me thought that I should do some more research on the firms listed, but then I told myself that since Gunnar and I were going to do this together it didn't matter who the firm was.

The actual truth was that the shame I felt from not being able to make our marriage work was so overpowering, I wanted to outsource the whole thing as quickly as possible so I didn't have to think about it. I was trying to impulse-buy a legal way out of my feelings. Lily, the lawyer I was finally connected to, listened patiently as I gave her the rundown, which was starting to feel like a speech.

"Well, I hope that you two can work it out between yourselves. That's always the best," Lily said. "You do realize though that in California, all assets accumulated during the time of your marriage are split 50/50, right? Which in your case backdates six years to when you became registered domestic partners."

"I've read that, but I don't think that's what we're going to do."

"Why's that?"

"I contributed more. A lot more actually. I mean, I'm not some bastard trying leave him destitute or anything like that. I want him to be OK. More than OK. But I want something fair too."

"Have you discussed this with your husband?" Lily asked.

"Not the details. Not yet."

"OK," she said.

In her tone, it sounded to me like she thought I was very green. Which I was. My anger started rising.

"He's entitled to half the house, half the investment and retirement accounts, half of all your household goods, even half of your frequent flyer points. That's the starting point as far as the law is concerned," Lily continued. "You said you were a screenwriter on the side? So, he also owns half of all the intellectual property you created."

"Well, there's some screenplay ideas that we worked on together," I informed her, "but not the other things I did on my own, right?"

"No, everything. Anything you created while you were legally a couple is using community time and is therefore counted as a community asset."

"That's insane," I blurted out.

"That's the law. Also, he's entitled to spousal support for three years, half the time that you've legally been a couple. Your registered domestic partnership supersedes the marriage here."

After getting some figures about how much we both earned, she used a standard formula called the DissoMaster and popped out an eye-watering number for the monthly alimony.

"You've got to be kidding me!" I exclaimed. "That's half of what I take home every month! He has a job! We don't have kids!"

"Listen, I'm just telling you what the law is."

I started rambling down the phone. "Obviously this was written for men and women. I mean, I don't want to sound sexist here, but you know, I could understand if he'd given up a career and raised kids and all that. And women don't get paid the same or get the same opportunities, and that's all wrong. And I guess these laws are written to compensate for that or something? But we're both men! Isn't there some gay divorce clause?"

"When it comes to the law, it's the same for everyone."

"So, we had to fight all that time to get equality in marriage, but we just got divorce equality for free?"

"I'm afraid so. And because you make more than him, he can ask the court for you to pay all his legal bills."

I took a deep breath. I made about seven times what Gunnar did. Sadly as men, we're raised to assess our male worth by what we do and how much we make—and in a gay relationship between two ambitious men, it could be a recipe for dynamite. Plus, I'd supported him through years of unemployment. We'd fought a lot about him starting work again. He'd finally taken a job at a charity startup. Which I was happy to support, they did great work. But surely Gunnar wouldn't take advantage of this and use it against me?

"Look," I said to Lily, "I appreciate that you have to tell every potential client this. But Gunnar and I are reasonable people. I don't think he's going to want things he didn't work for. And this will never go to court. It just won't."

"Karl, you seem like a nice guy. Let me be honest with you. I've seen this situation before, and I've had this conversation many times. Nine times out of ten, it ends up being lawyers vs lawyers. Even if it starts with mediation. I'm just warning you now."

"OK, well, he moves down here to LA in a few weeks and we'll be in your office mediating or ratifying a deal we've come up with."

"Great," said Lily. "I look forward to meeting you guys."

I said goodbye and hung up quickly. Lily was doing her job, talking from experience and trying to prep me for a very possible eventuality. Yet, the sudden rage that spewed up inside me was intense and violent. It scared me. I wanted to smash my phone on the desk.

As I sat outside the office on the concrete bench that overlooked the carpark and freeway, I remember thinking I just wanted this over fast. I didn't want to feel these things.

THE OFFER

Gunnar and I texted most days in August 2017, as we still had a lot to organize with the move before we could even get to our divorce. But of course, the two things bled together. After a few phone calls and text exchanges, not many of which were easy or pleasant, we decided I'd move back into the house in LA after our tenants vacated since I was going to be paying the mortgage and all the community costs. Also, I hoped to live there after Gunnar and I had come to a deal.

He was going to move in with an old friend till he found a place. Soon though, we had to start talking about how we would end things. I'd sent him a proposal that was a 70/30 split of everything and figured we'd probably end up with something more like a two thirds/one third. Our first conversation about it over the phone didn't go well.

We exchanged a few pleasantries, caught up about the dogs and the cat, but talked only a little about what we were feeling. This is the first thing we started to lose in our divorce—parts of the truth were now off-limits, feelings were kept out of the other's sight.

"You read the proposal I sent, yes?" I asked.

"Yeah," Gunnar replied coldly.

"So, what did you think?"

"I don't think it's going to work."

"All right. Well, it's a negotiation. We have to find something we both think is fair."

"I went down to the courthouse here in San Francisco and I spoke to the clerk,"

Gunnar informed me. "He told me I'm entitled to half of everything. Plus spousal support."

"I know that. But I supported you for five years. It's not like I want you to have nothing. But half isn't fair. You know that, right? And why alimony? We don't have kids."

As the conversation went on, Gunnar's answer to everything was, "I'm just telling you what the law says," like it was a stonewalling mantra. Exhausted, I asked Gunnar to just send me back a proposal in writing.

"I'm working on something," he replied.

The next day at work, I dropped by Joshua's office. He wanted to know how things were going, in particular, the math and cost of it all. I brought him up to speed on the conversations with Lily and Gunnar.

"I have an idea for you," Joshua said.

"All ears," I replied.

"Give him the house."

The rage rose fast. But before I could object, Joshua went on.

"Hear me out. He gets half the house anyway…"

"But that's not fair. I paid for it," I objected.

"Mate, based on the conversation you had with him, he wants half of everything and spousal. Law says he can have it. You don't have any wiggle room there. Back to the house, your half of it is worth less than three years' spousal support. So, you'd save in the long run. Plus, there's no real estate agent or lawyer fees. You just sign it over. If he sells it now, he gets a nice chunk of change. If he's smart and rents it, it'll be worth a bomb when he retires. You can save another deposit in a year or two for a new house because you're not paying spousal support. He's set up, you're set up. No fight. Everyone wins. The end."

Joshua was right. It was simple, quick, elegant. Kind of genius, actually.

My ego was kicking against it hard, but I knew I just needed a couple of days to adjust to the idea. I even ran it by my parents in Australia. My dad, who's a financial planner, had to agree it made a lot of sense. So the next day, which was a Friday, I called a real estate attorney and we made an appointment for the following Tuesday.

By Sunday morning, I was in love with the idea. It was going to hurt, but at least it would be done. We could both get on with our lives and still be friends. I was excited by the idea of us knowing each other in the years to come. I even had this future scene in my head of Gunnar introducing me to his new boyfriend when I was over for dinner at the house in a couple of years. If we couldn't make our marriage work, we could at least be a good example of how to do a divorce right.

Sunday night I was at a birthday party, having a great time. It was good to see friends. But I was also smiling because I imagined a simple and easy conclusion to me and Gunnar. And a new life starting soon after.

I texted Gunnar. *Hey, can we talk tomorrow? I have an idea.*

Tomorrow's busy, Gunnar texted back.

OK, well, let me know when. I think it's good news.

No reply.

That seemed odd.

Given the tone of everything lately between us, I thought good news would be welcomed. He still hadn't sent me back a proposal either.

Dread suddenly washed over me like a wave. I put my drink down, made my farewells, and went home, this feeling sticking to me like an oily shadow.

ONE RING TO WRECK THEM ALL

The next morning, my phone rang mid-meeting. Front desk told me there was someone from the American Automobile Association there to see me. That's weird, I thought. Then that feeling of dread from the night before ramped into sharp focus—Gunnar had served a summons on me. I could feel it.

Lily had told me that serving summons is an unavoidable part of the divorce process. Even if everything is amicable, one party has to serve the other to legally get the divorce in motion. Gunnar and I had discussed that we would need to pick a time and place for one of us to do it. He was still in SF, so I'd offered to use the lawyers I'd been speaking to, since I figured they'd be our lawyers when he arrived in LA. We'd agreed there'd be no surprises.

After a short, sweaty elevator ride down to the lobby, the man there asked my name, put an envelope in my hands, and said the words I'd only heard in movies and TV shows: "You've been served."

I took the elevator back upstairs, numb.

"What's wrong?" Joshua asked as I walked into his office.

"Gunnar just served me," I said, holding up the envelope.

When Joshua hugged me, that's when the tears started. The summons was a calculated sucker punch, and I was floored by it because I didn't think that's who Gunnar was. Or who we were.

Joshua told me to take the day and I called Lily from the parking lot.

"Karl, I'm really sorry to hear this. When's the hearing?" she asked.

"What hearing?"

"Have you opened the envelope?"

"No."

"OK. Look inside. A court hearing will have been set. That's what a summons is, summoning you to appear in front of a judge."

Phone propped under one ear and with shaking hands, I opened the envelope. Lily was right; a hearing had been set in San Francisco for October 24, ten weeks away.

"So he's hired a San Francisco attorney and served you," Lily said with an audible sigh, "which means he's been planning this for two weeks. We're already behind."

That meant during the conversations Gunnar and I had been having about no lawyers and no surprises, this had already been in motion.

"I can't believe he'd do this!" I spat out furiously.

"Karl, we have a saying in our field. 'If you really want to see who you're married to, divorce them.' How soon can you get here?"

It took me nearly two hours to get to Lily's office in the Valley.

When you first move to LA, you hear people waxing lyrical about "the Valley," an almost mythical land on the northern side of the mountains that ring the top of Los Angeles city—not unlike the Wall in *Game of Thrones*. The Valley isn't filled with white walkers, but it is the birthplace of the accent made famous by Valley Girls. It's also a long, long way from LA proper. And I worked south of LA, in Torrance. Making this same trip in Europe would probably get you across a small country. When I rang these lawyers the first time, I hadn't even bothered to see where they were located.

The drive did give me time to think though. Calming down from the shock, I wondered if I was making the right move by going with Lily and her firm. Now that it was lawyers vs lawyers, I had to reevaluate. If I'd asked around my circle of friends, I'd probably have found someone connected to a lawyer. And if they didn't handle divorces, they would know someone who did. A personal recommendation would have been a better idea than my knee-jerk reaction of picking the first name off the list. But the idea of calling people who'd been at our wedding two years before and having to explain that we were getting divorced and that it had already devolved into lawyers... I just couldn't do it. Pride, ego, and shame all kicked in and so I didn't do the first obvious thing.

Then I felt my wedding ring on my finger.

I had a habit of rubbing it when I was troubled; the metal under my thumb always had a calming effect. Now it felt like a cruel joke. Yanking the ring off my finger, I wound down the window. I wanted to hurl my wedding ring onto the freeway and have it crushed by ten thousand cars a day.

But I couldn't do that either.

I wanted to believe we could still find a peaceful way to divorce each other. And my finger felt naked where the ring had been. It now felt cold as the wind raced over it. I remember thinking that without my ring I'd just be a normal guy again, like I was losing a superpower. Sensing something, I glanced up to see the cars ahead slowing down. I jammed on my brakes and skidded, rubber and cement grinding against each other—the sound everyone in LA fears most. I only just missed ploughing into the car in front of me. The driver glared back at me in his rearview mirror.

Rattled, I slid the ring back on my finger and continued to drive north.

CHAPTER 3

*"You don't leave the first time you think of doing it.
You leave when you have nothing left to learn."*

— JOHN

THE VOICE AND THE CHORUS

THIS IS A PROBABLY A good point to talk about instinct vs panic, the little angel vs the little devil sitting on your shoulders, or—as I call them—the voice vs the chorus. We all have them, and we all know how the battle between them feels.

The voice always knows the truth, and what's right and wrong. And it always speaks first. The voice knew I was getting served a summons before it happened. The voice nudged me to look up on the freeway. The voice is the smartest part of me.

The chorus, on the other hand, drowns out the voice with a thousand ideas. From this panicky bucket of plans, I generally choose quickly and poorly then act rashly. The chorus's ideas feel great in the moment, but the chorus will also justify every bad decision till you're drowning in quicksand.

Malcolm Gladwell wrote a *New York Times* bestseller on this phenomenon called *Blink*[2], the basic idea being that the second you lay eyes on an object or a person, you instinctively know their true nature. It's something in our DNA, part of how we survived mammoths and cheetahs a few millennia ago. These days, however, a host of other influences kick in that are emotional, cultural, political, etc., and people convince themselves that they don't know what they already truly know. For years, I'd promised myself that I would be more attentive to the voice and tune my mind to trust it.

One day. But not that day.

THIS IS HOW NOT TO HIRE LAWYERS

I parked at the lawyers' offices, which were above a carpet store in a strip mall. I'd driven past it twice, thinking I had the wrong address. The voice told me to get back in my car and leave. Instead, I circled the building's perimeter on foot, unsuccessfully searching for the entrance to the firm.

I walked into the carpet store and asked a staff member who pointed to a staircase at the back, past the shag and flooring. As I arrived upstairs, I was comforted to see that it at least looked like a law firm from here. Wood, lots of wood. I asked the receptionist why there wasn't a separate entrance, and she cheerfully replied that the principal of the firm owned the building. Something about that didn't make me feel better.

As I sat in the reception, the voice reminded me that I still had a whole list of lawyers from Pride Legal I could call, that today could just be the first of three or four meetings like this.

I was led into the boardroom for a round of handshakes with what seemed to be the entire office. This included Butch, the principal of the law firm and owner of the carpet store, and Lily, who till that point had just been a voice. In real life, she seemed like someone I'd hang out with, like we would have been friends if we'd met socially.

When I described the details of the divorce as I saw them, Butch told me they could usually solve cases like mine in two phone calls. I was instantly, willingly, relieved. Butch went on to compliment me on how impressive I was, that most people who come through their doors are broken, in debt with no visible means of getting out of it. It seemed like he was stroking my ego on being an advertising professional, a screenwriter, and all-round good human being, and told me it would be a pleasure to have someone like me as a client.

And the chorus ate it up. I'd walked in there on one of the worst days of my life and my inner victim grabbed the steering wheel. Which is not to say that these lawyers didn't know the law—I learned some valuable information that day.

In Californian divorce law, the only things that can influence the ruling are physical violence and theft of community property. Basically, did anyone hit the other person? Or did anyone steal from the other? Nothing else can be entered in as evidence because it isn't relevant. No affairs, no lying, no past relationship histories, no emotional abuse, no he said/he said. Blood or cash. That's it.

So they asked not once, not twice, but three times in different ways if Gunnar had ever hit me. Of course he never had, but I felt how much the lawyers wanted me to say it.

Blood was out, so we moved on to cash.

The lawyers outlined how we could use private investigators to tail Gunnar, how we could send someone into his sports club to befriend him and pump him for information. They talked about using forensic accountants to check out his financial affairs worldwide, where he maybe had been siphoning off cash from our community funds. They talked about depositions where they'd grill Gunnar for information, and that doing this had saved other clients hundreds of thousands of dollars in the long run.

By the time they were finished, I was completely convinced that I'd been married to a sleeper agent. The pen was in my hand as the voice reminded me that there was a list of other lawyers to meet. But the chorus countered with the "fact" that it would only take two phone calls and anyone could make those. Next thing I knew, I was signing on the bottom line and giving them a retainer of $10,000.

The whole drive home, the voice berated me for taking no responsibility for my own actions. Or my own knowledge too. I knew Gunnar would be scared for his future.

And I knew how he acted when he was scared.

However, I just couldn't rise above it at the time. I had hired my lawyers because I thought they liked me. And because I was too ashamed and overwhelmed to do it the right way. But I didn't need new friends, I needed hired guns. Gunnar was scared and now I was scared, so everything was about to degenerate fast. I knew this, yet I listened to the chorus who backslapped me for hiring professionals vetted by Pride Legal and getting my defense rolling.

I arrived home after swinging by a liquor store and buying a bottle of scotch. After the day I'd had, I bought the nicest one that I could find. I never had liquor in the house. I'd never been much of a home drinker.

As I poured myself a stiff one, I got a text from John Hare.

YOU LEAVE WHEN YOU HAVE NOTHING LEFT TO LEARN

It had been just over a year since I'd met John Hare in Berlin. Since then, we had been in sporadic but meaningful contact. We texted every month or so, having intense chats about life, the universe, and everything that went over several hours. In the same way that we'd had that almost-psychic first meeting on Museum Island, we had an uncanny ability to reach out right when the other needed it.

John's text opened with a photo of the square where we'd first met. It was taken from his POV, looking back over to where I'd been standing that day.

I was walking through the square today, John's text read. *I felt that something had gone seriously wrong with you and Gunnar. Everything OK?*

We're getting divorced, I texted back.

Shit. I'm sorry to hear that.

Thank you. I wish I'd left him a year ago.

If you had, think of everything that you would never have learned.

John's text gave me pause.

True, I texted back. *I'd be repeating the same mistakes with someone else by now.*

Bingo! You don't leave the first time you think of doing it. You leave when you have nothing left to learn.

Still, I'm terrified. I don't know what happens next.

It's easy, he texted. *Operate on instinct. When you set out on a path, the universe sends the right people and right situations to you. You'll be guided.*

How will I know who they are? I asked.

You'll know. They just show up. Like I did.

It was getting late and I signed off for the night, thanking John for his help. I looked at my wedding ring again. I took it off and put it on the coffee table. Straight away, it felt like I was missing a limb. I rubbed the callous at the base of my finger that the ring had made over the years. Now it felt like a lie to wear it, but too big a truth to take it off.

I finished the glass of scotch and slid the ring back on.

MY DREAMS COME IN WAVES

I'm standing on a beach, chained between two poles. The chains are so tight I can't sit down. So I stand there in the cold, watching a small wave on the horizon roll toward me. Only the closer it gets, the larger it's revealed to be. I pull on the chains frantically but they hold fast. I yell for help, but I'm the only person I can see. When I turn back, the tsunami is as tall as a building, a dark-blue death knell casting its shadow over the beach.

"Karl? Karl?"

I looked up at the dozen faces staring back at me in the boardroom.

"Sorry. Where were we?" I said, refocusing on the deck I was presenting.

"You were taking us through concept two," the head of the account reminded me.

"Yes, right. Let's keep going."

The tsunami was a recurring dream that had begun to haunt my waking hours too. I often zoned out in the middle of whatever I was doing. But I didn't want anyone to know how damaged I was. Or that I was changing—a married man on his way to being a divorced man.

I hadn't realized how much of my identity was wrapped up in my ring, my husband, and my married life. Every time someone asked how the move was going and when Gunnar was going to arrive in LA, my heart grew spikes and stabbed every part of me it could reach.

But it was the rage that surprised me the most. What had been just a trickle in my first conversation with Lily was now a burst pipe that would explode at the strangest provocations. Someone who couldn't get to the point in a meeting. A pencil I couldn't find. A coffee machine that needed refilling. The rage would come fast and hard and I'd wrestle it down, hoping no one had noticed.

Gunnar and I had had no communication as per Lily's request. After nearly a week of no news, which didn't feel like good news, I checked in with her.

"It looks like we're in for the long haul on this," Lily explained. "They want half of everything, maximum spousal support, and for you to pay all his legal costs."

"I thought you were going settle this in two phone calls."

"They're determined," Lily replied.

"OK, so when you've settled these in two phone calls, what was the difference between those cases and mine?"

"The personalities."

While I sadly kissed the two-phone-calls solution goodbye, I still couldn't understand why I had to pay Gunnar's legal fees. Lily replied with a response I'd get very used to hearing as the one who earned more: it's the law.

"So, if he's decided he wants everything that the law allows and it's free for him to go to court and get it, what imperative is there for him to settle?" I queried.

"Karl, the court date is nine weeks away. We need to start prepping."

"Prepping what?" I asked.

Lily started listing off boxes to tick: preparation of finances, lists of all assets, statements concerning the nature of the marriage, the divorce, the agreements that we made about how we would handle it pre-summons and so on and so on. As she kept listing, I clicked through folders on my laptop wondering how much I already had and how much I had to find.

Joshua and I caught up between meetings that Friday, and he listened to me seethe over Gunnar's demands and Lily's list for the hearing.

"You should still think about giving him the house," Joshua counselled me.

"Over my dead body!" I exclaimed.

"Mate, despite what's happened, it doesn't change the fact that it's still the smartest, fastest, and cheapest plan."

"He started it! I was trying to do the right thing! He's abusing the law!" I protested, before diving into a detailed description of Lily and her team's plans. I ignored the sadness I could see in Joshua's eyes.

"Sleep on it," Joshua advised. "Get over the shock of this week and then revisit it.

You owe it to yourself. I don't like seeing you this way."

But I didn't revisit it. Instead, needing to be assured of my own rightness, I went on a recruitment drive. Over the next few weeks, I started tentatively telling a few people at work. They were sad to hear the news and sorry for what I was going through. Then, as I told them about Gunnar's antics, the way the law was written, and how I felt he was abusing it, their outrage on my behalf was intoxicating. It reinforced everything that I wanted to believe about my innocence. Their reactions became my emotional food and I gorged myself. Soon, I was telling anyone who'd listen, like a junkie chasing a high.

My firmly held belief at the time was that Gunnar had turned our divorce into a money fight. What I didn't realize until much later was that I was just as guilty. It started when I wrote my intention for the divorce to go as quickly and cheaply as possible. Even though that was still totally achievable by offering the house to Gunnar, I didn't do it.

Because I could give it to him, but he wasn't allowed to take it—which meant we were equally matched on ego, fear, and greed.

Let the games begin.

THE CRISIS OF IDENTITY

On the weekend, I had coffee with an Australian friend called Rooney—Roo, for short. I know what you're thinking, an Aussie called "Roo." But let's move on. Roo and I had met during my screenwriting days at Australians in Film in LA. It had been a while since we'd seen each other and there was a lot of news to catch up on.

We sat in a quiet café in Venice Beach we used to meet at, surrounded by screenwriter hopefuls tapping away on keyboards in the shade of palm trees painted on the café walls. I gave Roo what was becoming a very well-rehearsed speech about Gunnar and the divorce. He made all the right noises in all the right places, giving me my fix. Roo himself had also been going through quite a few life changes with the birth of his first child.

"What was it like when you found out the news?" I asked.

"Mate, the whole universe changed," said Roo, smiling.

"I bet. What was the biggest thing?"

I was expecting him to say he'd been wondering whether to marry his girlfriend, or figuring out whether to stay in the States or head home to Australia, or maybe whether to sell his car and get a family wagon.

"I had to figure out who I was," Roo told me.

At my perplexed look, he explained, "The day she told me the news, I realized that I've basically lived my entire life as an overgrown boy. In nine months, I was going to be a role model to a little human. I had to figure out what I stood for, what values I wanted to pass on to her—in a nutshell, what kind of man I was. And I found out that I didn't have a clue."

"I think you're selling yourself short, mate," I countered. "You've always had a pretty good handle on what you're doing in life."

"The filmmaking, the bicoastal life... all that is just surface nonsense. Everything that I thought was important wasn't, and everything I thought wasn't important was."

"How do you mean?" I asked.

Roo smiled. "I've spent my whole life comparing my insides to everyone else's outsides. How I felt was based on how everyone else seemed. And that's a crappy way to figure yourself out. So I just got quiet, went internal. Deep down, you know. Because no one else can tell me who I am. I have to."

While Roo was talking, I had a flashback to that conversation with John Hare about premature enlightenment.

"How's it going?" I asked Roo.

"Takes time. Longer than nine months." He laughed. "But I'm on my way."

Roo was renewed, clear-eyed. For a guy who'd devoted a big part of his life to the study of martial arts and the spiritual side of it, he was centered in a way I'd never seen before.

As I left, I thought about all my straight male friends who'd gone through what Rooney had. I was also an overgrown boy and a validation junkie who had spent his life chasing the next job, the next title, the next city, the bigger income, industry fame, clothes, and new men—all with the promise of a contentment that I never felt. It was infantile. Peter Pan-ish.

I ended up driving all the way down to Venice Beach and parking near the sand. I took off my shoes and walked to where the water lapped the beach. Staring off into the horizon and listening to the waves, I made a decision.

I may not have been having a kid, but—I thought to myself—why couldn't my divorce be my crisis of identity? I could use it to dig down and figure out who I was. Tired of running from myself and looking for anything or anyone else to make me feel good, I made a promise. I would do the work. I didn't care how much it hurt. If I was going to go through this, I wanted to come out the other side a far, far better man.

I just had no idea how I was going to do it.

But I had to start somewhere.

Holding up my left hand, I looked at my ring. I remembered the day that I proposed to Gunnar under the dappled forest light of the Muir Woods, thinking it would be the greatest thing I'd ever do in my life. We were so happy that day.

I kissed the ring once, slid it off my finger, and tucked it into my pocket. I thought of that old Buddhist quote, that the journey of a thousand miles begins with a single step.

Then I turned toward the shore and started to walk.

CHAPTER 4

"If he'd put as much effort into our marriage as he is into our divorce, maybe we wouldn't be getting one."

— KARL

AUGUST 2017

MY BROTHER GIVES ME THE GIFT OF TIME

AFTER MY TALK WITH ROO, I thought a lot about how I'd ended up where I was. I realized that I'd basically been chasing a rainbow my entire life. I'd followed the script for the gay world—even getting married—and I'd done everything the straight world said you were supposed to do in your career. But I was starting to realize that both were just ways of absolving myself of responsibility for my life. The world said, "Do this," so I did it. Can I have my happiness now, please?

Now the rainbow was going up in flames.

Despite all my searches on and offline, nothing had turned up on gay divorce. None of my gay friends could advise me either. Gideon's experience was the closest, and his had gone reasonably fast and agreeably. I had no idea how to write a new script for myself. I guessed I'd have to wait for more guides, like John had told me.

Standing on the precipice of being broke for years to come, I began to wonder: if I lost all my income, assets, and stuff, what would I actually have left?

Friends and family. That's it.

I'm ashamed to say that I'd only gotten around to tending those relationships when I wasn't busy with work, shoving the people I loved between meetings and business trips. What Roo had said—about how all the things that he thought were important weren't, and vice versa—was starting to make sense.

Then my brother Tony gave me the best birthday present of my life.

Two facts come into play here:

1. Tony is a year and two weeks older than me, and
2. I am useless at math.

After missing each other for a few days, Tony and I finally connected so he could wish me happy birthday. We got chatting about the two of us being a year older, not that I was feeling any wiser.

"So, you know, mate," Tony said, "now that I'm forty-seven, I've been thinking about some of the—"

"Forty-seven?" I queried, cutting him off.

"Yeah, forty-seven," he answered.

"No, mate. I'm forty-seven this year."

"What are you talking about, Karl? I'm forty-seven this year."

"You are?" I replied slightly lost.

Tony sighed. "Karl, I'm going to give you a hot tip. You take the year that you're in, subtract the year you were born, and that's how old you're going to be that year. And do you know why?"

"No. Why Tony?"

"Because math doesn't change."

The year was 2017. I was born in 1971. So that meant… Oh, I was forty-six. Forty-six!

"Karl, seriously. How long have you been getting this wrong?"

"Dunno, mate. Eight years maybe… Ten?"

"Bro, bro, bro…" Tony muttered under his breath.

After we hung up, I practically moonwalked. It was like a fairy godmother had granted me a whole year of my life back—a whole year to use for my divorce. This was better than a *Queer Eye* do-over.

Suddenly the pressure of solving this fast was gone. Instead of my divorce being a shameful sprint, I embraced the idea that it was going to be a marathon. A longer road meant that I wouldn't know everything that was coming, but that was OK. That I would make mistakes figuring it out on the way was OK too.

My friend Grant had a different reaction: "Can I have back that forty-seventh birthday present I bought you? I'll give it to you next year, you dum-dum."

EVERYTHING YOU POST CAN AND WILL BE USED AGAINST YOU IN A COURT OF LAW

Lily had told me to also keep all texts, emails, and every social post and message from any platform that I received from my husband. "And you post nothing, about anything, during your divorce," was the stern advice I'd been given. Even on professional sites like LinkedIn.

Even on dating and hookup apps like Grindr, Growlr, and Scruff.

I thought about some of my social media "friends" who would already extrapolate all kinds of damning interpretations of anything I posted. Then I imagined someone who's out to get me combing my feeds and being paid to do it.

Other couples I knew had gone through social media wars after breakups, posting pictures of themselves with a new hot guy so that they could get a dig in at their ex. But in the long run, they'd always realized that they'd been more harmful to themselves, their friends, and family. No post ever got enough likes to take the pain away, and the comments section was always a poisonous brew.

One friend told me about a drunken photo he'd posted in full anger one night that was the talk of the office watercooler on Monday morning. Later in my journey, I met another divorcing gay guy who, post breakup, had been hit up by a hot dude on Grindr. They quickly developed quite an intimate texting relationship over a couple of weeks, and soon he was telling this guy all about his lawyers' plans. Then one day the hot dude dropped a fact he couldn't have known about. This guy suspected, but could never prove, that it was his ex with a fake account. Like Lily had said, if you really want to find out who you're married to, divorce them.

So, shortly after my birthday, I went off everything. Cold turkey. All social media, hookup apps, the works. It was a relief. Firstly, because I'd quit the world's worst unpaid part-time job. Secondly, I didn't need to see what Gunnar was posting—if I wasn't in the boxing ring then the punch couldn't land. And thirdly, I had too much stuff to figure out and still no idea how to do it. I wanted as few distractions as possible.

Banksy, probably the world's most famous and famously anonymous street artist, once said, "I don't know why people are so keen to put the details of their private life in public; they forget that invisibility is a superpower."[3] So I became invisible.

This journey I was going on was not going to be a spectator sport.

THE FRIEND FILTER

In the weeks since I'd asked for a divorce and the news had started getting out, I'd noticed my friends were falling into four camps.

The first were the friends who were really, truly, got-your-back, call-anytime-day-or-night there for me. The Gideons, the Brians, and my biological family.

The second camp were friends who did care, but just couldn't be around for it. I found this confusing and a little hurtful at first. But divorces, and weddings, bring up a lot of stuff. When I heard of either happening to close friends, it would force me to open up all the dusty boxes of unresolved things from my own mental attic. So I had no judgments about the friends who had to fade out for a moment. I'd done the same in the past.

The third group were Team Gunnar, people who were friends of ours as a couple but sided with my husband as the divorce played out. I remember one text exchange in particular with a close friend of both of ours called Tim in San Francisco. Gunnar and I were beyond close with Tim; we used to joke that we three were in an unconsummated throuple. But reading between the lines of our decidedly cool exchange of messages, I knew it would be our last time texting. I was gutted that my marriage had been a failure. Losing Gunnar's friendship was awful but to be expected. Losing Tim hurt like a slap I didn't see coming. That said, I had to respect that he'd made a choice for one of us.

The fourth group were the tricky ones. "Binge-watchers." People who seemed remarkably hungry for all the gruesome details of my side of the divorce. And I was only too happy to serve it up to them. What hadn't occurred to me was that they were doing the same thing with my husband till one let slip, "Oh, that's not how Gunnar said it happened."

That pulled me up short. What had I said to them? What had they said to Gunnar? I shut those "friendships" down fast.

As August closed out, my default state had become paranoia. Gunnar serving me a summons, the law not at all in my favor, Tim, the binge-watchers—when you're a nail, everything looks like a hammer.

The grinding anxiety that sat in the pit of my stomach was a constant, exhausting companion who always left a bitter taste in my mind. I was sleeping fewer hours every night. Without enough sleep, your brain stops producing enough dopamine—the chemical that makes you feel happy. The less dopamine you have, the more negative and paranoid you become, and the less you sleep you get. So it goes, in a downward spiral.

When I did sleep, the dream was always the same. The tsunami was rolling closer and closer, the chains tighter and tighter.

SEPTEMBER 2017

THE FINANCIALS AND MY UNDERWEAR DRAWER

Whenever Lily's name appeared on my phone screen, I felt ill. The conversations were always about three topics: what Gunnar and his lawyers had done, what they might do, or what Lily needed from me now. Getting divorced was becoming a full-time job.

Large documents in legalese would turn up in my inbox, indecipherable to the average human. I'd call the firm and ask what they were for, and lengthy explanations would pour out about what this document was and why it was needed that often left me none the wiser.

The whole affair was starting to feel like I'd bought a sports team to compete in a game I knew nothing about. Only the players knew the thousands of confusing rules, yet they needed my permission to make every play. I had scant idea what I was approving with no alternatives to suggest. And until we got to court, which was still six weeks away, there was no umpire. Most of the exchanges with Gunnar's lawyers seemed to be pure process or a pure process of saber-rattling. And at $300 an hour, I was burning through the retainer. Every email I sent cost $50 for every person who read it. A twenty-minute phone call cost $100.

I'd pore over the documents, then email back any inaccuracies and spelling mistakes. These notes would be passed to a typist by my lawyer. The documents would come back, often with the same mistakes on them. We'd do another round. Same mistakes, and sometimes new ones. On the third time, I'd send a super-pissed-off email and then finally they would come back correct. These documents were always needed in a hurry, so I started checking my inbox every half hour to make sure I wasn't holding up the process. With nowhere to talk in an open-plan office, I'd started to make calls at what I was now calling "the divorce bench" outside the building.

"So we've received financials from Gunnar's lawyers," said Lily one day.

"OK, what does that mean?" I asked warily.

"I'm about to send you over a PDF. I wanted to be on the phone to talk you through it."

I opened the email and clicked the attachment. I watched the spinning wheel of death before the document finally snapped to life.

"A hundred and forty-eight pages!" I shouted in surprise. "What's in this?"

"This is a comprehensive list of every single asset you have and its value, according to them," Lily explained.

Scrolling through, I felt shock, then complete disgust. The list was more than comprehensive. It had all our joint bank accounts and credit cards with all their balances. To be expected, I reasoned. But then the house, its current value, loans, deeds, car leases, and the pets and the cost of their care. OK, fine. But it went on to list every single item we owned and its market value, from the furniture and electronics right down to our clothes and a rice cooker.

Gunnar had noted every single screenplay or TV show or half idea I'd ever talked about. The document went on to list every bank account I'd ever had in my life, in all the different countries where I'd worked.

"God," I mumbled aloud, "if he'd put as much effort into our marriage as he is into our divorce, maybe we wouldn't be getting one. I don't get what all these old accounts have to do with anything. I'd forgotten I even had these. How did they find them?"

"Forensic accounting," Lily replied. "Basically, they're setting up a case that you've got money hidden overseas that you made while the two of you were together. You'll have to call all these banks and get statements to show account activity."

"They're all empty," I protested. "I'm sure most have been shut down for inactivity."

"Well, you'll have to prove that."

"This is going to take ages, Lily. I don't have time for this."

"You have to make time, Karl. We need to prove you didn't withhold money from community assets."

"But Gunnar knows I wouldn't do this."

"Lawyers keep you busy with assertions that they know have no merit, just to wear you down," Lily explained. "This is pretty standard."

There were also assertions that Gunnar had been barred from the family home and that I'd cut off all access to community funds. I was being painted as a villain, like I'd thrown him onto the street, penniless.

"That's a lie. We agreed I'd move into the house," I moaned to Lily.

"Is it in writing?" she asked.

"No, we spoke on the phone."

"Then you can't prove it. That's what they're banking on when the judge reads this."

"But you told me to cut him off from all the credit cards," I stated.

"Of course. Otherwise he could run them up and you'd be liable for the debt."

"He has a job, but does it say in here if he's OK for cash?" I asked. "I could send him some money."

"That's really sweet," said Lily, "but there's no way you should do that. It admits liability and sets a precedent when we haven't agreed on a spousal support number yet."

"But that makes me look like a bastard, and the judge might think he deserves a higher number."

"I'm sure we'll settle this before trial," Lily asserted.

"What's the thing that convinces him to settle?" I asked. "He wants every single cent the law allows. So why will he settle for less? Especially since I'm probably going to have to pay all his legal fees?"

My disgust was threefold.

Firstly, that I was embroiled in an accelerating process which had every legal right to probe this deeply into our personal affairs. I felt violated, like many unseen people had gone through my underwear drawer and tried on every pair.

The second part was disgust with Gunnar, that he'd made such a Herculean effort to let total strangers into every part of our world.

And thirdly, my legal counsel seemed to be pushing me further down a hole that didn't look like it was going to resolve without a court date. I understood why this advice made legal sense, but it seemed like every move could also paint me in an even worse light.

I got off the phone, steaming. I'd never felt so helpless, taken advantage of, and exposed. The moment I got home, the scotch bottle was open and I drank through my rage, standing in front of the mirror, having imaginary fights with Gunnar.

LET THE LYING BEGIN

The next morning, hungover as hell, I started looking through the financials in greater detail. There were statutory declarations prepared by Gunnar and his lawyer about the life that we had led and the lifestyle he was therefore expecting to maintain.

In short, it was a work of fiction.

He had written that we'd travelled first class on round-the-world trips and owned a big home where we'd hosted monthly social events and parties. All of this was true. But the trip (singular) was a one-off special event for our honeymoon, paid for on points that I'd saved up for years and had decided to blow all in one go. Yes, we owned a great house, but I was probably going to have to buy him out of his half. And the lavish parties were a once-a-month potluck that all our friends came to.

So yes, the facts were true. But the way they were presented was not. Gunnar's account made it sound like we walked down the red carpet to our private jet and landed on our personal airstrip at the back of our home to attend the catered black-tie event that we threw just because it was Tuesday. More champagne please, butler.

And since he was campaigning for spousal support that would allow this imaginary existence to continue, it was unfair on me. Or was it unfair? Was he actually lying? Was I too? In retrospect, it became clearer how murky these questions really were.

Fairness is important. That's the whole principle behind the law. Yet people are cajoled by their friends, families, and lawyers to take full advantage of the law, and to paint facts in a certain light when it isn't necessarily the right thing to do.

Once lawyers are involved, the lying starts. Because, unlike using a mediator, talking through lawyers means you no longer have to look your husband in the eye. Demonizing someone is easy when they're not in front of you.

Dan Ariely wrote a book called *The Honest Truth About Dishonesty*[4]. According to his studies, he got to the bottom of why seemingly good people do truly dishonest things.

He discovered, it was because we can. Because all of us already do.

Dan puts it best in an interview from the *Hidden Brain*[5] podcast: "One of the frightening conclusions we have is that what separates honest people from not-honest people is not necessarily character, it's opportunity."

Big lies, as Dan found out, are made up of a series of small deceptions. Almost all of us speed on the highway because we tell ourselves a few miles over the limit isn't really speeding. We pocket extra change in a store that a clerk gives us by mistake because, well, he gave it to us so we didn't steal it.

Ariely calls it "the fudge factor." Honesty, he posits, isn't a character trait but a state of mind. He goes on to say that it's easy to do the first little thing. Then we have a chance to do the next thing. So do we? Yes, because the second time is easier. And the third. And fourth. The brain reacts strongly to the first act of lying. Then, in time, it fades into the background. It's our second nature to protect the way that we want to believe things went. Self-deception is something that we all do.

I believe the legal system encourages this.

When two people talk in a room together through a mediator, one says their version, and the other says theirs. Then both may concede that aspects of the other's account are more correct. Or one may realize they'd forgotten a specific fact.

With legal exchanges, conversations are all one-sided. These one-sided declarations are then signed to confirm they are the God's-honest, absolute, 100% truth. Later, if you realize it wasn't quite true or you've let your lawyers, friends, or family convince you to overpaint it, it's too late. To say you made a mistake means that all your testimonies will now be called into question.

The lie is now cemented and must be protected. The judge has to believe that you were right. So you can't admit you were wrong.

Going down the lawyer route is more than likely going to end up in the same place that it ends for most people: reading works of fiction by someone you used to love, who now you never speak to, wondering who they really are, or ever were.

Years later, I realized that the moment Gunnar served summons on me, he and I as we knew each other both died.

When you lawyer up and go to war straight away, the first casualties are whoever you used to be and all the great memories you'd had together. They get shot up and left by the side of the road. In Gunnar's place now stood someone who became more and more a two-dimensional villain, curling their moustache.

And I'm sure Gunnar felt the same way. Maybe even from the night I'd said I wanted a divorce.

I spent the rest of the day deleting every single photo of him off my laptop.

WELCOME HOME

Over the course of August and into September, my work had stepped up into high gear. The agency had recently won the account I was in charge of. The client had left a previous agency after only two years, and the one prior to us after just eighteen months. There was a lot of pressure to make this work from the agency and the client, but mostly from myself.

My marriage and life were total wrecks. I swore my work wouldn't be.

My hours per week leapt from the fifties to sixties. One day off was the most I was taking. And on that day, besides the normal adulting things, I was ticking off an endless list of items that my lawyers needed. I'd doubled down on getting all my financials done in response to Gunnar's lawyers, dutifully passing them on to Lily.

One workday, I sat on the divorce bench and spoke with Lily and Butch on the phone about how to prepare for the trial. The conversation turned to the house. The tenants had moved out two weeks before and Gunnar was back in LA, living with a friend. Somewhere. Our lives had been intertwined a few weeks before, and now we had both lost our orbits, like two planets whose sun had died.

I was still in the serviced apartment near work where I had a few weeks left on the contract. I had meant to move back into our house several times, but things were so crazy at work I hadn't got around to it. That's what I told myself. In truth, I had no desire to be living there again.

"So what's it like being back in the house?" Butch asked.

"I haven't moved in yet," I replied.

"Are you kidding?" Lily asked.

"No, I've just been busy—"

"Has Gunnar moved back in there?" interrupted Butch.

"No," I said. "I mean… no."

"But he still has keys, doesn't he?" Lily asked.

The anxiety mill in my stomach went into full grind mode, the rising panic twisting my voice.

"I guess so. But we agreed that…"

"You also agreed no surprises and he served a summons on you, remember?" Butch practically yelled. "You need to drop what you're doing and head to your house right now. And I mean now! Move in and change the locks today!"

With every sense in fight or flight mode, I ran to the parking lot and drove to the serviced apartment to pack my things. On the way, I dialed Brian and asked him to find a locksmith who could come to the house pronto.

I hung up.

Then I started laughing.

And I couldn't stop.

Suddenly, I was sitting in the passenger seat and looking over at myself driving. I watched myself laughing so hard I could barely keep my eyes on the road. I sounded sick, wounded, and unhinged. Another part of my brain was thinking, "Wow, this is the moment they're going to say that he lost it."

Just as quickly, I was back in my body again. Shaken, I pulled into the parking lot of the apartment building—half in my spot, half in my neighbor's. I raced inside, grabbed a couple of big, blue IKEA bags, and started shoving clothes, books, and food all into the same totes.

Then I stopped.

My body started to convulse uncontrollably with sobs and, after stumbling into the hallway, I collapsed. I was outside myself again, sitting on the bed and watching my body face down on the carpet from a small mental outpost of sanity.

Fumbling my phone out of my pocket, I rang Mitch. Mitch is someone I've known since my early days of living in LA. A power lifter, he looks like he could rip a phone book in two but is one of the gentlest souls I've ever met. For years, he had been a great friend and spiritual guide, always ready with an astute observation on any situation.

I cried at Mitch for a good thirty seconds before he could get a word in. I told him where I was, what the lawyers said, and that I thought I was losing my mind.

"Karl, you're just exhausted, that's all," Mitch replied. "This is overwhelming. But you have a job to do today and that's to get all your stuff in bags, in your car, and to your house. That's all you need to think about. So get up and get moving."

"OK," I said, standing up, grateful that someone was telling me what to do.

"Do you have a bed?" Mitch asked.

Everything was in transit from San Francisco. The house was empty.

"Oh God, Mitch. I'm forty-six and I don't have a bed," I replied.

"I'm going to Costco to buy you a blow-up mattress and I'll meet you at the house, OK? Now move. Drive slowly and don't crash."

With a telephonic push from Mitch, I packed up my stuff, got it into the car, and went Driving Miss Daisy all the way to Los Feliz. I opened the garage door of our house.

Empty.

Relieved, I parked inside.

Opening the basement door, I walked into the house I hadn't stood in since we'd moved to San Francisco three years before—a three-story concrete loft house that smelled like the stale ghost of someone else's life.

"Hello?" I yelled out, listening to the echo. No dog paws. No cat mewling.

I walked upstairs. The place was empty. The next-door neighbors had cut down the beautiful tree that had greened up the main fifteen-foot window. Now I could see right into their backyard with a decrepit empty pool, its bottom covered in dead leaves.

Then the doorbell rang and I nearly jumped out of my skin. It was Brian with the locksmith. Mitch turned up not long after with a blow-up mattress.

"It's got a headboard," Mitch pointed out. "That's really important, you need the support."

I was terrible at asking for help, and even worse at receiving it. One half of me knew I needed all I could get from good friends, the other half of me resented it completely. Every friend lately was seeing me at my worst. They didn't care, yet I was still ashamed.

The boys left as dusk fell, after helping me drag some garden furniture into the living area and spread a blanket on the floor for a couch. I was home, for better or for worse. In that large, empty, echoing, concrete bunker, I sat on the blanket, marinating in regret for every promise that our life in this house had never fulfilled.

I wanted to be anywhere except there, defending it against someone I had no defense against. For weeks after, I half expected to come home and find Gunnar there with his bags and the animals, telling me he had nowhere else to stay.

CHAPTER 5

"Your shoes are the only time machine you can climb into and they can walk in only one direction."
— THE EMOTIONS DIARY

I'VE CHOSEN THE EXPLORER'S LIFE

EVEN THOUGH IT HADN'T WORKED, Gunnar and I had spent eight years building something together. And I'd thought we'd be looking each other in the eye as we took it apart together. Then, suddenly, a piece of your life cracks off without warning—like a chunk of a melting ice shelf shearing away from the face—your fingers grasping hopelessly against the laws of divorce gravity.

Divorce is designed to be a long and drawn-out affair. From the moment you file, it's a minimum six month wait by law in California, regardless of what you've figured out with your spouse. You can't rip off the Band-Aid, mourn the loss, and get on with new lives. You're unable to build while you watch pieces of your old life fall away, and the panic that came with that took me completely by surprise.

I didn't want to be in that marriage anymore, I knew that for certain. But at least I was a part of something. Now, I was part of nothing. And a bad gay. On my finger where my wedding ring had been, there was a strip of pale skin. White like a ghost.

For many weeks, I would get up out of bed, shake off my hangover, go to work, go through the motions, go home, get drunk, and get up again the next day.

I was terrified and on edge most of the time. Losing everything and having no map, no timeline, and no idea what direction any of this would take was a terrifying new normal.

Yet I'd signed up for all of this. I hadn't given Gunnar the house when I still could have. I'd decided to use the divorce as my crisis of identity, which felt like the right decision and very noble at the time. Now that I was starting to see what this journey was really going to take, I wished every day that I could go back.

But go back where? Not to Gunnar.

A friend of mine called Jorge is an illustrator, and one day at work I was looking at his website when I came across a picture of an astronaut. When I saw it, I thought, "That's it! That's what you're doing!" A lone explorer, setting out into uncharted territory to seek out a new life. I printed it out and stuck it up on my bathroom mirror. Every morning, it would remind me that I'd chosen the explorer's life—leaving everything safe and familiar behind because the urge to set off into the unknown was greater, knowing there would be battles where you'd fight for your life with no land in sight, and that you might just go crazy in the process. That said, you might also discover a new world full of riches unimaginable.

For these are the voyages of the Starship Divorce. To boldly go where no gay man I knew had gone before. And on the upside, at least I wouldn't die of scurvy.

However, in September 2017, the explorer's path felt like it had a strange inertia. Bends in the road, dead ends, full-on collisions. There were a lot of personal realizations and lessons from guides in rapid succession, without nearly enough time to process them—let alone take them on—before the next pearl of wisdom was handed to me like a hot potato. To try and pretty up this part of the journey would be disingenuous to how it felt.

The disembodied moments on my moving day gave me a pretty clear indicator that depression was settling in. Everything had started to seem disconnected. I was on the path but getting yanked all over it, and suffering from emotional whiplash.

Perhaps not surprisingly, I was spending a lot of time looking backward. Not just because the present and future felt chaotic and terrifying, but also to try to remember the last time I was happy, to make sense of how I'd gotten here and why I'd stayed in my marriage so long.

It all started the day after I'd gotten engaged. I think.

YOU GOT ENGAGED?!

Way back in 2012, when I walked into the office on the Monday morning after I'd proposed, my work partner saw the ring on my finger and was instantly out of his chair.

"You did it!" he yelled, bear-hugging me off the ground. News spread and soon every other married guy in the office came over. Straight guys I'd only ever seen in meetings served up huge congratulatory hugs and smiles. Champagne and paper cups appeared out of nowhere.

I was taken aback by what a big deal it was for all the married guys I worked with. Then I realized we may never completely understand each other's lives, but every married straight guy knows what it is to get engaged. To buy that ring, organize the moment, get down on one knee, pop the question, and then slide that ring on the fourth finger of the left hand of the person they love more than anyone else on Earth. We had that in common now.

There were even a few good-natured laughs as one guy asked, "Wait, who proposed to who?" and I talked them through how I'd popped the question with a second ring in my pocket for Gunnar to put on my finger.

I can only speak for myself here, but I believe this would ring true for a lot of gay men my age: I've had a lifelong mistrust of straight guys. They were the ones I tried to imitate for years growing up. The bad ones beat me up in high school, and the worst ones write laws that make the whole LBGTQ+ community suffer. Ever since I'd come out, I'd always hung back a couple of degrees from hetero men till I knew I could trust them. I know there are lots of great ones—some are my best friends are straight guys—but even with them, I find myself envious of the ease with which they move through this world.

Then suddenly, those feelings were gone. For the very first time in my life, standing among all those straight guys in my office with that ring on my finger, I truly felt like I was their equal. One of the guys even said to me, "Now that you're engaged, you just made *my* marriage bigger."

I know I'm not supposed to say, or even think, that I needed straight men's validation to believe that I was as good as them. I know that's not PC. It's not what we gays say to each other in the fight.

But it was true. I loved how it felt. And I hated how much I loved it.

JESUS, ARE WE GETTING DIVORCED NOW?

Returning to 2017, it was the second Friday night since I'd been back in the house. My wedding ring sat in a box on the mantlepiece but sometimes, when its presence was so loud I couldn't ignore it, I'd take it out. That night, I palmed it gently, missing the superpower of equality it had once given me. Now I was a married man on his way to not being one. I was thinking about how there isn't even a word for it, like "un-fiancé" or something, when Brian called.

"You. Me. Drinks. Now."

"I'm not feeling it, Brian…"

"C'mon, man. Let's go. You're such a shut-in…"

When I continued hemming and hawing over the phone, Brian finally said, "Bitch, if you want to have a social life, that's gonna require you to actually leave your house and let people see you."

Couldn't really argue with that.

So I scanned my bedroom floor, put on a T-shirt that passed the sniff test, then tried to compensate by hiding it under my most expensive jacket. I fixed my hair, hated it, and gave up as I walked through the mess to the downstairs garage, past the dirty dishes covering the kitchen counters.

It was a vibey Friday evening at the Eagle, our local gay bar. And as Brian and I got drinking and chatting, I was surprised to discover that I was actually having fun. I breathed in the LA autumn night air from the bar's courtyard, watching the silhouetted skyline of stucco apartments, palm trees, and power lines. It felt good to be out of the house and out of my head. A good-looking guy came over and started chatting to the two of us. He seemed to be really into Brian and as they started talking away, I stared off into the distance for a minute. Then he turned to me. "So, Karl, are you single?"

I stared back at him like a deer in headlights. As the ever more uncomfortable silence stretched out, Brian had to intervene: "He's getting divorced."

At first the guy nodded in commiseration, but it was a reflex. Then his brow twisted up. "Wait... From a woman?"

"No, I was married to a man," I replied.

The guy put his hand on my shoulder. It seemed like he'd lost his balance. Then he looked me right in the eye. "Jesus! Are we getting divorced now?"

I said the same thing to him that I'd said to Gunnar. "I'm sorry, I tried."

The guy blinked a little.

"OK," he said shakily, and then wandered back to his friends. They all had "so-how-did-it-go?" looks on their faces. The guy said just a couple of words, then they all looked over at me like I had leprosy.

"You all right?" Brian asked.

"Yeah, I'm fine," I lied.

As I drove home, I realized the absolute, number one, shittiest thing about being the only gay man you know getting a divorce, is that you are the only gay man *anyone* knows who's getting a divorce.

HERE'S YOUR CAR, AND SOME TRUTH

LA is a car town. It's famous for it. The city is basically a collection of neighborhoods, walled off by the tyranny of distance and stapled together with freeways. Way back, it used to have one of the greatest public transport systems in America, all based on streetcars. Urban legend has it that the car and tire companies bought the transport system and then removed it to make the population dependent on cars.

I don't know if that's true—there are a lot of conspiracy theories around this phenomenon—but what is true is that "Metro don't go to my house," as the Angelenos say. If you live in LA, you need wheels.

Just pre-divorce, my husband had been down in LA on a trip and bought a car on impulse. He'd blown our budget for two cars on just one. We, of course, had an almighty row about it but he refused to take it back, handed me the keys, and I'd been driving it till he got back to LA. I was only too happy to hand it back.

My lawyers had advised me not to let Gunnar in the house, since he was still technically a fifty-percent owner. He could announce that he wasn't leaving and I wouldn't be able to get him out. So, we'd arranged to meet in the parking lot of the Gelson's supermarket down the street from our place.

It was the first time that we'd be laying eyes on each other since San Francisco six weeks before. I thumbed my hand where the ring used to be, cursing myself for this reflex. But I was hoping we'd be able to agree—or at least start the conversation—on pulling back from the lawyers, finding a mediator, and settling it ourselves.

Arriving early, I paced around an empty part of the lot waiting for Gunnar's arrival. The place smelled like day-old bread and commercial spice mix in the LA heat. It felt like such dirty business meeting there, like a drug deal.

I'd had the car washed and it was gassed up—I didn't want to give Gunnar any reason to complain. I couldn't stop thinking about how every tiny thing might affect the case. I noticed a streak on the side of the car, reflected back by the streetlights. I started frantically wiping it with my T-shirt as an Uber pulled up and Gunnar got out. I hoped he hadn't seen me doing that.

He'd lost weight. He was looking fitter. The chorus started on about him getting in shape to find his next boyfriend.

I'd rehearsed the whole opening of this conversation many times in my head. I had my lines all ready. I was about to begin when Gunnar approached me for a hug. That was the last thing I'd expected, and my throat was suddenly paralyzed. Taking my silence as a yes, Gunnar leaned in, stretching out his arms. I panicked, put my hand out and held him back.

"You've got to be kidding me," were the words that came out of my mouth. "After everything you did, we're a long way from even a handshake."

Genuinely hurt, he pulled back. "Oh, OK."

Great start, Karl, I thought. Well done.

"We agreed no surprises, then you served a summons on me," I continued.

"Because I thought you'd served a summons on me," Gunnar explained.

"What? Gunnar, if I'd served you, you would have been served. I told you we'd figure out who would do it to who, and where and when. So there'd be no surprises."

"Well, I thought you had."

"OK, look. Emotions were high back then. But now you know. So can we drop the lawyers?" I asked. "For all those years we had, can't we figure this out?"

"I'm only seeking what the law states I'm entitled to." Lawyer's words coming out of his mouth.

"Gunnar," I said, getting exasperated, "you're using laws that weren't written for us, to get a settlement that we both know isn't right. All I want is something that's fair. But it sounds like you've decided to take me for every single cent the law allows. Am I right?"

"I'm just doing what my lawyers told me to."

"Gunnar, they work for you. They do what you tell them. If you take me for everything, that's a choice you are making."

He said nothing and looked away.

"I'll take silence as a yes," I said.

He stared back at me. Silent.

I had my answer. So I thought I may as well throw a Hail Mary at the buzzer.

"Have you thought about what this will cost? My friendship, for starters. If you continue this way, we'll never speak again when this is all over. But also, everyone we know, regardless of whether they have a hundred in the bank or millions, worked hard for every cent of it. They all watched you sit around for five years and do nothing, and they all made comments to me about it. I'll cop to my part of allowing that to go on way too long. But do you really think they're going to respect you if you take me to the cleaners? You'll lose every single friend we have. Is it worth that to you?"

"I want you to come back," Gunnar said.

That hung in the air between us for a moment.

"Oh," I replied, stunned.

"This has brought up a lot of stuff," Gunnar went on. "I realize now I have a lot to work on. But I know if you're with me, I could do it. If you were by my side, I could get to the bottom of why I am like I am."

I imagined him and me living in the house again, with the animals. Industry breakfasts. Hugs. Being known again. I could have it all back. When it was good, it'd been great. The chorus was trying to rip through my skin and grab Gunnar with both arms. He stood there waiting for an answer.

"I don't want to hide anymore." The voice's words coming out of my mouth.

As startled by what I said as Gunnar was, I had to think about what I meant.

"You want me to come back to help you figure yourself out. But I'm trying to figure out who I am, Gunnar, and I can only do that if I'm not with you. When we're together, there's not enough room for me as well."

"Karl, please give us a second chance."

"We had it. It was after Vienna. And we blew it. And that wasn't even the second chance, it was the hundredth. You don't want my help, you just don't want to be alone."

As I said it, I knew it was the truth. Because the truth tastes different.

"Take a third, Gunnar. No spousal. I'll get a loan and buy you out."

I held out the car keys. Gunnar finally reached out a hand and took them. He was still wearing his ring.

"I'll think about it," he said. We both knew he wouldn't.

He was fuming by the time he got in the car. I watched him drive off, then I walked all the way back to the house.

The next day I leased a Prius. I didn't want it. But I couldn't walk to work.

THIS IS HOW IT FEELS TO BE KARL TODAY

Since early in the divorce, John Hare and I had started texting most days. He was something of a night owl, so even though we were on different sides of the world, we were more or less in the same time zone. I reveled in my chats with him—winding, philosophical, inspiring.

I'd been filling him in on Gunnar and the meeting we'd had in the parking lot.

Sounds like that day was a steaming pile. But it was only one day, John observed.

Problem is, all the ones coming look just as horrendous, I texted.

They look that way now, but each will be different.

I just feel like this thing will never be over. And I'm going to lose everything and have no money.

Then John wrote the line that ended up saving my sanity.

This is how it feels to be Karl today.

What? I texted back.

I had a period like yours. Different circumstances, but something I felt I'd never see the other side of. I got through it by just saying to myself, this is how it feels to be John today.

It helped? I replied.

Sure did. It's about acceptance, so you stop fighting what you're feeling. And it's a time limit. You only feel that way today. Tomorrow will be different. It might be worse, it might be better. But that's tomorrow. I'd say it on good days, I'd say it on bad days.

So simple. Nine words. But change things it did. I started saying it to myself every day. It was like a pressure valve would be released. Crappy days were contained to just one day in the many that would number my life. And on the good days, I'd celebrate a day of sunshine.

THE PAST HAUNTS ME. AND VICE VERSA

With no likelihood of a settlement between me and Gunnar pre-hearing, the court day preparations stalled. Which is not to say that September was quiet. I was doing seventy plus hours a week at the office. With that, plus the chaos of the divorce, I'd completely forgotten about the movers. I woke on one very hungover Saturday morning to a loud banging at the door. Then I hazily realized that was the day they were turning up with all our worldly goods.

Furniture lined the back alley of our house like a pack of lost designer dogs in a forest of a billion boxes. I didn't even know what was in most of them.

I had the movers bring in the bare minimum of stuff: sofa, coffee table, kitchen stuff, my clothes, the end. And definitely not our bed. It was bad enough being back in the house where it had all started to go wrong. I'd continue camping inside like I was in trench warfare.

The boxes, which took up half of the garage in piles that stretched from floor to ceiling, were like an ominous portal to a past life. It was after stacking them all that it happened. I smelled Gunnar. Somewhere between the mattress and the boxes, his ghost was in my nostrils.

I held my breath every day as I walked past them to the car.

I was brushing my teeth one morning when the thought struck.

I'm single.

Not in the legal sense yet, but there was definitely no ring on my finger. I stopped brushing and started taking an inventory of my body.

Oh dear, I thought.

Back in San Francisco, I was part of a cycling team that met up on weekday mornings. Early ride-outs were my jam. I felt like we woke up the city, our collective energy pulling the sun over the horizon. Since I'd been back in LA though, all that had come to a skidding halt. Add to that my divorce regime of post-work drinking, weed, and the late-night eating binges and I wasn't looking great.

Love handles. Big enough to be seen through jackets. Hmm, OK. I can probably cycle those off.

Posture. Not terrible, but I slouch too much. I thought I should probably get one of those posture-correcting straps I'd seen on Instagram.

Weird red things. What are these? Moles? I had five on my stomach. There were a couple on my shoulder. Poking them, I thought, aren't these the things that old people get?

Arms. They've shrunk a bit. I could get the muscles back. But what I couldn't figure out was when that old guy's crease appeared where my armpit meets my chest.

Ass. Wasn't terrible. But I didn't remember that crease line. When did I become spongy origami?

Hair. Perhaps I was being paranoid, but I thought it had thinned. Maybe the stress had made it fall out a bit.

Face. Actually, the face was pretty OK. But my eyes were sad. Even I could see it.

Chest. Still holding shape well. Then I counted a few gray chest hairs.

Crotch. I found three gray pubic hairs. Gray hairs on chest was fine. Gray hairs on the crotch, not fine.

Ever critical, I gave myself a six out of ten. And at forty-six years old—so, like, sixty-six in gay years. There was work to be done. The chorus was yelling at me like an infomercial: "Tomorrow, get up at 6 a.m. and go to yoga and then hit the gym every day after work and get back on a good diet and stop drinking and eating late and this will be your new normal and you'll have the body you had when you were thirty-six in just four weeks!"

Even the thought of it exhausted me.

Thirty-six. Life was good at thirty-six. It was the year before I met Gunnar and I was a screenwriter who'd left full-time advertising to pursue his dreams in LA. I was subletting a studio just off Venice Beach, hiding from the building manager and shoving checks under her door every month, driving a piece-of-crap car with paint chipping off the roof, and writing every day. I was living my dream, feeling invincible, and it wasn't a question of *whether* I'd win an Oscar, but *when*.

In the mornings I'd ride my bike down the coast road, the ocean on my left and the sun coming over the horizon to the right, salt air on my face and sunlight in my nostrils. I remembered feeling that I was exactly where I was supposed to be.

I was also seeing a bit of a lovely young guy called Niko.

Hmm, what is Niko doing these days? I wondered, back in my forty-six-year-old body. We'd been in sporadic Facebook contact over the years, but I hadn't clapped eyes on him in at least five. So, I rang Niko up, we talked a while, and we made plans to get together.

In the days before, I hunted down the fragrance I used to wear back then, pulled out some unfinished screenplays that I noodled around on, and even started listening to all the artists I was down with at the time.

Niko and I met for a bite at a vegan place in my hood, talked, caught up, had a few laughs. He was as I remembered him: handsome, funny, intelligent. It was like the last almost-decade had never happened. We ended up back at my place, with him leaving in the early hours.

Then I didn't text him again. The whole meeting with Niko confused me no end. It had felt good to see him, but I couldn't understand why I was avoiding him after.

Everything lately seemed to go like this: I'd feel bad, then I'd feel bad about feeling bad, then I'd do something I didn't understand, then I'd feel bad about that.

It was doing my head in. But now it was starting to involve people who hadn't signed up for it. After writing and rewriting an overthought text to Niko, my thumb hovered over the send button and then I deleted it. I wanted to take a hammer to my phone screen. So I took a breath and said to myself, "This is how it feels to be Karl today."

The crappy feelings got turned down immediately. In the calm, the voice prompted me. Crisis of identity. It was time. Full Myriam's Law. I was 100% responsible for making my life, so I'm 100% responsible for fixing it too. So get to it, the voice demanded.

For a change, I actually knew where to start.

THE EMOTIONS DIARY

There was a period in my life just over ten years before, where I'd gone through a pretty miserable stretch. A psychic friend had suggested keeping an emotions diary—basically, you write a question in it, wait for an answer, then write that down. When I asked her who was supposed to answer, she just replied, "I don't know. Someone always does though."

Naturally, with any kind of great advice like that, I ignored it. But I never forgot it.

And now, at what felt like an emotional rock bottom, I was ready to give anything a try.

So I bought a hardcover notebook, cracked it open to the first page, picked up a pen, and thought, here goes nothing. Then I wrote this:

I went out with Niko for dinner and we had a great time and now I'm avoiding him. But I like him, and I can't figure out why I'm paralyzed here. Why does the idea of calling Niko again feel wrong?

There it was. It felt wrong. Which made no sense to me. As I was dwelling on that, I heard a voice. Not really heard. Felt is more accurate. I started writing down what it "said."

You're looking back to a time you felt safe. You want somewhere to hide. But you can't hide in the past because it's gone. It doesn't exist anymore. All you have is now. You want yourself and Niko to be the men you both no longer are. Your shoes are the only time machine you can climb into and they can walk in only one direction. Niko means that you are ready and open for new things. But they have to be what's in front of you, not behind you.

As I looked at the answer on the page, I felt like Harry Potter casting his first spell.

That was it. That's what was going on. Not just what had happened, but *why*.

I texted Niko to thank him for the night and apologize for not being in touch since. Niko texted back and we chatted a while. It was like a window had been opened to let some fresh air into the room.

For over a year, this emotions diary became the single most important thing in the world. I kept it by my bed. I never left the house without it. I would forget my keys and wallet some days, but I always knew exactly where this book was. I would sit down at least once—sometimes a couple of times—a day, and write down what was going on with me.

After a few weeks, the work in the emotions diary started to find a three-step formula: What, Ask, Wait.

1. *What*
   I'd begin by writing down the most recent incident that had spun me out (I'd gotten an email from my lawyer, a text from Gunnar, someone at work had pissed me off, etc.) and how I felt about it. Not overthinking it, as writing from the hip helps access instinctive truths. This "what" would fuel a question.

2. *Ask*
   Every question is a good one. How? Where? When? Who? Often the question you conjure forth is a revelation in itself. But I found "why" questions revealed the most. By its nature, "why" asks you to look underneath.

3. *Wait*
   After the question, I'd sit quietly and listen. Then the answer would arrive and I'd write it down as it was explained to me. I don't know where the answers came from. Call it the universe, God, your grandmother's ghost, your spirit animal, wisdom that's buried deep inside you. It wasn't the voice; it was definitely its own entity. And it always came with the advice I needed.

With the emotions diary I became a student of my emotions, not a servant to them.

Over time, I got to know the diary well. Its tone changed depending on the question and situations. From a nurturing friend to a coach, and sometimes to a slap in the face. It could get genuinely pissed off when I was indulging a situation that I knew was bad for me, or I was asking a question it had already answered several times.

This may sound like the kind of thing that psychics do. Or crazy people. But years ago, there was a bestseller called *Conversations with God* written by a man called Neale Donald Walsch[6]. In the early 1990s, Neale suffered a series of horrific incidents: a fire that destroyed all of his worldly possessions, a divorce, and then a car accident that left him with a broken neck.

He recovered, but now alone and unemployed, he was forced to live in a tent, collecting and recycling aluminum cans to have enough money to eat. Understandably, he thought his life had come to an end.

Neale was angry at how much had been taken away from him. One day, full of rage at God, who he felt had betrayed him, he wrote a question down. And much to his surprise, an answer came. He kept asking, and answers kept coming. Elizabeth Gilbert talks about the same process in her book *Eat, Pray, Love*[7] and so too do many other people.

So, instead of trying to pick the emotions diary apart to nail exactly how it worked, I tried to not to dwell on it. It worked, and that was all that mattered.

We need more mysteries in this life.

THE HEAD IS FASTER THAN THE HEART

Catherine is a French woman I've known for two decades and a dear friend. She came to stay with me in LA on a work trip. We'd met in South Africa when we were both working in Johannesburg, drinking way too many ciders in the bar down the street from the agency. Lean, tall, with long dark hair and striking eyes, and exuding a healthiness I was severely lacking back then, Catherine also has that annoying French ability of being effortlessly chic all the time. In the ups and down of our lives and the times we'd shared all over the world, Catherine was like a sister to me.

Unfortunately for her, my depression was in full swing. I spent most mornings crying before work on my patio. Even though I'd embraced my divorce with Myriam's Law, and was trying to use it as my crisis of identity, armed with the emotions diary, the work was slow and hard. There weren't a lot of good days. Just slightly less crappy ones.

I was tired of looking like shit in front of my friends and so I almost asked her not to stay. But after a chat with the emotions diary, I realized that my ego and pride were in the way.

You're a train smash right now. Embrace it. No one's expecting you to be on top form. How about not trying to be cool for a while?

Forewarned, Catherine happily came to stay with me just as I was. And I'm so glad she did because she gave me two great pieces of advice.

We'd made plans to go and do yoga one morning but after another night of insomnia, the tsunami dream playing in IMAX 3D, I woke up and the tears started before I could even get my feet on the floor. Catherine came out to the patio, a yoga mat under one arm, to see me with wet, hollow eyes and a coffee I'd let go cold in my hand.

"Sorry, Catherine. I don't think I can join you at yoga this morning."

Catherine regarded me. "I'm not worried about you. You already want to be better in here," she said, touching my head, "but the head is faster than the heart."

The head is faster than the heart.

I blame it on being a Leo, but my patience levels are never lower than with myself. So out came the emotions diary to see if I could find out why I had to have this time lag between organs.

Why does it take so long for the heart to catch up to the head? I asked it.

Because otherwise you would act on every stupid plan you have. Right now, you're having a thousand ideas a day about your future, and most of them are rubbish. The time delay weeds out the dumb ones. Be grateful. It may take a while, but it's stopping you from wasting time and effort on dead ends.

Once again, it was right. At that point in time I'd been considering a new career path.

I'd found Buddhism when I'd lived in Japan. And while I hadn't acted like much of a Buddhist for a long time—I'd barely prayed the last year—after seeing an episode of *Chef's Table* about a Korean nun who'd lost her mother and walked into a Buddhist monastery in her early teens, I decided that was the answer.

I'd move back to Australia, leave all my worldly goods behind, and enter a monastery—little known fact, but the second largest Buddhist monastery in the world is in Wollongong, the next major city south of Sydney.

On a call with my lawyers one day, as I told them of my master plan, they gave me a reality check.

"Karl, while I think that's really admirable," Lily said, as indulgently as she could, "you can't resign from your job."

"Of course I can. In fact, I should resign. My doctor is seriously worried about my health. You know the hours I'm pulling right now."

"If you resign," Lily continued, "Gunnar and his lawyers can make a case that you did it to avoid spousal support. Then you'll still have the bill every month and no job. You'll go backwards."

I said nothing as I tasted the acid rage rising in my throat.

"Karl?"

"I'm here. So let me get this straight. I'm trapped in my job that I hate, that's probably going to put me in hospital, to pay spousal support to Gunnar and fund his lawyers so he can clean me out and take his time doing it. And then when the divorce is done, and he's got half of everything, I'll be handing him half my income for three more years. And the law gives me no way out of this."

"Karl, if you'd been together ten years or more, they can make a case for you to pay alimony for the rest of your life, as long as you're able to."

"Lily, I just want to go home to Australia," I said, surprised at how I choked up.

"If you do, Gunnar can put an arrest warrant out for you in California. You'd be avoiding a court order."

"OK. I'm hanging up now."

Sitting on the divorce bench, I stared out over the freeway.

I felt like an animal in a cage getting poked with a stick. Lily had explained that the spousal support was so Gunnar could maintain the life we'd had together. The irony was that I didn't want that life anymore. I'd realized it wasn't worth what I'd given up to have it.

All I could see ahead of me was working my ass to the bone and still being financially screwed till I turned fifty. I sat on the bench for half an hour, crying. It was the middle of the day on a Tuesday, and my phone buzzed as half a dozen coworkers looked for me.

LOOK FOR THE SIGNS

Hi John, you there?

Hello, my friend. How goes you? John Hare texted back.

Not well. I'm stuck and I'm lost. I don't see a way out.

Have you seen the signs?

What signs? I texted back, puzzled.

Remember when this first started, I told you that people and events conspire to help you. They show up and show you the path. It's like driving at night. You can't see the road in front of you, but you trust it to be there. Just follow the signs to get where you're going, even though you can't see the whole path. Make sense?

It does. Thanks John.

Go hard, Karl!

I fell asleep promising to be open to the signs. It felt good to know John was there and to think that forces were coming to my aid. I didn't know if I truly believed it, but at least it was something.

WHAT DO I DO WITH THE RAGE?

Over the next week, prompted by Lily's conversation, I start hatching plans for how to get fired. Should I lose it in a meeting with the clients? Should I insult them? Maybe I could yell at someone in the office publicly? But I didn't want anyone else to get injured over my mess.

So I considered enlisting someone's help at work and asking them to make a complaint to HR about me for an incident that never happened. But how would that conversation go?

How do you ask an African American or Asian coworker to say that you used a racist slur? Or ask a female coworker to say that you made a sexist remark? Would I do that for someone if they asked me to report them as a homophobe? Could I look HR in the eye and lie to them? Probably not, I thought. Plus, it was too much to ask another minority to risk being branded as someone who "complains."

Even if someone was willing to do it, I'd basically never work in advertising again, even as a freelancer. It'd be all over AgencySpy, the online gossip hub of our industry. I'd wreck my career and potentially harm someone else's too.

Then one day at work, I got a voicemail.

"Hello, this is a message for Karl Dunn, husband of Gunnar Magnusson. I'm calling from UCSF Medical Centre. Can you call us back ASAP on this number?"

Running to the divorce bench, I imagined Gunnar must have been back in San Francisco for work and had an accident.

A mental image of him bleeding flashed through my mind. I quickly called back.

"Hello! This is Karl Dunn, Gunnar Magnusson's husband! You rang me. Is he OK?"

"That's what I'm trying to find out," replied the doctor. "I was hoping you could give us Mr. Magnusson's new number."

"I'm sorry, I don't understand what's happening."

"Mr. Magnusson had a minor procedure earlier this year. I'm trying to make a follow-up call but his old number is disconnected. You're his emergency contact."

"Right," I said. "Yeah… I don't have his number."

"You don't?" the doctor asked, confused.

"We're getting divorced."

"Ah! Right! Sorry. You're the one listed here."

After the call, I sat on the divorce bench for a while. In the aftermath of the exchange, something truly awful was clear. I'd asked myself what I would feel if Gunnar had been seriously injured or dead. And the answer was relief. Because it would be over.

"You're disgusting," I said out loud to myself.

If you really want to find out who your husband's married to, divorce him.

One Saturday on the way to work, on a half-empty 405 Freeway, I saw this gap in the railing where they were doing some roadwork. The wall was being replaced where it crossed over the top of another freeway.

In my mind, I saw myself calmly turn my car into the gap, sail off the edge, and crash down on the side of the road below.

How funny would that be? I thought darkly. Gunnar is already counting all this money he's going to make out of me, and then I die. I imagined the look on his face.

I couldn't stop laughing.

At work, there was a guy I barely knew called James. But he was famous at the office for having gone through a particularly brutal divorce. People had mentioned James to me in hushed, almost reverent tones. I had a million questions I wanted to ask him, but we didn't have that kind of relationship. However, this particular Saturday, I got to the empty office to find him there. He'd had to duck in to finish something. Remembering John's advice, I took it as a sign.

"Hi, James," I opened nervously.

"Hey, man. What's up?"

"Sorry," I almost whispered, "I heard that you had a really bad divorce. Um, I don't know if you know but I'm getting a divorce too."

James turned around in his chair. "Dude, I'm so sorry."

Many people had said these words to me. But there was something about the way James said it. He just got it.

"I have a question," I ventured.

"Anything. What do you need to know?"

"What do I do with the rage? I'm so scared of myself. It comes out of nowhere."

"Oh, yeah. That," James said, nodding his head, looking off for a moment. "When you get in the car every morning, imagine that your ex is sitting in there with you and call them everything you can think of. Say it all, yell at the top of your voice. By the time you get to work, you'll feel ready for the day."

It was like James had handed me a magic pill. My body could feel that it would work.

"And you need to find some kind of sport where you hit things," James continued. "You know, martial arts, boxing, kickboxing, whatever. Just something where your fist meets a bag."

"Oh, I don't know, mate. I'm more of a yoga, swimming, cycling kind of guy," I said, not that I'd been doing much of those lately.

"Trust me, it helps. More than you can believe."

I thanked James for his wise words and on the drive home from work, I sat next to Gunnar. And I let rip. At first it was just great to say these things I'd been thinking and feeling out loud. Then I got super creative, kind of amazed at the insults I freestyled out of nowhere.

I didn't drink that night.

James started swinging by my workroom and, over the heads of all my coworkers, ask if I needed to go downstairs for a coffee. This was code for, "Do you need to talk?" James's wisdom is sprinkled all through this book. He gave me the download on lawyers, divorce tactics, feelings. But bigger than all of that, I never felt alone again. I knew that James was just a short walk away and ready to listen. And that he got it.

A couple of days after our talk about rage, a Groupon popped up for a kickboxing place around the corner from work. OK, universe. Message received and understood. I bought a week of classes, packed some gear, and before I could talk myself out if it, rolled up after work the next day.

I've striven all my life to be a man of peace, so when I arrived and saw everyone kicking, punching bags, and yelling, I was intimidated. I'd always had this idea that gay men are the peaceful ones. Straight men start wars, not us.

When they wrapped my hands like a boxer, though, something stirred. Like I was getting ready for battle. When my first punch landed on the bag, it felt good. Really good. Next punch, even better. Working the circuit, I did my first jabs, uppercuts, roundhouse kicks, and a range of moves I've only ever seen in films. The visceral explosion of energy hooked me hard.

By the end of the first class I was a sweaty mess, grinning from ear to ear. It had been a long time since I'd smiled about anything. I signed up, and five nights a week I emptied all my pent-up rage out onto the bags and mats.

Finally, the body under my skin did something I was proud of. Something new. Something that helped.

At first, it was about getting out all the anger I had toward Gunnar. Then, sometimes, a class would bring out surprise truths.

I'm a man of peace? I'd kicked off this divorce, hadn't I?

I was the one who wrote an intention that was all about money.

I could still have given him the house. But I had my stupid pride.

So, I'd hit the bags instead of hitting myself.

CHAPTER 6

"This divorce is happening for you, not to you."
— Ludo

OCTOBER 2017

CHARLES DARWIN AND THE THEORY OF DIVORCEOLUTION

By the start of October, life had settled into a routine. The routine, however, was chaos. "War is Peace," as George Orwell wrote in *1984*.

My work life was now a seven-day affair. Things weren't going well on my account. There was a cultural gulf between us as an American agency and an overseas client. These misunderstandings meant that there was an eternal redo on everything we were making. Add in time zones, pressing deadlines, curveballs, and late nights, and my team was burning out.

Plus, I was regaling them with divorce updates on the daily. Whether they liked it or not. Every night, hitting the bags at the kickboxing studio, I'd replay the day and regret it. But I couldn't help myself. If I was having a good day with it, I felt compelled to tell everyone. If I was having a bad day, they were definitely going to hear about it.

We were three weeks away from the court date in San Francisco and there was still no response from Gunnar to the financials I'd sent to my lawyers weeks before.

When I'd asked Lily about it, she said that lawyers used this kind of stalling tactic to allow little time to prep before hearings.

The anxiety mill was in high gear, newly filled by a suspicion that my client was thinking of jumping ship. Even though I wanted out of my job, failing at work after failing in my marriage was more defeat than I could handle. So I doubled down on my work efforts.

In the emotions diary, I'd had a strange answer to the question, *Why can't I have one win?*

You're not looking for a win. You're looking for a piece of solid ground to stand on. Wins come and go. Everything shifts. You're not going to have anything permanent under your feet for a while. Get used to it.

Catherine's presence made me clean up my home act: less drinking, earlier to bed, meditating more. Funny how other people can be a mirror you don't like to look into.

One day Catherine gave me her second piece of great advice. She shot me a text. It was just a photo of her hand holding the underside of a drink lid. There was this quote there from Charles Darwin that read, "It's not the strongest of the species who survive. It's not the smartest. It's the ones who adapt most readily to change."

I noticed two things. First was that Catherine has really nice nails. But it's that chic thing again. Second was that I didn't understand natural selection at all. I thought it was strength and smarts that were the deciding factors. And having been a gay teenager with no interest in team sports, I'd always hoped that intelligence would be the more valuable asset in a zombie apocalypse.

But there it was on the bottom of a bottle cap.

Adapt.

Change was all around me. Friends, family, work, sex, money, my body, and personal responsibility. I didn't think that I would ever see change as some kind of joy-filled jumping castle. But instead of grabbing frantically at the pieces that were falling away, I could try waving goodbye to something that no longer served any purpose.

I didn't have to be strong. I didn't have to be smart. I just had to be willing to adapt. That felt like something I could do.

A VISIT FROM THE HUSBAND AND A VISIT TO THE LAWYERS

Catherine returned to San Francisco and within days my good friend Uli had come to stay with me. Uli is a hilarious, gregarious, bearded and bespectacled German sass-bomb of a human being and the best dressed person I've ever known. We'd met years before working together in Amsterdam. I hated him the first three days I knew him. After seven, we were roommates. It was that kind of friendship. More like brothers.

Uli was freelancing with us at the agency and his energy in the room was a breath of fresh air. It was good to have another old friend around to talk with at night, and a brilliant writer to solve the never-ending problems we had at work every day.

Then one day a text from Gunnar arrived. We hadn't had any contact since I'd handed the car back. I hated corresponding through the lawyers. It was slow, expensive, and read by too many eyes before it ever got to me. That said, a message from him on my phone made me feel weirdly violated too.

Gunnar wanted to come over and get some furniture and things from the garage. He must be in his new apartment, I surmised. Good, I thought. The less of all that stuff around the better. We arranged a time and Uli made sure he was far away from the house.

In our garage on the underside of the building, Gunnar pulled up in his car. No one tried for a hug this time. He attempted a couple of jokes, but I was in no laughing mood. He'd decided to make it hell for me through his lawyers, so I wasn't going to fall for the nice-guy act in person. In retrospect, it was probably just as uncomfortable for him, maybe more. He was coming back to the house for the first time in years.

Gunnar had a guy with him to help out. He looked like Gunnar's type. But it could just have been a guy off TaskRabbit. At least I didn't have to figure out if I should help him or not. Seeing Gunnar in our garage, he was so familiar, yet so alien. Adapt, I told myself. This is not your husband anymore, he's your opponent. Be professional, courteous, but distant.

As they finished loading things up, the helper (or bedroom buddy) made himself scarce.

"Listen, this financials thing with the lawyers. This has dragged on long enough," Gunnar said. "Can you just get them to us?"

"What are you talking about?" I replied. "You're the one holding it up. I sent financials to my lawyers six weeks ago."

"We never got them," Gunnar said, puzzled. "I thought you were stalling so we'd have no prep time for the hearing."

I knew Gunnar's tells pretty well. It didn't seem like he was lying.

"Are you sure your lawyers sent it?" Gunnar asked.

The rage started boiling up. I've never had a great poker face and Gunnar watched the whole thing dawn on me. He saw me look weak.

"I'll call Lily tomorrow and get this resolved. Step out so I can close the garage."

Gunnar got in his car. I thought I caught him smiling to himself. I pressed the garage door button and listened and waited till I heard him drive out of the building. I called out for Uli, but he still wasn't back.

In the basement of the house, I screamed at the top of my lungs. I wanted to punch a hole through a wall, I wanted to burn my lawyer's office to the ground, I wanted to kill. I had three whiskeys just to try and knock myself out, but the night held nothing except staring at the ceiling, thrashing around my bed, and a couple of hours of sleep stolen sometime before dawn.

At 9 a.m. the next day I was on the divorce bench calling Lily. She said she'd check on what was going on.

An hour later, I received an email from Lily's office clerk with a bunch of new financial documents to review. As calmly as I could, I gathered the additional information they needed. Then I received documents with incorrect numbers that I had to point out with a return WTF email. I felt a level of anger I never had before. I went back and checked my emails; I'd sent all the financials on October 10th. It was now November 21st.

So I sent an email to the whole team at the firm telling them I'd be there in an hour.

On the whole drive up to the Valley, I went over the possibilities. Had we been the ones stalling? Had my team dropped the ball? Was Gunnar just psyching me out?

I practically handbrake-slid into a parking spot and stormed upstairs past the carpets.

But the conversation I managed to have in the boardroom with the team focused only on the trial that was taking place next week. It seemed that the six-week gap just went unexplained.

The hearing was about spousal support. They explained that Gunnar was seeking the highest number possible. So you go to court to set something called "interim spousal support," which is the amount the one who earns more has to pay the one who earns less, until a final divorce agreement is reached. The number is decided by a formula called the DissoMaster program. Basically, they put in what you earn, what your spouse earns, and then the DissoMaster spits out an answer. You would think that the whole point of it is to find a fifty-fifty balance between parties. But it's not.

We discussed how I would be up for almost half of what I took home every month, plus arrears from the time of our split and the exact date of that was apparently up for debate. For me, it was from the time Gunnar arrived in LA, since I'd paid everything up till then to wrap up our lives in San Francisco. They claimed it was much earlier, from when I'd left to freelance in LA and before I'd even said I wanted a divorce. Which made no sense to me. Plus, they would also be asking for me to pay all of his legal fees in arrears and going forward. From what I understood, they would probably get that.

One useful thing I did get from the meeting was that Lily and the firm would make an application for me to appear telephonically and have the case moved to LA County, since Gunnar, myself, the house, and everything to do with the case was there. Gunnar had apparently already been granted a telephonic appearance.

Leaving the firm that day, I felt ill. My finances were a disaster. I wondered who I could borrow money from to switch counsel. Then, afraid and utterly exhausted, I listened to the chorus instead—the laws were all written in Gunnar's favor, so it didn't matter who was representing me. I was screwed anyway.

I gave Uli the download from the day. But there was something different in how he listened, a reservation. I didn't ask. I didn't want to know.

YOU'RE ALREADY FREE AND YOU'RE MISSING IT

In the week before the trial, work continued at a breakneck pace. When an account is in trouble, as ours was with the impossible physics of workload vs bodies vs hours in a day, senior management start turning up in the room. Lots of opinions, lots of direction. We seemed to be reconcepting every couple of days.

I wasn't making it easier. I was running off at the mouth in terror about my impending hearing with no respect for my team's workloads, or how my diatribes were affecting them.

Then, the day before the hearing, I got a call from my lawyers.

"Your application to appear telephonically has been refused," Lily informed me.

"What?" I exclaimed.

"You need to appear in person in court tomorrow in San Francisco. So do we."

"How did Gunnar get his application granted and I didn't?"

"It's not up to us, but we need to get moving. You have to appear."

I hung up the phone and instead of taking a moment, I went straight back into my workroom. The team watched as I explained how I had to appear in person, that Gunnar didn't, that this was unfair, that my lawyers had probably not applied in time, that I was sure this was their fault, that I should probably sue them, that I needed to leave now and pack a bag since I had to fly up tonight. Uli spoke up first and said it was all good and that the team had this, and to go and do what I needed to do.

From the airport taxi, I texted some SF friends of ours, Ludo and Gerard. We arranged to have dinner but by the time I landed in the city where it all went wrong, I was in such a foul mood that I tried to cancel. Ludo insisted though, and ended up having to almost drag me by the hand to the restaurant as I railed against the injustice of having to be there in San Francisco. Once seated, Ludo set the ground rules.

"You are both our friends. We are not going to choose. Any advice I give you, I have given the same to Gunnar. Anything you say goes no further than this table. The same way, we will not tell you anything Gunnar has said to us. So please don't ask."

In the moment, that struck me as the model of good friendship in a tough situation.

But I also took it as a challenge. So I launched into my well-rehearsed victim's speech. I wanted them to hate Gunnar as much as I did.

Ludo instead interrupted with a question: "I don't understand. What are you so worried about?"

He went on to tell me about his ex-partner of twenty years who left him for someone younger, which he shrugged off by saying, "It was a wonderful time but when it's over, it's over."

Dragging out the big guns, I told him about the money and the spousal support.

Again with the shrugs. "I left a small fortune and a house on the table. But," Ludo said, making clapping, slicing motions with his hands, "I washed my hands of it. Seriously, why don't you give him the house and this will all be over?"

Seeing how angry that made me, he calmly took my hand. "You're free already and you can't even see it."

"Free? I'm not free. He has me over the barrel because of these insane laws."

"No, Karl. You are free."

"How? I'll be paying spousal support until I'm fifty!"

"You are not with him anymore. So you are free. The rest is just money. You were free the moment you said, 'I want a divorce.'"

I stopped my protests. Ludo smiled and nodded as he saw it sink in. I'd been thinking my freedom would start when the divorce was signed. Or when I paid my last spousal support check. However, it had already started and I'd been missing it.

"I would rather lose you as a friend than tell you, 'Yes, you're right,' when I know you're wrong," Ludo concluded.

HOW LONG WERE YOU HAPPY FOR?

By dessert, Ludo had really helped me flip my mental state on my current situation. "My parents divorced when I was young," he told me. "They often spoke about how long they had been together. But this metric is not important. How long were you and Gunnar happy for?"

Ludo's question made me think back to the week before, when I'd been getting my hair cut by a new barber. Barbers and hairstylists are all part-time psychologists. There's something about the sudden intimacy between two strangers that means people will offer up their deepest secrets in a salon chair. After hearing of my divorce, the barber told me a story in return.

He and his girlfriend had been together since high school. She was the all-American girl, cheerleader, and homecoming queen. He was the lead guitarist in a rock band that was getting some traction. They moved in together after high school, and he started touring with his band while she went to college to study graphic design.

Then the cracks started showing.

She didn't like him being away on the road so much. And she really didn't like his band's fans—tatted-up, leather-clad female rockers who screamed his name from the front of the crowd. He swore he'd never touched another woman, that he wasn't even into girls like that. But she never believed him and they'd fight about it constantly whether he was home or on the road.

Finally he left the band, learned to cut hair, and settled into a life with her as she graduated and started working in a graphic design studio. Then she became obsessed with moving to Portland. He was surprised by the suddenness and intensity of this desire, but he could cut hair anywhere.

After a couple of months in Portland though, she'd fallen in with a group of women who liked the hard party life. She started coming home later and later, drunker and drunker. She got her first tattoo. He wasn't mad, but shocked that she hadn't told him about it. This continued till finally she was starting to look and behave like the groupies of his old band that she'd hated so much. One day he'd had enough, broke it off, and moved back to LA.

She's now a full-time tattoo artist.

What he realized later, he told me, was that there was someone she wanted to be so badly, but she'd given it up to be with him. And he was a musician who'd become a hairstylist to stay with her. Then he said the thing I'll never forget.

"Every time you don't do something you want to do because of the person you're with, you're lying to them."

By that metric, I'd been lying to Gunnar for years. And probably him to me.

Back at dinner with Ludo and Gerard, I figured out an answer to Ludo's question. "I was really happy with Gunnar for the first six months. I was myself. Then I started changing my shape to fit him. I think he did the same." Gunnar and I had a lot of great times over our eight years together. But there was an undertow that started early and I guess had dragged us both down with it.

As we stood on the street saying our goodbyes, Ludo offered one last piece of great advice: "You're going to be in for some rough times. But always remember one thing—this divorce is happening for you, not to you."

EVERY DOG HAS ITS DAY IN COURT

Shakespeare wrote, "All the world's a stage, and all the men and women merely players." Nowhere does this feel truer than in a courtroom. It's like one big, expensive farce.

I turned up early the next morning at the courthouse in San Francisco and met Lily outside. We joined the line that stretched around the block like it was the hottest club in town that no one wanted to get into. The first major reality check of the day was seeing dozens and dozens of straight people there to get their cases heard; every class, race, religion, and language.

Divorce is the great equalizer. There were probably people in this line who'd voted against gay marriage. At least now we had something in common.

Inside, past security, the walls were covered in pamphlets and posters about how to take care of children during a divorce.

As we waited outside our courtroom, Eva, Gunnar's counsel, arrived. We all shook hands, then I stood to one side as Eva and Lily discussed a settlement. I say discussed, but it looked more like a pantomime, with grand hand gestures, shaking of heads, eye rolls, and no deal.

The part that made me prick up my ears was when Eva talked about the judge.

"In my previous experience of him, our argument sits very well. No deal. I'd rather go in the room."

Then it hit me. This was an away game. We were the visiting team playing on Eva's home court. Literally.

Oh no, I thought. We're toast.

Courtrooms look way better in the movies. Ours was harshly lit with rows of seats where you sit like grocery items waiting to be scanned—meaning you have to witness all the cases being heard before yours. I felt ill. Not just because the anxiety mill was on full grind or because of Eva's home advantage, but now I knew our dirty laundry was going to be on full display to yet more strangers. Whatever hope or dignity I walked in with died on the industrial carpet.

One couple had a kid and she was seeking child support. Both worked minimum wage jobs. They were arguing over $250 a month. I felt like such a dick comparing their situation to mine.

Then it was our turn. We took our seats in front of the judge, Gunnar was patched in, the room did the greetings and ceremonial blah-blahs, then Lily and Eva started their dance. They puffed and objected before the judge, but it all seemed so canned and over-rehearsed. Finally, the judge had heard enough and we arrived at what you could call "the Vegas Moment." Lily had warned me that you can put the exact same facts in front of two judges and get two completely different rulings. I prayed that our judge's sports team hadn't lost a game recently, that he'd gotten laid that morning, that his coffee had been just right.

No dice.

Once the numbers were put through the DissoMaster, I was stuck with the full monthly amount possible. He didn't lower it one cent. I had to pay arrears back to the date of our separation, and the judge took Gunnar's version of that over mine. Plus, I had to pay all of Gunnar's legal bills in arrears and going forward.

"Lily," I said, panicking, "if we're splitting the income fifty-fifty, why do I have to cover his costs too? Do something! Tell the judge!"

But she didn't. She put her hand on my arm to quieten me. The gavel came down with a bang. Case closed. Next.

I left the room in daze. Eva and Lily shook hands like it was some kind of a staged boxing match, a foregone conclusion and we'd just been going through the motions. I hated them both—Lily for not getting at least a fifty-fifty split of our combined net incomes and costs, and Eva because she'd done better than Lily. On the street outside, Lily assured me that it had been a really good outcome.

"How?" I asked. "We lost on literally every point."

"We did get the case moved to LA."

"So now getting completely destroyed in a courtroom will just be a short drive away? How handy."

Not rising to my sarcasm, Lily continued, "Once the first hearing is over, it's like a pressure release. Everyone calms down, and we usually settle pretty soon after. What are you doing with the rest of the day? I'm going to visit some family I have up here."

"Really? Have fun," I said, shaking her hand quickly and walking away. I was acting like an ass, but I didn't care. If they were going to get rubbish results, putting up with my black moods was part of the deal.

On the plane back, I had trouble making sense of what had happened. The result in the courtroom, the dance of the lawyers, our story on display to a room full of strangers, the injustice of the laws. But then I thought of all the other people I'd lined up with, the couple whose case had been before ours, the homeless people everywhere in San Francisco—the sum total made me feel so exhausted, angry, and depressed, yet grateful that my situation wasn't worse. I hit the emotions diary hard when I got back to the house, then hit the whiskey bottle with equal gusto.

STRAIGHT DIVORCED GUYS ARE YOUR NEW BEST FRIENDS

If I had thought being married was like getting into an exclusive club, the brotherhood that I found with straight divorced guys was unlike anything I'd ever experienced. There is literally nothing one divorced man won't do for another guy going through it.

It had started with James. And over the next couple of months, I'd had more and more chats with straight, divorced Lyft drivers, bartenders, guys in queues in the supermarket, men outside music venues. The sense of being part of this invisible but incredibly strong community was a comfort I hadn't seen coming. When a divorced guy hears you say that you're in the middle of yours, they give you a look of understanding and compassion that is the thing your heart has been craving—somebody, please understand what this feels like.

All of them had handed over advice, wisdom, and many also their numbers with an "If you ever need anything," before a bro hug and best wishes.

I have this theory about us as human beings. Yes, we bond through shared joys, triumphs, and love. But it's nothing like how we bond through hardship, tragedy, and disaster. Being divorced has no symbol, no ring, but the experience binds us like survivors of the same shipwreck.

One of the most memorable moments of this phenomenon played out at the divorce bench one morning.

James and I were sitting there chatting when Ash arrived. James introduced us; Ash was in the club. He was keen to hear about divorce from the gay perspective, so I gave him the low down on the hearing.

"Man, your husband is really letting the guy side down," he said, lighting a cigarette.

"I don't follow," I said.

"OK," Ash replied, his gestures leaving smoke trails in his wake. "I'm a guy. I met my ex-wife. We had kids. She gave up her career to raise them. We split. I have to pay for that. There's no question about it. We fight about the number, but there has to be one. Now, your dude. Are there kids?"

"Nope."

"Did he give up a career for you?" Ash continued.

"No. I mean, he was offered a sideways move by his company in the transfer to LA."

"So he's got a job, in his industry, here in town?" Ash concluded. "It's not like he's an actor leaving LA for Delaware for his husband's career?"

"No, nothing like that."

"So why is he acting like a total bitch then? And I don't mean a woman. I mean a bitch. It's 2017, that's a unisex insult now."

"Um, OK. Because he can. The law lets him," I replied.

"But that's the point!" Ash half yelled, jabbing the air with his cigarette. "All you get as a straight guy in a divorce is to act with integrity so you can leave with your head held high. That's it. You're going to get fucked, it just depends how hard. You have to act like a man so that afterward you haven't blown the one thing you get out of it."

James nodded in agreement.

"But your guy," Ash continued, "just took that away. Our one thing. He's just ruined it. Because he's being a fucking little bitch. I've never met him and I already hate him."

I'd never thought about my divorce that way before. I remembered the coworker way back who'd said that my engagement just made his marriage bigger. Seems like we also have the power to make every straight man's divorce smaller too.

YOU NEED TO SHUT THE DIVORCE UP

Gunnar's birthday was the week after the divorce hearing. Seeing it looming on the calendar, I'd decided to take a trip to NYC and hide out. I wanted space in case I had a meltdown. My ad career had allowed me to accrue a lot of flight and hotel points. Which was lucky; I couldn't have afforded it otherwise.

As I packed a bag the night before I left, Uli sat me down on the sofa for a sobering chat. "Karl, you need to stop talking about your fucking divorce."

While I reeled from the verbal slap, he continued.

"You are making the workroom toxic. Your job is to support the people who work for you. Instead, they are having to support you. And no one else can say anything, because you're their boss."

I knew he was right. Everyone in that room had been caught in the crossfire of my poisonous ramblings, shifting moods, and lack of focus. A few days before the hearing, I'd cried in front of a few colleagues over my inability to keep our volatile account on track.

Grateful for his honesty and full of shame, I landed in New York to find gray skies and rain. It was perfect. Walking the streets, I replayed the last three months from the trip to SF when I delivered the news all the way through to the disastrous hearing. There was so much I wish I could have changed. But the fresh scenery gave me some much needed quiet and thinking time.

Cutting myself a break for how I'd behaved up to then, I reframed my divorce and counted my tools.

Ludo was right about many things, including this divorce happening for me, not to me. It was basically Myriam's Law in different words. So, no more victim stuff.

Understanding now how unpredictable everything could be, I would adapt as fast as I could. But the head is faster than the heart. It would be OK to know something to be true even if I couldn't feel it yet. With the emotions diary, I could delve into the important work, which was what was going on inside me.

But I had some bridges to repair.

DO A FOURTH STEP. THEN A FIFTH. THEN REMEMBER YOUR GOLDEN MOMENT.

Walking the streets in NYC, I passed a church with the Alcoholics Anonymous symbol in one of its windows. It's almost impossible to live in Los Angeles and not know people in AA. In my group of extended friends, a few were in recovery and vocal about it. So I'd heard about the 12 Steps program, but had no idea what the actual steps were. Taking it as a sign, I googled it and was immediately drawn to steps 4 and 5.

Step 4 involved doing a searching moral inventory. Step 5 was about admitting the exact nature of your wrongs and making amends. I spent the time in NYC working on these two steps, making lists of every grievance I had committed in the last three months, and the people I needed to apologize to and set things right with.

But the list kept going. I started noting incidents that had happened over the last few years in my life. It felt good to get my mental house in order.

The next day was Gunnar's birthday. When I woke up, I lay in the hotel bed a long time looking at the ceiling. My birthday had been tough. His was worse. This was the day I'd always celebrated the best about him.

I wanted to hate him.

Instead, I missed him.

I missed his hugs. I missed his kiss. I missed his smell. I missed walking down the street and holding his hand. I missed how he made me laugh. I missed having someone by my side who understood me more than anyone else on Earth. I missed holding him when he'd had a bad day.

I wondered what he was doing—if he was with someone new, if he thought of me that day, if he hated me or if he missed me too. Then I remembered that friend's wedding where we'd headed hand-in-hand to the dance floor. So I got up, opened the curtains and flooded the room with gray light from the overcast day. Whatever else was going to happen, we had been those two people that day at our friends' wedding. And on the days where I wanted to kill him, I'd hold on to this one golden moment instead.

So I decided to celebrate us on his birthday. I bought a slice of my favorite cake, said thank you for the good times we'd had together, and toasted the new life I was making without him. After all, I was already free.

To great memories and new beginnings. And even if the memories had been shot to pieces by what we'd done to each other, without Gunnar there wouldn't have been this new beginning.

On my first day back at work in LA, I took everyone to one side individually and apologized for how I'd behaved, how I'd let them down, and told them that I'd never speak of my divorce at work again. People reacted coolly but were happy I was owning it. I would have to earn everyone's trust back again. After that, I spoke about the divorce at work only if asked, with tweet-sized responses.

At the same time, I tracked down everyone else on my list and called them up to apologize for the times I felt I'd done them wrong. Most were surprised. Their memory of the incident was totally different, to the point where it actually wasn't even an incident. But everyone appreciated the gesture to make something right.

It was progress. Those first three months had been awful. But I felt like I was finally using this divorce not to excuse my bad behavior, but to behave better. To become the human I wanted to be.

Little did I know, I still had much farther to fall.

CHAPTER 7

"For you, not against him. This is how you must make all your decisions."

— LUDO

NOVEMBER 2017

VEGAN SPECIAL AND A BROKEN LEG

THE UPTICK IN MOOD AT the end of October fell like a crashing stock market on November 1st. I organized the first spousal support payment to Gunnar, the first arrears installment, and a check to his lawyers for all his legal costs to date. Two thirds of my savings went out of my bank account in a couple of clicks. James had warned me that writing these first checks would be a sucker punch.

My finances had already been depleted by the move, my lawyers, and the overlap of rent on our San Francisco place, the serviced apartment, and now the mortgages.

Then Lily called to tell me they'd need another retainer. Why not? I thought. Everyone else is getting paid. In one more click, I was in debt.

It was a Friday and I thought all day about how drunk I was going to get that night. Propping up the bar at the Eagle on my own, I had stopped counting my drinks when a young twink guy made a direct line to the stool on my left.

"Are you the one getting a divorce?" he asked.

"Uh, yes," I replied, feeling that my drunken privacy had been violated by this sudden ambush.

"Seriously? Well, thanks for that."

"You're welcome." I have never called another gay man the F-word, but I was very close.

This nasty little queen cast his eye over my line of empty shot glasses, passed judgment with a raised eyebrow, and got up and left as fast as he'd arrived. I looked around the bar. Wait, I thought. Is this what they're all thinking?

The gay scene in any big city is like a small-town sewing circle. Everyone knows everyone else's business. I hate to talk down about my people, but queens love to dish the gossip—an early-days gay divorce was a juicy piece to throw around, I'm sure.

Drunk and paranoid, I slapped some bills on the liquor-stained bar and headed for the door. On the way out, a guy propositioned me and I ended up crawling back into my own bed a couple of hours before dawn. I felt cheap, drunk, and ashamed. Uli had headed back to San Francisco and I was alone in the house again. At least there was no one to witness me at my worst.

The tsunami dream returned. Only this time there were no chains holding me on the beach. I just sat down on the sand, waiting for the wave to come. There was nowhere to run to anyway.

When I came to that morning, I decided to give Gunnar the house.

I had no fight left.

I lose, Gunnar wins.

The end.

Maybe a week before, I'd been to the hardware store to buy some paint for a wall in the house. Just to try and make it feel different. While I was there, I bought a can of red spray paint as well. I didn't know why. Just seemed like a good idea. Then, that blurry morning, I found myself in the living room listening to the metal bead clank inside the spray can as I shook it back and forth.

"You stole this house from someone whose only crime was to love you." That's what I was blocking out on the wall in my head, wondering whether to add, "You lying piece of shit," on the end. No, I thought, brevity is better. I approached the wall, can in hand when my phone rang.

"Hello?" I said thickly.

"Hey, man. Wondering what you're up to. Want to get some brunch?" my friend Daniel asked, upbeat.

I looked at the can.

"I'm buying..." Daniel added into the silence.

"OK, yeah. Thanks," I replied. I could deface the house later, I thought.

"Sunset Junction Coffee Shop?" he asked.

That was the place Gunnar and I had eaten at every Saturday morning. It was the place we'd been sitting when we saw the house for sale on an app.

"How about Millie's?" I offered.

"Done. See you in thirty."

Daniel was in fine form when I arrived. With wiry, spiky black hair and tattooed all the way to his knuckles, Daniel's favorite word is "Fuck." He once told me it's the only word in the English language that is a noun, verb, adverb, pronoun, adjective, and pretty much anything else. I was happy to see Daniel's crooked-toothed smiling face. But the smile faded fast when I told him about giving the house away.

"Don't fucking do it."

"Daniel, I'm over it. I just want out."

"Listen, buddy. By the smell of you, you're in no fucking shape to be making life decisions," he said as my face went red, and I realized that I probably reeked like a brewery. "I hope you Ubered here."

"Lyft. I think they treat their drivers better."

"Fuck Lyft, fuck Uber, and fuck you for thinking about that this morning!" Daniel said, thumping the table. "Your fucking ex-husband is trying to steal your shit. Wake the fuck up!"

Trying to angle my breath away from him, I explained how I was legally over a barrel and that this may just be cheaper in the long run.

"For starters, you need better fucking lawyers," Daniel began, "and you also have no idea how this is going to end. Let's say you give him the house, it's all signed over, then he gets hit by a bus and dies. Which I wouldn't be fucking mad about. Now what? His family gets your house? Fuck that shit."

"I know. I just… I don't know…" I trailed off.

Daniel looked at me for a moment then leaned in, dropping his voice. "Does someone just need to have a talk with Gunnar?"

"We've done all the talking we can do. He's made his intentions clear. The lawyers—"

"No," Daniel said, cutting me off. "Does someone need to pay him a visit? Explain to him how things need to go?" He stared at me, waiting.

"Dude," I said, sobering up. "Are you…?"

"Not me. Someone."

The offer hung in the air.

Daniel had told me a little bit about how he'd grown up. It was in a bad part of a bad city north of LA, where you had to do bad things to get by. *Sons of Anarchy* country. Several people had said words to the effect that if they ever ran into Gunnar again… That kind of thing. But this wasn't that.

Daniel waited. I knew what I should say, but I didn't want to.

"Scrambled eggs, side of bacon?"

I jolted round to see our waiter, and he jumped in response.

"Jesus! And the vegan special," he said, setting down our meals. Looking at me, he added, "And no more coffee for you."

Daniel was still waiting.

"Thank you. But I don't think that's what I want to do," I said.

Daniel shrugged. "OK. Let me know if you change your mind. Pass the salt."

FOR YOU, NOT AGAINST HIM

I'd love to say that I never thought about Daniel's offer ever again. But I did. For a few days. Like Gollum stroking the ring and whispering, "My precious," I would wake up in the morning and think about what might happen to Gunnar if I pressed the button. I loved the feeling of power it gave me when I felt so powerless. At the same time though, I was more horrified by the thrill I got playing with this dark toy than anything Gunnar had done up to that point.

In those shadowy few days, I watched my humanity break away and sink beneath the waves.

It was a check-in call from Ludo that brought me to my senses. Without telling him what it was, I admitted that I'd been debating doing something really dumb. I think he could hear a strange tone in my voice.

"What I am going to give you is the same piece of advice that I gave Gunnar. *For you, not against him.* This is how you must make all your decisions. Do you understand what I mean?"

"I think so."

"I told him and now I'm telling you—if you do something to try and hurt him, you will only hurt yourself."

Ludo had no idea how right he was. In that moment, I said goodbye to Daniel's offer forever.

I went on to tell Ludo about how I'd had this grand plan to use the divorce as my crisis of identity, but that it wasn't going very well. In fact, I'd only succeeded in hitting a personal rock bottom.

"It doesn't matter. You're in the right mindset," Ludo replied. "Remember what I told you, that this divorce is happening for you, not to you? So your decisions must be for you, not against him."

I called Lily and told her to just take Gunnar to court and get this over and done with.

That night, I crunched the numbers three times, but couldn't find a way to make a buyout of the house work. My AA friends had told me there is a point when you hit rock bottom, where you just have to take your hands off the wheel.

So I sent Gunnar an email telling him I thought we should sell the place. I pressed send and it was like the entire weight of this concrete, three-story block lifted off my shoulders. He wrote back almost straight away in agreement.

And I had my best night's sleep in weeks.

I DON'T CARE WHAT HAPPENS TO ME

In the ad world, they often say that you need to be out by the time you're fifty or running a global network. I was damn close to the first and nowhere near the second. Before the LA job had come up, I'd applied for a lot of positions in San Francisco to be a Creative Director at start-ups and apps. I was told flat out that I was too old. This was coded as, "We're looking for a digital native," meaning that because I hadn't been born with a phone in my hand, I couldn't know the digital world well enough.

Facing down the idea that I would be working in ad jobs till I was fifty to service an alimony that would ruin me financially, only to be free of it as I reached my career obsolescence, kept me up at night. It was like the second wave in the tsunami dream.

I looked back over my life at moments where I could have made decisions that would have had me set up financially and career-wise, if I'd just followed my instinct at the time. The conversations in the car became ones that I was having with myself. The bags I hit at the kickboxing gym were my own past stupidities. Gunnar faded into the background as I got stuck into the man that had let him in in the first place.

Around this time, I started to get very worried about my mental health. I noticed I was saying strange things in meetings at work. Having outbursts that were borderline reportable. I wanted to have fights with everyone about everything. The downside of the kickboxing was that I now assessed people based on whether I thought I could take them out in a fight.

Plus, the out-of-body moments were increasing.

One night in November, Uli and I went to a concert. It was one of our favorite bands and I'd wanted to see them live for years. So, of course, there was a young woman sitting behind us who would not stop talking.

Not. Stop. Talking.

She was Cali Valley in full effect, speaking every half thought loudly over the music so her male companion could hear. Uli and I had asked her to stop talking and she'd just waved us off. This kind of spectacular disregard for other people makes my blood boil on the best of days. In my current state of mind, I was struggling for self-control.

Then the band started playing my favorite song. We hadn't even gotten to the chorus when she piped up again. The next thing I knew, I was out of my seat, facing her and unloading in full force.

"What the hell is wrong with you?!" I screamed. "No one came here to listen to you talk on and on about absolute bullshit! Just! Shut! Up!"

"Go find another seat," she yelled back. "I've got just as much right to enjoy this concert however I want."

Gesturing to everyone seated around us, I yelled, "Everyone came here to have a good time and you are ruining it for all of us. *You* go find somewhere else!"

Uli had joined in now as well. Her male companion was trying to play it all down. But then everyone around her started yelling at her too. She finally got up in a huff, dragging her guy with her. Our small group, with its newly found quiet center, high-fived each other then turned back to enjoy the rest of the night.

But as the concert went on, I wondered who I was turning into. There were a dozen ways I could have handled that better. What if her guy had wanted to have a fight? Would Uli have got pulled into that as well? And she'd behaved horribly, but did she deserve that? Had it opened an old wound? I cared about these things.

On the way home, I thought about her guy. What if he'd really laid into me outside the venue afterward? What if I'd lost teeth or an eye?

Then I realized that I didn't care about that at all.

That scared me.

I stood back from that feeling, not wanting to believe it was there. I'd swapped the idea of harming Gunnar for harming myself instead.

DO I STILL HAVE A PULSE?

John, are you there?

Hi Fella, John texted back. *How are you doing?*

Not very well. I think I'm losing it. I don't care what happens to me. I'm scared.

OK. Well, this is how it feels to be Karl today.

But it's every day. It's the same, it just gets worse, I lamented.

Do you have any up moments at all? John texted.

Not really. I used to. But not now.

I watched three dots pulse on my phone screen as John formed his thought.

Let me guess. Every day starts out bad, gets worse at work, you rise again at kickboxing, it finishes at home with the cat on a high, and then you lie awake overthinking everything till you fall asleep.

Yes, exactly, I texted back.

And sometimes, do you have a couple of better days in a row, think you're improving, then for no reason you wake up and feel like a train smash all over again?

Yes. I texted back, sitting up. *How did you know?*

You know what that sounds like?

What? I asked.

A pulse. If the line was flat, you'd be dead. Your pulse might be weak, but it's still there. I'm not worried about you. Get some sleep, and go hard tomorrow.

That's when a furry paw knocked the phone out of my hands.

MY GIRLFRIEND FRANCINE

Way back in 2009 when I met Gunnar, he came with a zoo. Two dogs, which I was thrilled about, and a cat. Not so thrilled. I didn't love cats, I didn't hate cats. I just didn't have any strong feelings about them. Francine, or Frannie as we mostly called her, was a bossy, calico little thing. And she worked some kind of black magic on me, because after a month I'd become completely obsessed with her.

During the divorce, Frannie had come to stay with me at the house. With my work schedule, I couldn't be home to walk the dogs. Gunnar had regular full-time hours, so they stayed with him. But Francine and I would talk up a storm the minute I walked in the house, anytime day or night.

The ritual would go like this: she'd hear me come in through the garage door and we'd meet on the middle level of the house. She'd yell at me for being gone all day. Then I'd have to chase her up and down the stairs till she'd finally hide under the bed. Then her paw would swipe out at the duvet cover that I'd make ripple with my hand. When she got tired of this, I'd head downstairs and make dinner. She'd jump up on the kitchen counter and start telling me all about her day.

She'd snuggle up next to me on the couch as I watched TV and then, in bed, the real festivities would begin. Frannie would sit on my chest, knock the book or phone out of my hand, then I would have to hold up both thumbs so she could lick them. My job then was to clean her face, and I could not do this hard enough. She liked it when her eyeballs bulged. Once she was satisfied, Frannie would pat my hand away. Then she'd paw through my beard, straightening out the hair. Bedding down on my chest and sticking her head under my chin, I'd put my hands over her body and we'd go to sleep. Every night.

Days would go by where Frannie was the only other living being that I touched. I had support from many people who were only a phone call away. But to drive home knowing she was waiting for me made everything OK.

LET THE REAL DIVORCE BEGIN

Everything else before now in the divorce had just been paperwork and chess.

What I'd learned through the emotions diary and encouragement from the voice was to sit still. And after Daniel's offer and the concert fight, I realized my biggest problems now were inside me. So that's where I had to go.

It seemed like I'd felt more emotions in the last year than I'd felt in the rest of my life put together. I didn't understand how all these enormous monsters could exist inside of me. By the end of every day, they'd worn me out in a way I'd never experienced. My bones were tired.

Months earlier, I'd been hatching an ill-thought-through scheme to go home and become a Buddhist monk in the Wollongong temple. That hadn't come out of nowhere. In the early 2000s, when I'd lived in Tokyo, I'd discovered Buddhism and devoutly read up on it. I'd prayed every day and gone to the temple every week to make offerings.

As a gay man brought up to be spiritually curious but not religious, Buddhism made sense to me. It had no firm stance on homosexuality and, I felt, was a kinder way to connect to a power higher than myself.

However, in the years after I'd left Japan, Buddhism's presence in my life had waned. I'd become a Sunday Buddhist at best. And in the last couple of years, the prayer beads had gathered a lot of dust.

Now that I wasn't looking at Buddhism as an escape plan, it seemed like a good place to restart and a good time to try and pick up where I'd left off.

Two people were very helpful at this early stage of the emotional work I embarked on.

The first is a Buddhist monk called Thich Nhat Hanh. He's written many books and toured the globe, speaking to tens of thousands of people. In his book *The Miracle of Mindfulness: The Classic Guide To Meditation*[8], Thich Nhat Hanh writes, "When a feeling or thought arises... The intention isn't to chase it away, hate it, worry about it, or be frightened by it. So what exactly should you be doing concerning such thoughts and feelings? Simply acknowledge their presence."

Then I wondered, if volatile emotions were going to continue being guests who turned up at my home unannounced for the foreseeable future, what if I invited them in? Made them tea? Basically got to know them?

The second helpful person is a man called Andy Puddicombe, another Buddhist monk, who started a very popular meditation app called Headspace. He has a beautiful analogy in one of his meditations[9]. Andy talks about the mind being the sky, and thoughts, feelings, and experiences being clouds. When storm clouds appear, it can feel like a hurricane is coming. What he points out is that the sky never changes. It's always the same. The clouds pass and then the sky is there again, unchanged.

My emotions weren't me. They were just something I was feeling at that moment. And soon wouldn't be. The cloud analogy helped a lot because it gave things a speed that I could understand. Clouds might move slowly, but they move.

Gradually I learned how to step back from my emotions and observe them. I'd still feel them. But instead of being a victim of them, I became a student. And by paying attention to them, they hurt less. I started to understand how I was wired inside.

When an emotion took over, I could step back, take a breath, and say, "OK, I'm feeling *this*, which is making me think I should do *that* to compensate. But I know after I do that, I'll feel worse. So, I'm going to sit with this feeling because it'll pass at cloud speed." Then a couple of moments later, it would have. It would come back again. In an hour, a week, or even a year.

However, instead of finding myself balls-deep in some bar or sex club, pulling out my almost maxed-out credit card in some designer store, or looking at two empty pints of Ben and Jerry's in front of me at 2 a.m., I'd catch myself before any of this happened. I'd say, "Karl, you know why you're about to do this." And then I wouldn't. Instead, I'd learn something new about the emotion each time I sat with it on the couch and made it a coffee.

When I got my first tiny taste of that skillful sense of self-mastery, it felt like an *X-Men* superpower.

This growing understanding of myself *was* the light at the end of the tunnel. This was my divorce. This was what I'd set out to discover when I'd decided to use it as my crisis of identity.

Not surprisingly, I started thinking a lot about explorers again. If ever there was a great unknown to head into, this was it.

Me.

But now, I wasn't afraid of the journey. I'd lost sight of land. There was nothing in front of me but dark, churning seas, but there was nothing left to do but sail through them—one eye looking inward, the other on the horizon.

ROAD TRIPS AND REGRET

I woke up with my nose stuck to the pillow. Feeling it crack off the pillowcase as I rolled my head, the adrenaline hit my brain and I was in the bathroom fast.

Once I'd realized that it had just been another nosebleed, I washed my face and nostrils. I hadn't had one in my sleep before. I took a good look in the mirror as I toweled off my face. I did not look well. I'd been getting nose bleeds for a few weeks. My gums, which had always been a little sensitive, hurt all the time and often bled too. Ulcers on the inside of my mouth stung when I ate or drank, and I'd been wondering if my breath smelled like blood. My hair was definitely falling out. I could see how it had thinned. My hairdresser had even commented on it. Migraines and insomnia were a part of most days. Under my eyes looked pretty dark too, but I'd forgotten what I'd looked like before.

Since I wasn't going to die that morning, I got ready to go to the airport.

My brother Tony had a convention to go to in the States, so he and I had hatched a plan to go on a road trip for the week before it started. In all the times that I'd threatened to jump behind a wheel and see America, I never had. And Tony and I, in our late forties, had never had this much time together in one chunk, just the two of us.

Despite how close we were in age, Tony and I couldn't have been more opposite. We had completely different interests growing up and vastly different skills. He knows how old he is for starters. Tony is also mechanically gifted in so many ways I envy, has a voracious appetite for news and current affairs, and—I suspect—is a lot smarter than me. Or maybe it's just the little brother syndrome. Older brothers always seem so impressive.

Physically there's almost no family resemblance. Tony is my height, barrel-chested, strong as an ox, thick set, with sparkly eyes. When we'd tell people we were brothers, you could see their eyes flick between the two of us, trying to figure out the story. "Yes," we'd say at their unasked question, "same parents." And he and I would laugh.

Then I got the travel bug. Leaving to work overseas at twenty-five, my only regret was that Tony and I were just starting to get to know each other well. Intensely different as teenagers, as young men we were just discovering how much we liked each other's company. I thought I'd be gone five years, ten at the most. Then somehow more than twenty had gone by. Tony arrived at LAX, we bear-hugged, grabbed his bags, and hit the road. Hearing his voice with his thick Australian accent was such a welcome taste of home for my ears—and a contrast to the American visuals of fast-food chains, strip malls, and nut farms that zoomed past the window as we cruised two hours straight north on the 99 to our American aunt and Australian uncle's place. It was going to be a rare gathering of the clans in Bakersfield.

On the way, we caught up on family stuff: Mum and Dad, his wife and kids. Two hours later at our aunt and uncle's, we cracked beers, sat around the lounge, and got talking more about the Dunns and where we'd all come from. My aunt is big into genealogy and had been piecing together the history of our family for nearly two decades.

My dad and uncle's side had left Lebanon in the early 1900s in search of a better life and met up with the Scottish side of the family in Australia. It's one thing to know theoretically that your ancestors came from a land you've never seen. It's another thing to see a family tree with all their names and pictures. To know they were once truly alive, filled with hopes and dreams, and crossing what a hundred years ago were incredible distances one-way in search of a better life.

Somehow, looking at this chart of names and history gave me an unexpected feeling of comfort, like I came from a family of explorers. People who'd put everything on the line to see what was out there for them, their children, their grandchildren, and finally me, Tony, and our two cousins. Looking at the ancient photos of my departed family in their best clothes, I felt like I knew them, at least in spirit.

Apparently, we used to be Barrakats. And Donas. Then somewhere along the way, it was anglicized to Dunn. And now there's a dozen Dunns in this world with an Irish name given to them by their Lebanese ancestors—which maybe just shows that no one can tell you who you really are except you.

The next morning, Tony and I took off on Route 66 (no, really, the actual Route 66) and started heading east. The basic plan was to meander across the country and end up in Nashville, where I'd fly back to LA and he'd go north to Indianapolis. Along the way there were waffle shacks, swim holes, small towns, two incidents with the cops over speeding (both me), a helicopter ride over the Grand Canyon, burger joints, diners, motels, and lots and lots of wide-open spaces. The days went by listening to podcasts and staring out over fields of grass with wind farms.

And we talked. About everything.

Most of what came from my side was regret. Things that I didn't do, and things I should have done/said/bought/stuck with/invested in. Not to mention when I should have left Gunnar.

These thoughts had spent a lot of time in my head but hearing them all come out over one long stretch made me realize just how many I had. I was a walking pile of regret.

Tony had an interesting perspective on it all.

"You know regret is totally made up, right? It's bullshit," he said.

"Feels pretty real, mate," I said, staring back at the cows in the fields.

"Yeah, but that's because it's all based on a fantasy, that if you'd only done this other thing back then, today your life would be infinitely better."

"It would have been," I said, turning my head back toward him.

"Karl, you have absolutely no clue if that's true. None! That's what I mean by regret being made-up bullshit."

He went on to explain that I could have made a fortune on the stock market if I'd just bought that stock back then, sure, but imagine the kinds of friendships I would have made. All born from comfort and not adversity. Or I could have stuck with screenwriting and been a forty-seven-year-old washed-up writer who'd never got anything made.

I nodded. I was catching on.

"Maybe you would have been hit by a car on that holiday you never went on. Put all your money into an industry that crashed, or left Gunnar earlier only to do exactly what you did with him with some other big, hairy dude with a beard."

"You're right, mate. I definitely would have."

"Like it or not, Karl," Tony said, slapping his hand on my leg, "you're exactly where you're supposed to be."

That night, I couldn't sleep. Tossing and turning in my bed over what Tony had said in the car, I gave up and walked around this one-road town we'd stopped in, lit by three streetlights—

only two with bulbs that worked. Dust blew in from the desert and danced through the beams. It was then that I came across a piece of graffiti, spray-painted on the side of a small building. For a moment, I thought I was imagining things.

It said: *You're exactly where you need to be.*

I burst out laughing.

"OK, universe," I said out loud, "I get it. But you did make a typo. This says 'need' and Tony said 'supposed'."

Then I realized. It wasn't a typo. I was *supposed* to be here, because I *needed* to be.

Whatever direction my life could have gone in, I would have found some way to meet the wrong guy, screw it up, and lose it all. Again. Because that's who I had been. Every serious relationship I'd had since leaving Australia ended with me financially and emotionally broke.

Somewhere, in the middle of America, I felt better. I was right where I was supposed to, and needed, to be. With a divorce happening for me, not to me.

Fuck regret. I'd wasted enough time on that too.

The trip finished up in Nashville where my great mate Buddy hosted me and Tony in his lovely home. Buddy took us out on the town for some honky-tonking—which basically means doing the strip in downtown Nashville—drinking, and watching an array of super-talented local acts play. It was a great way to finish the trip, laughing and joking with my brother and an old friend on a mild autumn night under the stars on a rooftop in the American South.

I took my favorite photo I have of my brother that night, smiling that big boyish smile of his, laughing at a joke Buddy had made.

Next morning, Tony dropped me off at the airport and we hugged a long time at the gate.

"Thanks for everything, Tony," I said, a little wet-eyed.

"No worries, mate. You're gonna be fine."

He headed north and I headed home. It was December 1st, and while I sat in the airport waiting for my flight I transferred half my wages to Gunnar, paid his latest lawyer bill, took care of all the community bills for our stuff, and paid my car lease and cell phone bills. I looked at what was left and wondered how I was going to make it to New Year's.

CHAPTER 8

"Gunnar was dead to me. There was someone else living there now."

— Karl

DECEMBER 2017

WHY KEVIN DIED

The road trip was supposed to be a turning point. I'd told myself that this was where things would start to pick up again. But December was another rollercoaster month—where I had no idea who was driving it, and I couldn't see the tracks. Every twist, drop, and hard turn came faster than I could process.

The moment I was back in the house post road trip with no one else around, I hit my old habits hard.

And I couldn't stop thinking about Kevin.

Kevin was a guy I'd dated way back when I was nineteen and still in university. He was twice my age and I thought he was God's gift. Kevin was handsome, funny, had a great job, wonderful friends, and a beautiful little apartment on the east side of Sydney that I moved into. But Kevin had demons. There were days where he was lost in thought, in some dark place. Being nineteen, I thought that I could just pull him out of it by hugging him, having sex, making him laugh, cooking for him, showing him what a good life he had.

After a year I couldn't take the darkness anymore, so I left him.

Six years later, he killed himself.

I was so angry with Kevin that I didn't go to the funeral. I was living overseas and thought, "I'm not flying home to commemorate this event." As far as I was concerned, it was the most selfish thing he could have done. After I received the news that Kevin had gassed himself in his car, after I'd cried for a couple of days, I promised myself that I would never shed another tear for him. You can't handle life, Kevin? Then fine. Good riddance.

But I did cry about him again. It just took over twenty years.

As I lay in bed the day after I got home from the road trip, I thought about all the judicial systems that had allowed Gunnar to legally create this situation. As my lawyers kept confirming, there was little I could do. But there was something I could do. That spot on the 405 Freeway with the roadworks over the bridge. I could go late at night when no one was around.

This thought was my new dark plaything, like a kid hiding in the garden shed and lighting matches.

But that morning, laying there in bed, I remembered Kevin. Everything about him. The shape of his body, his smell, his laugh, that Roman nose. And I felt a kinship with him.

Because now I finally understood why he killed himself. He was exhausted, and he just wanted it over. Taking his life was the one thing that was one hundred percent within his control.

I'd been angry with Kevin for over two decades because I thought that he'd taken the coward's way out. Now I realized that he'd taken the only option he thought he had left. There was one big difference between me and Kevin though. I had told people I was having these thoughts. And they had told me they were to be my first call.

In a text exchange, John Hare had even said that he knew I wasn't going to do it, because I'd told him about it. Most people I've heard about who actually kill themselves never tell a soul. Mum and Dad had said that everyone at Kevin's funeral couldn't believe that he hadn't phoned any of them. The ones who'd had a hunch that something was going very wrong with him were racked with guilt that they hadn't asked.

I hugged the pillows, pretended they were Kevin, and said sorry to him for all of it.

BYE FRANNIE, IT'S BEEN AN HONOR

Brian had been able to house-sit Frannie when I was on the road trip with my brother. December was another story. I was going to be away for most of it on shoots. Try as I might, I couldn't come up with a combination of people to be in the house while I was away. December is the month when LA starts emptying out and everyone goes home for the holidays.

So I had to do the one thing I didn't want to do. I texted Gunnar and asked him to come and pick her up. He would come that night. It was a Sunday. I spent the day with Frannie hanging out. I went for a nap so we could do our bedroom routine one last time. As she settled her head under my chin, I felt two tiny jets of breath from those impossibly small nostrils. The doorbell rang too fast.

I buzzed Gunnar in. We hadn't seen each other since he'd come to pick up furniture. He looked out of place, like an actor visiting the theatre when his play wasn't on. He was thinner. We didn't hug or shake hands. I didn't want to touch him or be touched by him. But I made tea and we sat at the table.

"So have you had a look at the latest offer?" I asked.

"Yes," Gunnar replied.

"And?"

"My lawyer's asked me not to discuss the case with you."

Then it just came tumbling out of my mouth. "You're not going to stop until there's nothing left of me, are you?"

Gunnar stared back at me. A dreadful silence stretched out. Then something broke.

I started crying. And I couldn't stop. It just poured out in wails, like a dam wall that cracks and then explodes.

"Your nose," Gunnar said in horror, pushing himself away from the table.

I wiped my nostrils with the back of my hand, and it came away covered in blood. Then I started yelling at him. About the bleeding nose and gums, the migraines, the insomnia, my hair falling out. That my job was killing me, and he'd made it so that I couldn't resign. When he tried to turn away, I demanded that he look at me, to look at what he'd done. Then I begged. I begged him to stop with the lawyers. I begged him to remember we'd loved each other once.

Then I sat down in the middle of the kitchen and looked at the ground, blood dripping off my nose onto the floor.

Gunnar was sweating now. I could see the stains coming through his clothes. He feverishly started looking for Frannie. I got up, found her, and put her in the carry box he'd brought.

He announced he was leaving, and I followed him outside and watched him put Frannie in the back seat. She was mewling hard. Then suddenly, I couldn't breathe. I gulped for air, ragged and heavy. Gunnar, half in the car, asked me if I wanted him to call anyone. I waved him away. Released, he took off fast. I knew that was the last time I'd ever see Frannie. She was his again. The last huge chunk of what we'd had sheared away and went underwater.

I walked back into the great echoing house that had never felt so empty.

Her food bowls were still in the kitchen.

I was hyperventilating.

The car keys were on the counter.

I thought about the 405. It was the dead of night on a Sunday. I could be there in twenty minutes.

I picked up my keys, closed my eyes, and thought I could feel Kevin's arm around me for a moment.

Then I opened my eyes.

No.

"You have to keep going. You have to keep going. You have to keep going," I said to myself, mantra-like. I repeated it maybe a hundred times as I paced the house, my breathing returning to normal. Even when you don't know why you're alive anymore, you have to keep going.

I went upstairs, packed a suitcase, had a shower, and headed to the airport for my early morning flight. Asleep before takeoff, I was awoken by the flight attendant just before landing in Japan. It felt like I was coming out of a really bad dream. If I ever got that low again, I promised myself that I would get help. I was OK once. I wouldn't let there be a second time.

Looking back, I wish I'd handled this entire episode very differently. I wish I'd gone to a therapist and gotten time off work. I wish I'd taken some short-term medication. I didn't do either of these things because I'm stubborn as hell and terrible at accepting help.

I learned a lot from standing on the edge and looking into the abyss. But I wish now that I'd been kinder to myself.

FREEDOM ISN'T FREE

On the shoot, I felt alive again. Casting, wardrobe, locations, tech run-throughs, dealing with the clients, and making sure everything was moving on course, on time, and on budget. I always feel in my element on set, all creative and practical parts of my brain firing.

That night in LA, when I came as close as I ever had to killing myself, felt now like the worst mistake I could have made. I doubled down on my promise to keep an eye on that specter.

Suddenly I was aware of every small detail of this day I might not have seen.

Every mass-ordered bento-box meal we ate on locations I would stare at, marveling at the colors, the tiny marinated fish, the umami flavors, the wooden grain of the disposable bamboo chopsticks. A sunlit wall pasted with dayglow posters covered in Japanese writing, peeling at the corners. That electric sweet smell of a streetside vending machine. Everything looked brighter, smelled better, tasted incredible. What the hell did I almost do to myself?

At night, I'd walk the city—a rare treat when you live a car-bound existence in LA. This particular night, Roland, the design director, joined me for a stroll. He'd had a front row seat for my first three months of meltdown at the office. But I liked how our relationship had changed since I'd taken step 4 and 5 of my self-imposed program.

"What are your plans when the divorce is over?" Roland asked.

"A friend told me I was free as soon as I'd asked for the divorce. That the rest is just money. My head gets that, but my heart is still catching up to that idea."

"You going to stay at the agency?"

"If we keep the account."

We shared a look. We both felt the tide coming in on that one.

"We'll see, right?" I said. "But with Frannie gone, I don't really have any obligations in LA anymore."

"So, you're free to do whatever?"

"Yeah," I said heavily.

"You're not happy about that?" he asked.

"Here's the thing. I always thought that freedom was some green field with unicorns, bunnies, and permanent sunshine. But actually it's this gaping, black hole that you have to fill."

"That's a good thing though, right?"

"Sort of. Yes. But I can't blame anyone anymore. Whatever I do with it is my responsibility. And it's sad to say, but I'm not used to flexing that muscle."

"Well, since we're in Japan, let's go to the 7-Eleven and fill that black hole with some cool Japanese shit."

We walked back to the hotel with bags of crazy-flavored snacks tucked under our arms, along with magazines we couldn't read.

EXPECTATIONS WILL KILL YOU

On the crew bus to the final director meeting before the shoot, my email pinged. It was Lily. The voice told me not to open it. The chorus clicked on it. Timing be damned—I wanted to know what I was in for.

Lily's message said only, "Call me." I waited as the PDF downloaded, then clicked Gunnar's lawyer's letter open. The final offer was the full legal amount of spousal support. No more negotiations. Even after that night at the house where the blood came out of my nose, I thought. Even after I'd begged.

I was surprised to find that I wasn't surprised at all.

The crew bus pulled up to the hotel lobby. I pulled Roland to one side to tell him I needed thirty minutes. That it was "divorce stuff." It was our shorthand now, no questions asked. He gathered the group up while I walked off to a quiet corner of the manicured hotel garden and sat under a tree. Checking to see I was alone, I started to sob, letting out a sound that was something animal. The birds flew away from the branches above me.

It wasn't the money anymore; I'd resigned myself to being broke now. It was that I'd hoped, right up till this point, that Gunnar would come around. That he'd stop pushing his advantage and remember that we loved each other once. That he'd be fair.

But he didn't. Because he didn't have to. This was the moment that our marriage, friendship, history, and future were truly over.

Gunnar was dead to me. Someone else was living there now.

I rang Lily, and as she talked through next steps and going to trial, the alchemy inside me shifted. I felt so calm, like a stone in a river that the water flows around.

"It's OK, Lily. We were always going to end up here. I see that now. Actually, I've always known it, I just didn't want to admit it. So any expectation I had that he'd do something different was a fantasy. It's not your fault. I have to go. Get the trial going."

"OK," she replied, perplexed by my Zen state.

I hung up and looked around at the garden, laughing quietly to myself. I don't think I would have done the same thing in his shoes. But who knows? If this divorce had shown me anything, it's that neither Gunnar nor I were the men I'd hoped we were.

Shortly after I asked for a divorce four months before, I started keeping a video diary. Just for myself. If I had a thought, or a revelation, or just heard something from someone that I thought was helpful, I'd make a short video of myself talking about it.

Later that night on the shoot, I watched them from the beginning in my hotel room.

It was like watching a tragic TV show. There were ones where I'd confidently talk about how I thought the divorce would be wrapped up in the next two weeks, that we'd settle a certain way, that everything would be fine. Rainbow after rainbow. My expectations were based completely on my desires and needs during a physically and emotionally insane time. They had nothing to do with reality and its box of matches.

I thought about Gideon's advice way back about writing an intention of how you want your divorce to go. Gunnar had written his at the start, been following it loud and clear, and I just hadn't been listening.

All the nights that I'd spent crying on my couch with a whiskey in one hand or blubbering down the phone to a friend, it was because I'd had a delusional expectation that was once again not met.

100% my fault.

In the videos, I'd noticed that I was very fond of the words "should" and "then." I'd used them almost mathematically. There was a formula.

Gunnar *should* (insert expectation here) so *then* I can (insert how my life improves here). In the videos and in my thoughts, I'd been writing hundreds of these.

Gunnar *should* agree to using mediators so *then* I can stop hemorrhaging cash on lawyers.

Work *should* hire more staff for my team so *then* I can keep saner hours.

Gunnar and work *should* just lay off me so *then* I won't need to self-medicate as much.

This equation always equaled zero. Because I'd been relying on someone else to do the *should*, so I'd never move past *then* and actually do something about making my life better. It was classic victim mentality, absolving myself of all responsibility for my life and handing it to others.

I'd been an idiot. But it was my first divorce, I told myself. Even Neo in the Matrix couldn't make it to the other building the first time without falling. And he was The One.

I vowed to try and have absolutely no expectations of what was fair, just, loving, or amicable after that. It wouldn't be easy, but I knew it would make my life easier. I wasn't going to lower my expectations. My goal was to literally have none at all.

As I contemplated that this would take some practice, the chorus came up with a plan to postpone all that.

I'M DREAMING OF A WHITE POST-XMAS

Hi mate! I texted John. *I have an idea.*

Yeeeeees...?

What about I come to Berlin for New Year's?

Seriously?

I'm broke, but I can get there on points, and a friend has said I can use his apartment while he's out of town. So, are you around? I asked.

Am I ever! It'd be great to see you. What's it been? John asked. *A year?*

Year and a half, I replied.

Christ on a bike! Send me the details, I'll pick you up from the airport. Go hard, Karl!

LONELINESS VS ALONENESS

As I was setting up travel plans to Berlin, a friend called Minh sent me a piece of writing he thought might be helpful. It's by a spiritual writer called Osho, an excerpt from his book *Joy*[10]. Now, to preface this, Osho is the former Bhagwan Rajneesh, the leader of the Orange People. Make of that what you will. But the piece did indeed help me.

The theme of the piece was becoming authentically happy on your own. To be alone, to start enjoying that, and eventually to love yourself. So that if no one else ever came along, it wouldn't matter. "Now you move like an emperor, not like a beggar."

That line struck me hard, as I realized I'd been a beggar most of my life, waiting for someone to rescue me.

Osho goes on to say that when you truly are living this way, you will attract another person who has also taken the same journey, and that when "two masters meet—masters of their being, of their aloneness—happiness is not just added, it is multiplied."

All the work I'd been doing in the emotions diary, tuning in to the voice and ignoring the chorus, sitting back and observing my emotions... I knew it was for a good reason, but not one that I'd put into words. To feel better about myself would have been my best explanation, or to use it as a crisis of identity. But to what end? I couldn't have said.

When I read those words though—"the master of your aloneness"—it all made sense.

That's what this whole thing was about. If I was ever with someone again, I wanted it to be because I wanted them, not because I needed them. And also, I wanted to not have to be with anyone; I could be perfectly happy with just me.

My crisis of identity had a destination.

I GET A SECOND DIVORCE

I was driving to work. The tirades of yelling at Gunnar or myself in the passenger seat had subsided. Instead, I was listening to a podcast on spirituality. Osho's piece had shown me that I was really at the start of a much longer journey than I'd first thought. I was climbing a mountain and thought I was near the top, then the clouds part, and I see that the peak is much further away than I'd bargained on. Depressing on one hand, good to know on the other.

My coworkers gathered in the conference room for a meeting I'd called. I wanted to make plans with everyone before I left on my Berlin trip.

Sebastian, the head of the account, looked at me puzzled. "What do you mean?"

"I'm going on vacation. I want to make a plan so all the projects keep moving while I'm gone."

"But you'll be available," he stated more than asked.

"Sure, if there's an emergency. But I'm going to turn off my phone while I'm away."

A ripple went through the room.

"What are you talking about?" he said. "You're the creative leader of this account. You have to be available twenty-four-seven. I don't care where in the world you are."

Shocked by the response, I took a moment to gather my thoughts.

"I don't think it's any secret that my life is a bit of a shambles right now," I said, "and to be perfectly frank, I've been deeply concerned about my mental health. Between my divorce and the hours I pull here, I'm losing my mind. Oh, and it's Christmas, by the way."

"I've worked the last four Christmases," Sebastian said with pride.

"What on? Do you even remember?" I asked.

Following his silence, I went on, "What I've never understood about this country is that the minute there's a death in the family, or someone's in the hospital, the attitude is, 'Take as much time as you need.' I'm trying to make sure that doesn't happen to me."

"You took this job. You knew what was involved," Sebastian responded.

He wasn't wrong. However, I'd always thought that if the machine could see I was going to get ground up, it would stop before that happened. But Sebastian, myself, and everyone else in the boardroom that day were just cogs in that machine. In America, when you break, you get thrown out and replaced. You are literally a human resource. I couldn't even be mad at him.

I'd had an expectation. I knew better. This one was on me.

"Well, then. Meeting's over, I guess," I said, then got up and left the room.

The unwritten rule in corporate America is that you leave your personal life at home. But when you are going through a divorce, or the breakup of a long-term relationship, it bleeds over every other part of your life. You can't help it. You're only human.

64% of Americans go through the breakup of a long-term relationship in their lives[11]. 90% of employees say their work was adversely affected when they went through a divorce[12]. I would imagine that the only other life-changing catastrophic event that's more common in the mental health sphere is the death of a parent. While there's leave for bereavement and long-term illness, and for joyful events like maternity, paternity, and even sabbaticals, there's no such thing as divorce leave. Plus there are currently almost no companies that offer services to help employees through one.

On my walk back to my office from that meeting, I resolved that I might have to work in a job like this for another few years to serve out my alimony, but I would live like a student, save as much as I could, then resign from corporate America as a full-time employee forever.

I'm getting divorced from this life too.

JEALOUSY, XMAS DINNERS, AND LAND MINES

LA empties out over the holidays. There are actually only twenty-seven people who were born and raised in LA, with a rumor of a twenty-eighth. Everyone else is a blow-in from everywhere else. The exodus at Christmas is unnerving. You wake up one morning and it feels like half the city is gone. You can literally do donuts in the middle of the 405 listening to Mariah Carey's "All I Want For Christmas Is You."

An emotion that had been on heavy rotation over the preceding weeks was jealousy. I had started noticing people in loving relationships everywhere. Walking down the street with their partner. In a restaurant together. Or even just laughing on the phone. How had they managed it? How had they succeeded when I'd worked so hard at it and failed? I'd spent most of December the darkest shade of green.

Master Of Your Aloneness 101 had a tough first semester. The worst night was Christmas Eve 2017. Brian was going to a dinner at a restaurant with a bunch of guys he knew and had very kindly managed to wrangle an extra spot. I was relieved that I had somewhere to go.

When we arrived, we were greeted by a whole table of gays. Eight couples. Twelve rings. As I sat at the table, I rubbed the finger where mine used to be. The guys were great though. Gregarious, generous, warm, full of yuletide good vibes. The conversations ranged from work to movies to families to wedding plans for one couple in the new year.

I didn't talk much that night. But being near them all was like warming my hands at a campfire. I just watched everyone else chat around me. Not so much the words though; I was looking at all the other things they were saying to each other.

A hand on a back, a side smile to each other, a gentle caress of a hand, a laugh at a private joke, an eye roll as an embarrassing story is told by one about the other. It all looked so effortless. When things were good with Gunnar, it had been effortless.

They were all so well dressed too. I had nice clothes. I just hadn't thought to wear them. Then I looked down at my stained jeans. And kaboom. Land mine.

One of Frannie's hairs was stuck in the fabric, staring up at me.

Very gently, I nudged the hair free, holding it on the tip of my finger. Waves of loss and isolation drowned me. Looking around at the table of happy faces, I just wanted to get up and leave.

Taking a breath and a mental step backward, I observed all the emotions I was cycling through. Then I smiled to myself. It was a classic case of something Roo had said. I was comparing my insides to everyone else's outsides.

The folks at that table could have been super in love that night, or they might have just had a fight. One might be really into this relationship, the other is having doubts. The couple showing the least attention to each other might be the most contented. No one knows what's going on in a relationship except the two people in it. I was jealous because I imagined my interpretation of what I saw that night to be a fact, and then beat myself up because they had something I wished I still had.

But I did have it.

I turned to my left, and there was Brian. One of several friends who were with me all along the way. I was sitting at a table of lovely people, who'd welcomed us into their special night. I was surrounded by love and all I was thinking about was the one piece that wasn't there anymore.

Looking at the hair again, I felt honored to have known Francine Fishpaw. I made a wish for her and blew her fur off my finger.

Love felt like an endangered species. So, after that night, I started counting how many loving things I saw every day, using the emotions diary to write down "Three Things I'm Grateful For." Tiny things: a cookie, a sweet dog, a neighbor waving. Sounds gooey, but it really made me feel better. From then on, when I chose to smile instead of scowl in love's presence, I felt like some rubbed off on me.

One of the guys turned to me. I was probably staring into space.

"Are you OK?" he asked.

"I'm great, mate. Just thinking how lucky I am."

He smiled, rubbed my shoulder, and invited me into the conversation with his husband.

The next day, I found a box and walked round the house. Top to bottom, I went through it with a fine-tooth comb. I found every single potential land mine that reminded me of Gunnar, Francine, the dogs, or any other part of my old life. I'd hold it in my hand, think of a good memory attached to it, then put it in the box. After an hour or so, the box was full. I took it down to the garage and put it high on a shelf.

Then there was just one last thing to do.

I went to the drawer where I'd been keeping my wedding ring. Since the day I took it off at the beach, I'd had no idea what to do with it. But now I did.

With the ring in my pocket, I went to a favorite green space in LA. I dug a small hole in the ground and then pulled the ring out of my pocket. It was so much lighter than I'd remembered it being.

Closing my eyes, I thought of the day I'd found it. The day I proposed. Watching Gunnar dance at our friend's wedding. Our own big day surrounded by friends and family. The first time I said the words, "my husband," to a stranger. The way I would play with this ring when I was stressed, and think of him, and feel better.

I kissed the ring once, put it in the hole, and covered it with earth.

CHAPTER 9

"You can still be rich, but like a chocolate cake."

— JOHN

BERLIN

ON THE PLANE, APPREHENSION SUDDENLY descended like a sharp drop in cabin pressure. Berlin had made so much sense back in LA. But now that I was on my way, it was the first time I'd stopped to think about what I was doing. John was someone I'd met when I was in a bad emotional state eighteen months before, when Gunnar and I had had our falling out in Europe. Since then, we'd shared a lot over texts and he'd been an amazing support and source of knowledge since the divorce began.

But I hadn't seen him, or even heard his voice, in all that time. Part of me wondered if I'd made him up somehow. Or if my idea of who he was was based in no way on reality.

And I was single now. That first time John and I had met had been affectionate, intimate, playful even, but not sexual. I was hoping that would be different this time. I wanted it to be. But I had no idea if he felt the same way.

Oh, well. Too late now.

I landed in Berlin, walked out the gate and scanned the crowd. I'd pulled up a photo of John on my phone but didn't see anyone like that around. Then he walked up. His black beard was longer. Ah, that smile. He was shorter than I'd remembered. In my mind, he'd become a giant, mythologized as this great virtual voice from afar that spoke in my hours of need. Sauntering over in pink combat boots, he reached into his Rastafari backpack and pulled out an apple.

"Hello, Karl Dunn. I brought you an apple because I thought you might be hungry and God knows what they put in plane food." And we're back.

I smiled, took the apple, and we hugged. He pulled away to cough.

"You OK, John?" I asked.

"Yeah, just this thing going round Berlin," John said, waving my concern away with his hand. "I'll have this knocked on the head in a couple of days. Right, let's hit the road."

We jumped a bus, headed into town, and caught up. Even though we knew the broad strokes of each other's lives—him more than me—we swapped the details that are too rich for texting. Berlin was under a blanket of snow. The black, leafless branches of trees needled the gray skies. The sun was white and milky. It couldn't have been more different to the palm trees and perma-sun of LA.

John talked about his school and the ups and downs of teaching kids English. He had a very animated way of talking. When he'd tell a story, he acted out all the parts and did all the voices, like I was watching a one-man show. A show interrupted by several coughing fits. Eventually we got back to the collective – the grand lady was still standing, still defying the creep of gentrification. John insisted on carrying my bag up the three flights of old, wooden stairs to his place. It was then that I noticed he'd sweated through his clothes. In the middle of winter.

His room was enormous, bigger than a lot of studio apartments. Back in the day, this had probably been the dining and living room. There was a bed, couch, dining table and chairs, and still enough room to hold a small rave under the chandelier and dozen paintings of landscapes that crowded one wall. And there were books—piles and piles and piles of books. With a penchant for vintage, all John's furniture was from the 1930s. The whole effect was like coming to stay with a punk English professor in the Weimar years.

The plan was to crash for a night or two with John, then grab the keys to my friend's apartment. But by the time John had gotten back from the kitchen with the tea he'd made us, he was turning an unhealthy-looking green.

"You don't look very well, mate," I said to him.

"I am feeling a little under the weather," he replied.

"Maybe you should throw yourself in the shower and grab a nap?"

"Would you mind?"

"Not at all. We have all the time in the world."

Soon John was clean, dry, warm, and tucked in. He had apologized half a dozen times in the process. But now, seeing him drift off, I lay down on top of his covers and gave him a cuddle that he snuggled into. I was a little worried. All his roommates and friends were out of town. Berlin, like LA, had also emptied out over the season.

I sipped the tea he'd made and looked out the window to the white street below, four black lines slicing it up where the car tires ran, John's sleep sounds filling the room.

MONEY MAKES THE WORLD GO DOWN

And so it went. I lived in that large room with him, did a little shopping for food, made soup, found that the wi-fi was strongest in the giant bathroom (that had a couch in it!), and clicked away at the keys, their sounds bouncing off the ancient, ornate cracked tiles as I kept everything in LA rolling along. As angry as I'd been that I'd be working through the break, I was glad to have something to do.

One day when John was feeling better, we were half napping, half chatting in his bed. All the sheets smelled of his cologne and sweat.

"So are you going to resign when you get back home?" John asked.

"I wish I could. If I did, Gunnar will make the case that it was to avoid spousal support. I'll have no income and still have the support to pay."

"They can do that?"

"Sadly."

"Is it a lot? Like could you just get another job, but doing something you like?"

"Advertising is the only thing I know how to do to make the kind of cash I have to send him every month."

When I told him the number, John sat bolt upright in bed.

"Jesus, Karl! How much money do you make?" He was genuinely angry. But not at Gunnar. At me.

"I don't understand you at all," John continued. "You're a good person. I know this. You have a good heart and that's hard to find in this world. Yet you have made choices that have you backing up industries that destroy the planet, extort human labor, and feed people's insecurities. You're better than that. But you have allowed them to buy your conscience. Don't tell me you haven't thought about it, because I know you have. And if *you've* made choices like that, what kind of hope is there for the rest of us?"

My jaw had gone slack. I watch him fuming. It took me a minute to gather myself.

"Wow," I managed, "I don't know what to say."

"Me either."

"I'm going for a walk," I said, and got out of bed without waiting for a response.

Screw that self-righteous artist, I thought as I angrily paced a wintery Berlin, kicking rocks and leaves.

After half an hour, when I'd finally managed to step back from my emotions and observe them, I realized what I was angry about. It's that John was right on some level.

At its best, advertising changes national conversations. Sometimes, you even find yourself in a position to tweak capitalism, working for companies that are putting out revolutionary products. But the industry that I joined, the one that I first fell in love with, had changed a lot over twenty years. And I'd spent a good chunk of that chasing the rainbow of my early advertising days.

In my jacket pocket, I found the keys for my friend's apartment. That had been the original plan, I mused. Calmer, I went back to John's place, took off my coat and boots, and went into his room where he was reading a book.

"Listen," I began, "I know my life is a mess and I'm the one that got it here. I want to change it into something I like, and I'm still figuring that part out. But you also have made choices.

You've chosen to make just enough money to cover your bills and allow yourself the maximum amount of time to pursue your writing and your art. And I truly, deeply respect it. But you've also said more than once, when you see something beautiful that costs a bomb, that you should have gone into advertising. I know you're joking. But it means you've also thought about it too. And all those grants that are there for artists to do the great work that they do are paid for by people like me. You are the yin and I am the yang."

John took that in, cocking his head in thought, shrugging a half agreement.

"I'm also a disaster area right now," I continued. " I want your help, I welcome your counsel. But that doesn't mean you get to sit there on a moral high ground and pass judgment on my life. OK?"

John smiled.

"OK," he finally said.

We were silent for a moment.

"Fancy a cuddle?" I asked.

"Go on then."

WRITE YOUR MANIFESTO

The next day, I was typing on my laptop in John's room. He was pottering around in the background. He was still running a fever but had a little color back in his face.

He set a cup of tea by my side. "Black, no sugar. Yuck."

"Never short of an audible opinion, are you?" I said. "Thanks. For the tea."

"Pleasure, treasure. What are you writing?"

"A manifesto."

"Wow! I thought you just wanted to change your life. You're starting a revolution?"

"No, John, it's not a real manifesto. It's for my client. Like a mission statement."

"Oh, OK," John said quietly.

Advertising often co-opted words like this and turned them into boardroom tools. Saying "manifesto" in those rooms felt fine. Saying it to someone who'd probably not just read, but studied, written papers, and had heated debates on the actual manifestos of revolutionaries, queer theorists, feminists, and other intellectuals made me feel like a fraud.

"Well, I'm popping out to the supermarket," John said. "Anything you need?"

"No, I'm good."

"OK. Back in a tick," said John, leaving. Then he stuck his head in the room again. "This manifesto thing…"

"Yes," I replied, waiting for the barbed comment.

"You ever written one for yourself?"

I stopped typing.

John shrugged. "Just a thought. Back soon."

I listened to the front door close.

I closed the laptop. I had no idea how many manifesto-like objects I'd written for clients, but I'd never thought about writing one for me. I'd made lists of things I wanted to achieve, sure. But they were results, not a code to live by.

I'd just bought a new emotions diary in a Berlin bookstore since the first was filled. I cracked it open and inhaled the smell of paper, ink, and possibilities.

Don't think, I told myself. Just write.

I picked up a pen and closed my eyes. Then I opened to the first page and wrote down, "I won't do anything for the money ever again. I'm only going to work on things I believe in."

I looked at what I'd written. This came from some part of me I hadn't been to in a long time. It was a place deeper than where I wrote the emotions diary from.

Next thing, the pen hit the paper again and I wrote out a set of values that I'd never put into words before. When I read it all out, I thought, "Yes, this is where I want to live from. This feels like me. Or the me I want to be."

John came back and I walked into the kitchen where he was unpacking groceries.

"I want to read you something," I said, holding the book in my hand.

"Hit me."

"One—I won't do anything for the money ever again. I'm only going to work on things I believe in."

John stopped unpacking groceries and turned to me, motioning for me to carry on.

"Two—I want to write and tell stories that help the most amount of people possible. Three—My body is the most important thing I will ever own. I vow to take care of it. I will tend to it, knowing that the physical and mental are equally important. Four—I won't tolerate any person who's taking advantage of my good nature. They have no place in my life. Five—I will listen to my intuition. It's always right. I vow to stop ignoring it. Six—I want to make art. Things that please me that I make with my hands. And seven—I will speak my mind and not hold back or try and make it sound nice for the other person. Clear, direct, honest, and kind."

I waited, watching John's face.

"So it is a revolution after all," he said. "Let's celebrate. I bought cookies."

JANUARY 2018

NEW YEAR, OLD ME

New Year's is always filled with such promise. For some reason we all think that the final tick of the clock in one year releases all the bad juju from the world—that with the flip of a digit, we are suddenly transformed into pristine beings, able to realize everything that was impossible the year before, only to discover a few days in that we are the same people we were last year. The same old habits have followed us. The same old patterns emerge.

John and I were lying in bed, hugging, on the first day of a new year. Now that he was feeling a bit better, I'd started sleeping in his bed instead of on the couch. We hugged a lot, and that was all. But it was nice. And a hug is a great way to start a new chapter.

There was still a lingering smell of sulfur in the air. In Germany, Silvester is the traditional meal at a family member or friend's house to ring in the new year with roasted meat, red cabbage, and knödel, a kind of round dumpling. Then, at the stroke of midnight, you do a shot of liquor and run into the streets to let off fireworks. We'd had a blast of a night.

It had been at a friend of John's, with some of his closest people, that we saw in 2018. They very kindly talked in English most of the night, but when the conversation switched to German, I got the feeling that I was the topic. I'm sure they wondered who this person was that was staying with their friend, and what the deal was between me and John. I don't know exactly what he said. But I felt it wasn't quite what I'd been hoping.

At the table, eating our New Year's meal, I ached for him to put his arm around me. At the stroke of midnight, I wished he'd kissed me. But instead he'd hugged his friends first, then me.

Because the other thing lingering in the air besides the sulfur was desire. I had a real attraction to John. I knew that now. And that a big part of my hopes for this trip was that he was going to feel the same way. It seemed so obvious in retrospect but it hadn't been to me till I was standing in front of him.

And I wasn't getting that feeling in return. So, it didn't take long for a sense of rejection to manifest, because that was my way. And that made me want John more, because that was also my way. Shoulds, thens, and expectations.

It might have been a new year, and I might have been a little smarter now, but I was still the old me. Head faster than my heart.

WHY DID I GET MARRIED?

After a few more days, John was well enough that we ventured to one of his favorite local cafes with rococo-red flocked wallpaper, where we chatted about art surrounded by East German furniture and lights from the sixties. They even had a breakfast plate option called "The Marx" that was served with a thin cigar. We were in full flight when John suddenly changed the subject.

"Karl, I've been meaning to ask you something. Why did you get married?"

I shrugged. "I was in love."

"Yeah, but you didn't have to get married to be in love. And from what you described about being registered domestic partners, it doesn't sound like you got any extra rights as a married couple."

"True."

"So why did you do it?"

"Because we finally could."

"Hmm. But again, doesn't mean you have to."

I thought about it for a moment. "You know, I don't know why I got married. No one's ever asked me that."

"Forget everyone else, ask yourself," John said.

John soon went back to the house for a nap and I opened up the emotions diary. I reread my manifesto, closed my eyes, found that place of honesty again, then let the pen fly.

TOP FIVE REASONS WHY I GOT MARRIED

1. I was in love and wanted to spend the rest of my life together with this man.

OK, so that was a good one. But did I really need to get married to do that? We were already registered domestic partners. Legally, there was absolutely no difference in the eyes of the law in California between RDPs and married couples. I didn't want to be with anyone else. We were living together and sharing a life. I didn't need to get married to continue any of this. Gay men had lived for decades, centuries even, in long-term, committed relationships without any legal recognition.

And I was the one who proposed. So I did this of my own bidding.

2. I did it for the cause.

We got marriage equality in California. Then they took it away. Then we got it back again. Now that we could get married forever, I felt it was my duty. The more of us who did it, the more normal it would become—just like the battle that mixed-race couples had faced in America back in the 1960s—and I felt that would be great for future generations of gay men everywhere. I was being a good gay and embracing our new possibilities.

But this was a terrible reason. Future generations didn't have to live with my husband. Or me, for that matter. Or with our fights about money, careers, respect, and partnership. Fights where it seemed we both thought we were the one hard done by. Doing something for the cause, hanging in every day when you just wanted it over, is a terrible reason to stay. And when you're married, there is no easy way out.

3. I did it to be anti-gay.

There is a thing that gay men do that drives me crazy. And I include myself in this. When you haven't seen a friend of yours for a while, one of the first things gay men ask each other is, "Are you and so-and-so still together?"

There is a culture of loneliness and isolation in the gay community. It starts when we are wondering if we are gay in our teens or even earlier. Because straight parents have queer kids, we aren't born into houses where our culture is on display.

Instead, the time we spend between wondering if we are gay and then finally coming out is some of the loneliest of our lives. Then we're bullied. Some of us are rejected by our family, friends, and everyone we love. But even if you come from a loving family in a liberal city like I did, you still modify your behavior to avoid suspicion and slurs being thrown your way.

Yet when we finally come out and find "the gay community," we discover that it's a jungle. All these men with all the same baggage are clumped together, and guess what people who've been rejected their whole lives do? They perpetuate that rejection. Now though, it's because of your height, or race, or age, or income, or body, or clothes, or perceived femininity. The apps make it ten times worse.

I wanted to be anti-rejection, anti-disposable relationship. I got married on some level to be counter-cultural to my own people.

4. You get better tax breaks when you're married.

How romantic, right? But why is getting married rewarded by governments in the first place? Tax breaks weren't my main reason, but they were great back-up dancers. However, the cost of a divorce vs those tax breaks is like a comet vs Earth. And that had worked out so well for the dinosaurs…

5. I have incredible insecurities about finding someone I'm attracted to mentally and physically who would love someone like me.

When I wrote this one, I stopped and stared at it for a while. There it was. The darkest, most honest reason why I did it.

I have always been attracted to big, hairy men. And when I was a young gay man in Sydney, I copped a lot of crap for it. All my friends would say, "Why are you with that fat, ugly, older, hairy guy? He's gross."

It took a long time for me to not be embarrassed by what I liked. The heart wants what the heart wants. Being into guys who look like Alec Baldwin or James Gandolfini in the narrow-minded gay world of 1990s Sydney was like coming out all over again.

Then I was in a relationship in the early 2000s for a few years and when I came away from that, suddenly there was the term "Bear." I was thrilled. At last! All these guys I'd adored for years for their size, shape, and hirsuteness had finally worked out that they were hot and there were lots of them. And they gave it a name! Then I discovered that it was a party I wasn't invited to. I'm 6'3", 185 pounds, built like a swimmer. And what I discovered moving to LA in 2006 is that it was Bear for Bear. I was suddenly invisible. And it hurt.

Generally, I wasn't attractive to the men I desired. Which did nothing for my confidence. LA in those early days was a dry, lonely time for me, punctuated with unrequited love and getting stood up a lot.

But ever since I was a little kid, my dream had been to move to America, become a successful screenwriter, and find a hot Bear guy—maybe a producer or studio exec—who adored me. And we were going to live happily ever after. We were going to be *that* couple.

So I was husband-hunting like crazy in LA. Fresh from every passionate disinterest, every time I got stood up, every time I became too attached to a guy in an open relationship, I'd cry about it for a few days, go buy a new outfit, get my hair cut, tell myself I was new again, and the hunt would continue.

Then I met Gunnar. The sexiest man I'd ever seen, who liked guys that looked like me, who was single, and who actually wanted to date. Smart, funny, worldly, charming. And he couldn't get enough of me. When we started going out together, the unanimous reaction was, "Oh my God, where did you meet this guy?" It was widely considered that I was dating a supermodel of the Bear world. I was over the moon.

Because also, when we went out, and I saw guys that had toyed around with me staring at Gunnar, I'd smile to myself. When they tried to make moves on him and he'd introduce me as his boyfriend, and later his fiancé or husband, I'd look at them and think, "That's right, queen. That's what I've got at home."

On really special nights, I'd wait till my husband had gone to the bar to buy a round, so that myself and the guy that liked Gunnar were alone for a few moments. On several occasions, it wasn't the first time we'd met. I'd mention this to them, often getting a blank stare in return.

"You stood me up on our first date."

"You stood me up on our fifth date."

"You told me you were sick and cancelled, then I saw you out with someone else."

"You and I talked three times on Bearwww about getting together, then you never committed to a time. But you insisted I send more pics."

"You took me to a street festival, said 'Let's get drunk because you can stay at my place,' and left me there with no way to get home after you picked someone else up."

Then, as the realization dawned on them, I'd deliver the killer blow: "Something tells me you're going to remember me this time."

This is, without a doubt, the number one most insidious reason for why I got married. Because I wanted this kind of power on lock.

Rather than dealing with my insecurities and finding value in myself on my own, I'd used Gunnar to do it instead. I'd had it validated by onlookers, and worse, used my relationship as a kind of revenge. I got married because I thought marriage would make the shame go away and prove to the world—and myself—that I was loveable. What an insane amount of pressure to put on my husband.

In that café in Berlin, I leaned back in my chair and read these five reasons again. No wonder it hadn't worked. Gunnar probably had a list just as bad as mine.

MONEY CAN'T BUY YOU CHOCOLATE CAKE

As the trip wound down to its last couple of days, we lay on the floor of John's room, listening to old cabaret songs on an ancient gramophone that John had been gifted by a friend.

"So, what happens when you get back to LA?" asked John.

"Go to trial at some point. Gunnar wants full spousal support for three years. I'm trying to get that reduced. But it's a total roll of the dice. A trial could potentially cost me $40,000, because if the judge rules against me, I have to pay for his and my lawyer fees. Honestly, part of me is thinking just to pay the max and be done."

John whistled low. "Glad I never went into advertising. I think if I end up in a trailer somewhere with a nice view, that would work."

"I might be in the one next to you," I quipped.

"Karl, question for you. Say the first thing that comes to your head. Why did you move to America all those years ago?"

"To be a rich and famous screenwriter. Win an Oscar. Marry a handsome American Bear guy."

"And how'd that work out?"

"I worked hard at the writing. Got paid. But none of it ever got made. I'll never win an Oscar. And as for the man… You know how that went."

"So why did you go back into advertising?"

I sighed as I listened to some long-dead cabaret star sing in German about an old love. I told John about how I wanted to be a rich and famous Global Creative Director but that my last three jobs had eaten me alive. Like my current one. And now I was broke, didn't have a life, and had probably missed my chance to ever hit those upper echelons of the business. I stared at the chipping plaster on the roof above as John sat up and changed the record.

"OK," said John, recranking the gramophone, "so why don't you try doing something that makes you happy instead?"

"I was planning to," I reflected. "But I guess I thought I'd do it after I was rich enough. That sounds really sad when I say it out loud."

John came and lay back down on the floor next to me.

"I think you think that there's some magic number," he said, "an amount in a bank account, or a number of houses, or something. And then you'll be safe. You'll be happy. You'll kill yourself to get there, then find out that the money was never the answer anyway," John said, leaving a pregnant pause. "Or you could do things that make you happy today."

I nodded, clueless about what those might be.

"Seriously though, you've said several times you always wanted to live in Berlin. Why don't you just move here when all this divorce shit is over?"

I turned to look at him, laying my arm across his chest.

"I could actually do that now, couldn't I?" I said. "Well, not now, but maybe in a couple of years."

Moving somewhere just because I liked it and not for a job was a radical idea for me. My mood brightened enormously. This jacket felt very good to try on.

"You can still be rich, but like a chocolate cake," John offered.

"John, you are without doubt one of the most amazing people I've ever met."

John blinked his eyes demurely and we laughed.

"Why thank you, kind sir," he said.

Then I put a hand over to touch his thick head of black hair, leaned in, and kissed him. He stayed in the kiss for a moment, and then pulled away.

Mortified, I sat up.

"Sorry—" John began, but I cut him off.

"No, it's fine. You've been sending the signal loud and clear and I was just pretending I hadn't seen it. Sorry."

John stared down at the floor.

"Karl, I was really excited that you were coming out here. I wanted to see you again. But showing you around, all the talks about your life while battling this illness, it's exhausting. I can't be the holiday fling as well."

Then I started tearing up. Embarrassed, I stood up to get away from him.

John stood up, came to me, and put his hands on my shoulders. Now it was my turn to look at the floor.

"That day that we met on the square here," John said quietly, "when we looked at each other, it was like some sort of electricity passed between us. I didn't see anyone else around, it was just the two of us. I don't know what it means. But I know it means something."

I looked up, nodding. "I felt it too. So now what?"

"It's not really up to us. The universe will decide all that stuff. You go home in a few days. We'll keep in contact. And I guess all will be revealed."

"I guess so." I looked at John's face. "I wish I was better."

John shrugged. "You're doing OK, all things considered."

I shrugged back. We giggled.

"Fancy a cuddle?" he asked.

"Go on then."

YOUR FLIGHT BACK TO THAT UNHOLY MESS IS NOW BOARDING

I'd woken that morning next to John, pulled him in, and cuddled him as his warm body readjusted in my arms. I am so lucky to have met this man, I thought. Of all the guides who'd popped up on my journey, John had been the most significant by far.

The conversations, the disagreements, and the hard truths had brought me face to face with a lot of demons I'd have to contend with over the next couple of years. But at least now I knew where the work was to be done.

I'd packed my bag the night before and insisted that he not come to the airport in his condition. Instead I got dressed, hung my keys up on the hook in the hallway, and hugged his sleepy self by the front door as he stood warm and malleable in my arms.

"I'm going to miss you, John Hare."

"I'm going to miss you, Karl Dunn."

"I'll text you when I'm back in LA."

"Yes, you will."

I kissed him on the forehead. "For everything, mate."

"Pleasure, treasure."

I rolled my bag to the front door, stepped out into the hallway, closed the door, and left the building.

On the way to the airport, my phone buzzed. It was a text from John.

Just so there's no misunderstandings before you leave, if you and I ever find ourselves living in the same city, and we're both amping on our lives, maybe we could try dating each other and see if we're a better team than we already know.

I stared at the screen and smiled.

It's a date mate, I texted back. *See you at the café on the corner for breakfast in 2020.*

Deal. Go hard, Karl.

As I arrived at the airport, my heart got heavier. Why didn't I just stay in Berlin? Not for John, but for me. Or fly home to Australia? I could do it, I thought. I could change my ticket right now and disappear. But I'd made this life in LA and I had to go back and clean up the mess of my divorce. For better or for worse.

So I fastened my seat belt.

CHAPTER 10

"Be happy Gunnar has someone else, it gives him less time to think about you."

— Ludo

PRIMARY AND SECONDARY EMOTIONS

After ten days in Berlin, looking in a lot of mirrors, writing a personal manifesto, and getting glimpses of my true self, I knew my emotions were the dark churning sea that I had to now dive into. I also felt like I'd been out on parole and was now back in my cell in LA.

Life returned to its routine. Wake up either angry, sad, depressed, jealous, afraid, or some combination of those, then drive to work seven days a week, kickbox, come home to an empty house, have dinner alone, go to bed. On the upside, the drinking was ebbing away. After the decision that I was going to move to Berlin at some point in the distant future, I finally had something to live a better life for.

I kept a picture of the Berlin skyline as my screensaver.

And even though I was working on becoming a master of my aloneness, LA was pretty lonely.

John and I texted most days now. But because of my work, it was rare that I was able to connect with friends in town. No one wants to go out at 9 p.m. on the spur of the moment on a Tuesday because you suddenly have a window. Early in the divorce, that hadn't bothered me. I'd just start drinking or getting high at home. Now that both of those hobbies were subsiding, I had time on my hands each night. So I started delving more into the subject of emotions and how my brain worked.

For things that ran my entire waking life, I'd spent less time investigating the foundations of emotions than watching YouTube clips about my favorite actors. Bradley Cooper wasn't with me every second of the day, yet I knew way more about his career than even the most basic stuff behind the science of how I feel.

Turns out, all emotions are made from the same basic ingredients.

The American Psychologist Robert Plutchik writes about how there are eight primary emotions: anger, sadness, fear, joy, interest, surprise, disgust, and shame[13]—what he called the Wheel of Emotions. These are the basic eight that we are all born with, the ones we developed over millennia, so we didn't get eaten by wild animals or eat poisonous berries.

It's like music. There are only twelve notes in Western music. That's it. And yet because you can combine them in millions of ways, with their order, timing, emphasis, genre, etc., the canon seems infinite.

Another way to think about primary emotions is like a color wheel. Just like combinations of red, yellow, and blue create almost every single color on the planet, these eight primary emotions are the basic colors from which every other emotion is mixed together.

Primary emotions are directly connected to an event or stimulus. You get a letter from a lawyer, you read it, you feel anger. Easy. Secondary emotions are much more complex because they often refer to the feelings you have about the primary emotion.

If primary emotions are what you feel, secondary emotions are how you feel about what you feel. Secondary emotions are very individual as we learn them from our parents, our friends, our culture, society, language, movies, books, and other things that make up our environment.

Back to the lawyer letter example, I'd read one and feel anger. That subsides in a couple of minutes. But it's replaced by all the secondary emotions: frustration that I can't control my anger, shame at failing in my marriage, resentment at being caught in a process I never wanted to be in, fear that I'd end up financially ruined, and so on, all of which I'd ping-pong between for hours after the initial rage was long gone.

Someone else could have gotten the same letter and felt gratitude for their anger because it kept them focused, delight in how they were going to respond, smugness for the way they would outmaneuver, satisfaction that they'd won ground.

This piece of knowledge on primary and secondary emotions boosted my work in the emotions diary, because I now had a better framework to break down my emotional episodes. The new work moved from *what* I felt about the way I felt, to *why* I felt about the way I felt.

And I'd soon have a perfect example to work on.

MY HUSBAND HAS A NEW BOYFRIEND

LA has 18.7 million people spread out over its greater metropolitan area of nearly 34,000 square miles. But sometimes, it's just not big enough. One night out, I ran into one of the binge-watchers that I'd cut out early in the divorce.

This person took the greatest pleasure, poorly disguised as friendly concern, to let me know that Gunnar had a new boyfriend. I truly hoped that all those years of acting classes I took while I was a screenwriter had paid off, and that I hadn't given anything away at the time. But I immediately felt surprise and sadness. Then, after about a minute, the secondary emotions kicked in. Anger, frustration, and jealousy all came out to play. Not long after, I was in my car driving home, eager to be in front of the emotions diary.

Pulling into the driveway and garage, I guessed that this moment was inevitable. At some point, we'd both start dating again. Which meant that one of us would have to be first. Still, six months seemed fast to me.

Diary open on the dining room table, I started with anger.

I was angry that Gunnar had jumped right into the next relationship while the dead body of our marriage was still warm. It felt like he'd brought a trick to the funeral. I was also angry that it seemed like he was living an unexamined life. I was willingly wrestling with every demon I had, and I was annoyed that he wasn't going to go through the same pain I was—which then I felt stupid about. Who's to say he wasn't processing it? Maybe he was already further along than me.

As I turned my attention to the frustration, I wrote how I was more of a mess than I'd realized and that I was angry with how slow this whole process was. If I couldn't win the legal battle, I wanted to win the spiritual war.

As for jealousy, that was easy. Gunnar had me over a barrel legally, was getting a financial reward I thought he didn't deserve and I couldn't afford, and now he had a new boyfriend.

And then the part that made no sense at all was that I felt jilted, like a jealous lover. I hated that more than the rest combined. There was no part of me that wanted to get back together. We didn't even talk now.

So I ended up back in anger again, but with myself.

Then I remembered that when we went on our first date, Gunnar had been separated from his then husband for only six months. They were in the middle of their divorce when we had first started seeing each other.

I looked up from the diary and laughed. This was Myriam's Law in full effect. How could I be angry with Gunnar for doing what I already should have known he would do?

And then, the emotions diary read me nicely: *If John and you were in the same city, you'd be trying to date him. So Gunnar is just doing what you would have done if you'd had the chance.*

I rolled my eyes at myself.

On a phone call with Ludo, I told him about the new boyfriend and he made a great point. "Be happy Gunnar has someone else, it gives him less time to think about you."

MY DICK DOESN'T WORK

Like a lot of gay couples, my husband and I stopped mating in captivity. The passion dies after the first year and you just don't do it for each other anymore. The sad part of it was that he was the only one I ever really wanted. But again, I have to take responsibility for dating a series of men who'd lose interest in me early and look outside—or who I made feel that way.

Adding a divorce on top of that with all the volatile emotions it brought up, plus Gunnar's new partner and a hypercritical evaluation of my own age and body, and I was feeling fairly unfuckable. I'd failed to be attractive to my husband, who at one stage couldn't get enough of me, so why would anyone else want this? In short, I hated myself. And my dick had basically shut up shop.

Crazy thing is that every morning I'd wake up with morning wood. Every damn day. I knew everything still worked. I just couldn't make it work.

Convinced that I would disappoint every man I tried to have sex with, I avoided all offers. Which fueled the downward spiral. And that's how it had been going for many months.

Flipping back through the emotions diary and rereading all the reasons that I'd got married and how little I regarded my ability to keep someone I liked, I realized that I'd been treating sex like an audition and/or performance. For a long time. Maybe twenty years.

Like the emotions, what if I just owned that? Invited that knowledge in and made it tea? Be honest and vulnerable about it?

One night, I was out with friends when a lovely man started chatting me up. He was a good kisser and he was keen to come back to my place. Then, on the way to my car, I panicked. All the fears about disappointing him came flooding back. I felt like I couldn't go through with it, that I'd be that weirdo that flakes at the car door.

"Hey, mate. Just so you know, I'm in the middle of a divorce. From a guy. It's messed me up pretty good. And, um, I sometimes have performance issues now which I'm working through. Anyway, I just wanted to let you know that if I don't get it up, it's not you. But I can definitely guarantee excellent hugging and superb kissing. So, if you want to bail, I get it. But it's too exhausting to pretend to be something I'm not right now."

The guy stared at me for a couple of seconds. "I don't think anyone has been that honest with me in a long time."

We looked at each other for a moment longer.

"I kind of prefer just kissing and hugging anyway," he continued, "but most guys don't think that's very cool."

"Oh, I'm super uncool," I said.

He smiled and climbed into the passenger seat of my car.

HAPPINESS ISN'T A RIGHT OR A RECIPE, IT'S A HABIT

As I went through the first couple of months of 2018, the one emotion I struggled with the most was happiness. Life at that point was a sky of light-gray feelings with frequent thunderstorms. Writing down three things I was grateful for each night brought on a short-lived soft glow. But sometimes, happiness would pierce the darkness so suddenly, I would hold my breath. If I moved, I thought it would disappear.

My first reaction to happiness was, "That feels amazing."

Next would be, "How did I do that?"

Then I'd try to grab it tight, only to feel it evaporate.

Frustrated, I'd retrace my steps to see if I could find the PIN combination that had brought it about.

Then I'd be sad that it was gone. Like a castaway waving at a ship that passed right by the island but didn't stop. I could feel happiness. I just had no control over it. So I started to just simply notice it, not grab at it, when it came by. And say thanks for popping over.

I started to have whole good days. Amazed, I'd run with it, getting something done that the depressive feelings had stopped me doing. Like laundry. What did screw me up though, was having two happy days in a row. Two! I'd go to sleep happy and wake up feeling good. And the feeling would last all day. Then, sometimes, it was three days. Three!

I got fooled a few times into thinking that this was the new normal, telling people I was feeling better, that I was coming out of it. Then I'd wake up after a winning streak to find I was as sad and depressed as ever. No warning, no trigger, just back in the hole again. The experience was like snakes and ladders with someone else's hand moving my piece around the board.

John was right; it was a pulse. Up and down. It was going to take time, the one ingredient that I couldn't fake.

Happiness, though, was something I'd had an elusive relationship with my whole life. It had always been about getting that next job, or title, or living in that neighborhood, or that country, or owning that jacket, or bagging that guy, or having this much money in the bank. Then, and only then, could I be happy.

However, as soon as I'd achieve any of these things, they became immediately meaningless. I didn't even stop long enough to look at this glittering jewel in my hand that I'd had to work hard to achieve. The moment it was mine, I threw it on the ground and set my sights on the next thing.

Alan Downs is an American psychologist and the author of the book, *The Velvet Rage: Overcoming the Pain of Growing Up Gay in a Straight Man's World*[14]. His client base was predominantly white middle-class gay men, so a caveat here that his research came from a very particular view of the world. That said, Downs heard the same things coming up again and again.

He makes the point that as we are growing up, we get validation from society and our families for being a version of ourselves that we aren't. As kids, we all want approval. Even if that means getting approval for pretending to be someone we're not. We continue living this way, getting validation that feels hollow, till it feels like we're living a huge lie. Then we come out.

The problem is that due to these behaviors becoming so ingrained from such an early age, all validation continues to feel false and worthless. So the never-ending hunt continues.

That was me for sure, waking up in my bed in my early forties with this wonderful life and not understanding why I never felt good. I felt happiness was owed to me. I'd moved to America for the pursuit of my happiness.

In early 2018, what I was only just beginning to understand was that happiness wasn't a right. It wasn't a recipe. It wasn't about things. And it certainly wasn't a person either. After listing all of the reasons I'd gotten married and discovering how much pressure I'd put on my husband, and on John while I was in Berlin, I was embarrassed that I'd been handballing my problems into the lap of any man I was interested in, hoping they would figure it out for me.

Real happiness was a personal, active choice.

Looking back over the lists of three things I was grateful for, they were mostly tiny little things I'd noticed around me. Like something small someone had done. Or something I'd done for someone else. Or a kindness to myself, cutting myself a break for a negative tailspin. Instead of it being an elusive state, I began to understand what happiness looked like to me, and that it was a habit that I could create.

This seemed so fridge-magnet-philosophy obvious. But something else I was finding was that the really obvious, most basic stuff had started to mean something deep. The stuff your grandparents told you were the really important things.

Between the emotions diary, a meditation practice, the kickboxing, vulnerability, and reframing time, I was finding a slow but steady way out of my perma-funk. By the time I jumped on a plane for another shoot at the end of February, I was seeing the way ahead. It wasn't going to be some magic pill, handsome stranger, or genie-in-a-bottle-style ending. Instead, it would be something I'd build on my own.

YOU NEED TO DO SOMETHING WITH ALL THIS UGLY

When I got back from the shoot, it was time to put the house on the market. So I rang my friends and got some recommendations for real estate agents, including a man called Dana, who was the final one that came to the house to have a look. I liked him because he didn't act like every other real estate agent, who tried to get me to sign on our first meeting.

Dana told me that place was a slam dunk to sell.

"But you need to prop this place up," he said, looking at my scant furnishings. "It's practically empty. Do you want me to call someone to get some things in here?"

"No," I replied. "I have a whole garage of furniture."

"What's it doing down there?" Dana asked.

I suddenly realized how big the echo was in my house.

"Just didn't feel like decorating."

"OK. Well I can have the photographer come early next week. Can you do it by then?"

"Sure, no problem."

I knew if I called Brian, he'd be over lickety-split to bitch-slap me into prettying the place up. However, it felt like something I needed to do myself. So, completely out of character at the time, I started the moment Dana left.

Artworks, paintings, cushions, lamps, tablecloths, desks, chairs, and knickknacks emerged out of a cloud of garage dust over the weekend. I got to work with the drill and soon everything was up on the walls, rooms were rearranged, vacuumed, tidied, and completely made over. I was on a roll. Three loads of laundry were washed, dried, folded, and put away. The patio was scrubbed, the outdoor furniture cleaned, the plants trimmed and watered and brought back to life.

I sat back and looked at the house. Oh my God, I thought, this place is beautiful. I'd been living there for five months and this was the first day that I was actually happy to be there.

Inspired, I went through my wardrobe and Marie Kondo'ed a ton of stuff to Out Of The Closet. By the way, if anyone reading this got that black Issey Miyake overcoat, I'd love it back. I went a little overboard.

I went out and got my hair and beard cut. Then a mani and pedi. And when I got back home, I did something I hadn't done in months. I got down on my knees in front of my statue of Buddha and I prayed. And I said thank you.

In fourteen hours, my life turned around. My world was suddenly beautiful. And because I felt beautiful for the first time in months, my attitude to everything changed. On Monday at work, people even commented on how great I looked and how up I seemed.

I wished I'd done this months ago. But the head is faster than the heart.

Brian popped over one day to have a look at the transformation. He walked around nodding his head.

"This is real nice, man. You should have done this a long time ago."

"I know," I said. "Still, it's done now."

"Can I be honest with you? I'm glad you're selling it. I never liked this place."

I was shocked and a little hurt. "Why not?"

"I never thought I was good enough to be here."

"Really?" I asked.

"Your potlucks and parties here, uh-mazing! Like when twenty, thirty people are round. But like this, one on one... Uh-uh. Like sitting in a gallery."

Brian was right. I also never felt like I belonged here either. I realized in the days after, it had been a way for Gunnar and I to say to ourselves and everyone else, "Look at our fabulous life." A validation-seeking exercise. My favorite houses have always been older, craftsmen-type places. Wood beams, fireplace, super comfy, a bit kicked around. This house was like an expensive venue, not a home.

Dana sold it the first weekend it was on the market.

CHAPTER 11

*"You need to be careful with your heart...
You could fall into old habits very fast."*

— MARTIN

MARCH 2018

PACK YOUR BOXES. ALL YOUR BOXES.

I ROLLED INTO WORK THE NEXT Friday pondering what part of LA I'd live in. I still had a week in the house, and Brian had offered to let me crash on his couch till I figured out my next steps. Maybe I'd look at some rentals over the weekend.

The first email in my inbox was from management, asking if I could come upstairs to have a chat as soon as I got in. I sat down with a couple of people who I had only seen as I passed their office doors on the top floor of the building. I didn't know what they did, but they were important. And they very nicely offered me a coffee when I sat down.

My client was leaving the agency.

There was no way they could afford to keep me.

My last day would be at the end of March. In four weeks.

The news was delivered quickly, professionally, and without emotion. And I received it the same way. No one in the agency could know yet, I was told. I also couldn't share this with anyone outside; word could not get out in the industry. We stood, hands were shaken, follow-ups were promised as details were generated.

I went straight to the elevator, down to the divorce bench, took a seat, and started giggling.

I don't think there has ever been a person in the history of California so happy to lose their job. I was free. Free from the job that was killing me. Free to start again.

Free to go to Berlin?

By the time I got home, I'd already picked a leaving date. April 10. Just over five weeks away. One-way ticket.

Walking into the house, I looked around and thought, I'll take my clothes, some art, my books, kitchen knives, and that's it. Gunnar was coming the next day with a van to get his things. He could have it all.

Lily was happy for me, though she had concerns about me leaving the country.

"Lily, I'm not going to stay here just to wrap up my divorce. I'm tired of being a puppet on a string that everyone gets to yank around. I'm going to live my life."

Then I wrote Gunnar an email. I informed him that the client was leaving, I was finishing at work, and that I no longer wanted to live in America. Since we'd already arranged that he was going to come the next day, he could take all the stuff he wanted. Plus we'd also have to figure out how we'd wrap up the divorce before I left.

I was giddy. This could all be over in five weeks with me living in Berlin and the proceeds of half a house in the bank, I thought. I'd be set. Putting on some loud music, I jumped and ran and danced around the house. Let this old rainbow burn to the ground.

Gunnar arrived on the weekend with a big truck and two guys to help him. He was wearing different clothes. I wondered if the new boyfriend had been taking him shopping. As they packed everything up that wasn't in my pile, we thrashed out how spousal could work.

I'd be lying if I said that I didn't love watching him struggle with losing his checkmate. He'd had me over a barrel and expected to for years. I'm sure he'd already made plans for how he was going to spend all that alimony. And he'd lost it in a day.

"Did you look at our new offer?" I asked.

"You're cheating me out of what I'm owed," Gunnar said.

"What you're owed? You're getting half a house that you didn't pay for, all the furniture that was in it, and some alimony. It's not as much as it would be if I was full-time, but it's still more than most people's take-home pay."

"This isn't fair," he complained.

"Gunnar, we have no kids, you have no debt, and you have a full-time job. You get to go and live the new life that you want. And now so do I. Could you not be happy about that?"

"I'm only following the law," he maintained.

"And so am I," I retorted. "It's different for freelancers, look it up."

"I'm taking you to trial," he said furiously. "I'm getting what I'm owed."

Being nice had gotten me nowhere. Begging had gotten me nowhere.

"Gunnar, you're psychotic. You play perpetrator through your lawyers, then you play victim in public. You don't love people, you just love what they offer. I can't believe we slept in the same bed for eight years. I heard about the new boyfriend, by the way. You have no idea how to be alone, do you?"

The chorus cheered as I dropped the mic. The voice shook its head in disappointment. Gunnar stared back quietly. Then he got up and went to the front door, pausing once to turn back around. He gestured to the house.

"I'm sorry you thought you had to do all this for me, so that I'd love you," he said quietly, looking at me in the eye. He got to see how hard this punch landed as he closed the door behind him.

I had a dream that night that Gunnar and I were kissing in the forest where I'd proposed to him. We whispered passionate things in each other's ears. Waking up with his dream smell in my nostrils and the taste of his kiss on my mouth, I rolled over and reached for him, snapping awake as my hands pawed empty sheets. Climbing out of the glue of sleep, I remembered the night before. Today was meant to feel like a victory. Again with my expectations.

The part I hated most was that Gunnar had hit the bullseye. I accused him of only loving me because of this life I provided him with, but I had also believed that that was the only way I could keep him.

I should have picked up the emotions diary. Instead I picked up my phone.

John. You're not going to believe what happened.

WHY AM I MEETING YOU NOW, MARTIN?

Two days later, for the very last time, I left the front door of my house—which was going to be someone else's the next day. I'd taken one final look round and tried to squeeze out a tear, but couldn't. I smiled at my melodramatic attempt at a scene. I was done with the house and this life. This was a good day. I pushed the keys through the postbox for Dana to pick up, loaded up my car, and didn't even look back.

I was now living with Brian while I was wrapping up LA, and setting up Berlin. John was sending me a wealth of links and information ahead of the move. I started gathering pieces of paper I'd need from old employers, embassies, landlords, etc. I often wrote back saying I didn't know what I would have done without his help. When I asked if this was too much work, John always waved my concerns away with a "Pleasure, treasure."

Being roommates with Brian was fun and with the weight of the house sale off my shoulders, the end of my job less than a month away, and Lily working hard to finalize the divorce before I left the States, I was feeling younger than I'd felt in years. Brian and I hung out on the sofa at night chatting, watching TV shows, making dinner. And talking about men.

"You should put a profile up again," nudged Brian.

"Dude, I'm not feeling it."

"C'mon, man. Have some fun on your way out!"

"Gunnar's probably got profiles up. I don't want to see him. And my lawyer told me not to have any social media presence."

"What, Gunnar's going to take you to court 'cos you're having sex? He's got a boyfriend already! If you see him there, block him, and don't talk to anyone about your divorce—a) for legal reasons, and b) not sexy. Just be, like, a guy on his way out of town. You're a short-time-only offer!"

Without a lot more arm-twisting I had a profile up.

First message popped up. A young guy. I opened the message to see he'd written, "Hi Daddy."

"What…?!" I exclaimed.

Brian looked over my shoulder and burst out in a belly laugh.

"It's not funny, mate!"

"Karl, he's…" Brian leaned in to look at the guy's stats. "He's twenty-two! You're forty-six. You could, not just technically but in the state where I grew up quite legitimately, be this kid's dad. Honey, it's science."

"Yeah, but…"

"Sweetie, the world didn't stop when you were with 'He Who Shall Not Be Named' for eight years. Y'all need to look in the mirror, see what's up, and embrace that shit. You're in the 'Daddy' box now, happened to me when the first grays started coming through. So if some poor kid needs to work out unresolved issues with his father in your bed, that's community service right there."

"OK. I'm not saying he's wrong, I just need a second to catch up here."

"Take your time. But not too much, y'all only got weeks now."

While I was thinking about how to reply to the kid, another message popped up.

"Ooh, look at them scramble for that fresh meat," giggled Brian.

The next guy that messaged was handsome. Really handsome. Also close to my age. Good. We texted a little back and forth. There was a rapport. We arranged to meet on the weekend for a coffee.

And when I walked into the café, there sat Martin. Even better in real life. And the feeling was mutual. It was one of those, "How have we not met before?" moments. Martin had moved to LA the year before I did. He lived centrally. We were into the same museums, artists, fashion designers. We really liked each other's style. It was a meeting of minds. Of course one of us is about to leave the city, we laughed. Martin was curious about the move.

"Everything has come to an end here in America for me," I explained. "My marriage is over, my client is leaving the agency, I've had three jobs in a row that have ended abruptly and weirdly. I just think the universe is telling me it's time for a new chapter somewhere else."

"Be careful," Martin said.

"What do you mean?" I asked.

"When you go through times of great change, you are open to lots of new things. Good and bad will come. Take us, for instance. You're leaving, I'm staying. We're never going to be boyfriends. But maybe good friends. Meetings like this are a good sign for you. But you need to be careful with your heart. I can see how damaged you are. You could fall into old habits very fast."

Martin went on to tell me about how he'd been married and divorced years before, when they first made it legal. He and his ex were still on very good terms. Even so, he'd spent a long time developing the ability to be in the present and accept things for what they were in that moment.

"You will do yourself and other people a lot of damage if you try to make things into something they aren't right now. And maybe never will be. This isn't a time to get to know someone else. Get to know yourself. It is both the simplest and hardest thing in the world to do."

I nodded my head, taking his advice in.

"And one more thing," he said. "Get ready for the crash. It's going to come. You're riding on adrenaline and it'll run out."

"I think I'm already there, mate."

Martin smiled. "You'll see."

Martin and I did stay friends and saw each other a couple of times before I left. But after that first meeting, I thought a lot about what he said. I told myself that's what going to Berlin was about: getting to know myself, having time, making space, becoming a master of my aloneness. Even the voice agreed with that.

As for John, I was planning to do all these things with him as a friend. Then we'd look at it in a couple of years. That didn't pass the voice's lie detector test.

THE WIND DOWN

The last few weeks in LA felt like I was killing time in the departure lounge.

My job was tapering off dramatically. Meetings were called that I wasn't needed in. Fewer people were looking for me. I came in later and left earlier and it made no difference. My phone was quieter. Work was taking on a new Karl-less shape.

Soon it was my last day. A round of handshakes, a cleared desk, a farewell meal with my team, the last hugs in the parking lot.

All I did was count the days. And think.

I'd come to Los Angeles twelve years earlier with my sights firmly set on being a screenwriter and winning an Oscar. I'd changed back to advertising again and had a pretty stellar career, done things I never dreamed possible. But now didn't know how I felt about my industry.

I'd met the man I was going to spend the rest of my life with. Then asked for a divorce.

What had it all been about? I wondered in those last days. A whole chunk of my life spent in a land where I'd always dreamed of living, and yet I'd achieved nothing that I'd set out to do. Plus, Berlin was starting to scare me. It's all well and good when something is a desktop screensaver fantasy. Now it was becoming real. It was the first time in my life I was moving somewhere without a job or any idea of what I was meant to do when I got there. I wondered if I should have just been going back to Australia. But I had to follow my instincts. It was Berlin or bust, for whatever reason.

I was energized, and exhausted.

Everything I was taking to Berlin fit in two boxes and two suitcases. However, I had a shipping container full of lessons and an abyss of freedom I was staring down into. It was terrifying all over again. This huge gaping space to fill with I didn't know what.

As I hugged all the wonderful people who came to my leaving party—these magnificent men like Brian, Gideon, Mitch, Minh, Martin, Joshua, and a dozen more who'd been such pillars over the last eight months—I knew that this was the start. Family and friends. They'd take first place in my freedom. Everything else would have to fit around them.

THE THREE-LEGGED DOG

Ever since my divorce began, I'd thought a lot about a woman who'd walked her dog in the park with me back in San Francisco. She had this gorgeous golden labrador, happiest dog on the planet. Then one day she showed up at the park with her dog, who now had only three legs.

She told me he'd been hit by a car. When her dog came out of the anesthesia, he went to stand up and fell right over after trying to rest his weight on the leg that was no longer there.

Then the dog did the damnedest thing, she said. He looked at the place where his leg used to be. Then he wiggled his three remaining legs. With his new inventory and bearings, he figured out how to stand up and take a few shaky steps. After a minute of test-running his new 3 Series, he went over to the corner, had a pee, then came to lick her face with a "So, what are we doing?" grin.

As she told me this story, I looked over at the dog. Apart from the missing leg, he was exactly the same. Running around, hanging with his friends, huge smile on his face. No drugs, no therapy, no support groups, no movie-of-the-week deal, no standing around waiting for someone to ask him about his missing leg so he could tell his sad story.

As my relationship, finances, and sense of self fell away, I'd try to think of him running around the park, the breeze blowing around his fur, totally in his happy and joyous element. He needed nothing more than what he had. He was fine. I wanted to be like him. He did it in five minutes. It was taking me a little longer.

Lily and I had made two more unsuccessful attempts to settle the divorce before I left. The money from the house sale was in escrow, but Gunnar wouldn't sign any documents about how to divide the money up, so I couldn't touch it yet. I still didn't know how this whole divorce was going to end.

With only half a paycheck left in the bank for Berlin, I went to a tattoo artist and had a three-legged wolf running with a big smile on his face tattooed on my right forearm. It was to remind myself that I would always have everything I needed, even if it was just my skin and what was underneath it.

THE REST OF YOUR LIFE IS NOW BOARDING

There's always a hiccup. In the days before I left for Berlin, the place where I was going to stay there fell through. I had to scramble to find something fast.

Hi John. You there?

Sure am. How did the leaving party go?

It was great, mate. Thanks for the playlist of German songs.

A moving to Berlin party isn't complete without some German rap and a bit of Cabaret. How's your last few days? he asked.

Hit a pothole. My place in Berlin fell through. If you hear of anything going anywhere, let me know.

Kismet! Maybe it's our lucky day. I'm moving into a different apartment in the collective in three months, but the people there left early. My new flatmate's already there, and we need someone for the short term to cover the rent.

I'll take it. If it has a roof and a bed, I texted, *I'll figure the rest out.*

Brilliant! John texted back. *But there's no bed.*

If it's got a roof, I'll figure the rest out.

Ha! Then it's a deal.

Mate, you are saving my life again, I wrote.

Not a problem, I'll get the paperwork rolling to have you registered in the building.

My last morning in Los Angeles, Brian and I drove to LAX in his car, parked at the curb, and got my suitcases out of the trunk.

"Well, this is it, Brian. I'm off, mate."

"I'm gonna miss you, man."

We hugged a long time.

"Thank you for that night in the diner," I told him. "You said the shit that had to be said. You're a true friend."

We hugged again.

"Go on, man. You're gonna miss your flight."

"I love you, Brian."

"I love you too, man."

And with that, Brian got in his car and drove off. I looked over the view from the airport and remembered the day in 2006 when I'd landed there and thought, "God, this place is ugly. But I'm going to own it by the time I leave."

Oh well, I thought, I made a good run at it.

I took one last look, exhaled, and said goodbye to everything I'd done and didn't do. Then I rolled through the doors of the airport and left America behind.

CHAPTER 12

"Get ready. This is about to get ugly."
— The Emotions Diary

APRIL 2018

BERLIN. AGAIN.

"Surprise!" I said to John Hare's smiling face as we met at Tegel Airport and hugged.

"I have to say," John replied, "I've not met many people who can turn the universe around so fast. You're a Class-A Manifester."

Soon we were carrying my stuff up five flights of stairs and putting it all into what would be my new room. John had been a true champion. He'd borrowed and found enough furniture to make the bedroom livable, including a writing desk and chair. The one thing the place didn't have was a bed.

"But I figure that you can sleep with me at my place till you buy one," John offered.

"That would be grand. Thanks, mate. You're a lifesaver."

This is when I met Adnan properly. Adnan, John, and another friend of theirs called Taina all lived in the collective in different apartments but wanted to have a place together. Taina would be moving in in a couple of weeks. Adnan was already there.

Adnan was a tall, lean guy with a short beard, who dressed like a total academic. Taina had a dramatic streak of gray through her dark undercut, and was always clad in a mix of thrift-store and mystic clothes. A notebook, where she composed new poems, was always within her reach.

Adnan was from Syria, had come three years earlier as an asylum seeker, and was now a fluent German speaker, working at the university he'd studied at. Our arrival stories couldn't be compared at all, but the thing we had in common was Berlin. It's always been a beacon for people everywhere seeking new lives.

John took me on a tour of the hood, pointing out where all the essentials were. Then, after a nap and a bite to eat, we headed out to see a band. As we watched them play in a weathered cave of a venue, a haze of cigarette smoke hovering above us, I felt charged up. I'd made it. I was in Berlin. Whatever the future held, this city was my first step. Berlin would let me find out who I was now. Everything seemed possible. I could be an artist, I could start a consultancy, I could become a yoga instructor. I couldn't wait.

We got back to John's place in the wee small hours, and I ended up lying next to John in his bed. The bulbs he'd planted on the windowsill had started to bloom, perfuming the room.

The moonlight cast a wide diagonal line across us in the bed. We smelled faintly like sweat, alcohol, and smoke.

"Good first day?" John asked.

"Great first day," I replied.

"I'm glad you made it back," said John. "Even though it was sooner than we thought."

"Same."

Then we kissed. Then it became deeper. Our bodies started intertwining. And then something from the worst and most desperate part of me climbed out. I grabbed John Hare like a man clamoring for a life raft. It got very weird very fast. John sensed it and wound things down. "Let's get some sleep."

"Yeah, good idea. I'm exhausted," I said quickly.

As John drifted off, I lay next to him wondering what the hell had just happened. I scared myself with this need that burst out like an erupting volcano. I told myself I was just tired and not to worry. Eventually I drifted off too.

Late next morning when I woke up, John was already gone. I made coffee and texted him. He was out running errands and would be back later. When he returned, he was carrying an airbed with him. "You have somewhere to sleep now." I thanked him and we silently made an agreement to not talk about what had happened the night before.

Instead, we got busy with paperwork for getting me set up in the building, registering with the authorities, and officially being on the radar in Berlin. Like most countries, there's red tape. But German bureaucracy is something to behold. There are so many rules that no one knows them all and they always change. And there's always a new one that you only hear when you are at the counter again, talking to the same person you spoke to last time, who denies ever telling you what they previously told you.

Also, everything is always your fault. You hear, "Everyone knows this," way too often, accented with an eye roll or a deadpan stare. The widely used term "Berlin service" is not a compliment.

Over four intense days of running around Berlin with John, I finally had an Anmeldung, an official registration at an address. This is the single most important piece of paper you need to start a life in Berlin. From here you can organize your visas, apartment hunt, get a bank account, and so on. John was amazingly accommodating for all my newbie needs. Overaccommodating. I wondered if I was taking too much. He answered every question asked and not asked. If he thought of something I'd need to know, he'd send links. In those first days, he took me around Berlin almost like a tour guide. He was a wealth of information about the city and its artistic, political, and queer history.

While doing all this, John was also prepping to leave for a three-week trip. It was for a writers' residency he'd been accepted to in Stockholm, and he was excited to workshop some new pieces. We talked at night on the floor of the apartment's unfurnished living room about writers, thinkers, and the history of art in Berlin. Whole parts of my brain were coming to life again.

The night before he left, we hugged on the doorstep of my place and he went down two floors to his apartment. I didn't ask, but I'd really wanted him to sleep over. It was a bad idea. The memory of that desperation that lurched out the first night we'd had together still haunted me. As I lay in bed, I could feel that all was not well. I pulled out the emotions diary and made my first entry since arriving in Berlin.

This desperation I'm feeling for John isn't rational. I can feel myself grabbing at him like a life raft. What is going on?

Get ready. This is about to get ugly. You have been on survival mode for so long, you haven't had this much quiet in an age. You've got some PTSD to deal with now. No one can help you. Not John, not anyone. This shit is coming out of the box and it's not going to be pretty. Try not to let it splash up on everyone around you.

I was angry with the diary. This was the first time I ever remembered feeling that way about it. I was fine. Damaged, sure. But not as bad as it was making out. Maybe I didn't need the diary anymore, I thought. Maybe I'm in my post-diary stage.

The next morning I had some fun business to attend to. My favorite thing in the world is to be on a bike, riding in the sunshine. People wish they could fly, but birds wish they could ride.

Cycling had been my main sport for years. I did all my best thinking out on the road. It was cheaper than therapy too. For years, I'd wanted a fixie as a commuter bike but that wasn't possible in the hills of SF or with the clueless drivers of LA. Berlin, however, was built for it—flat, with bike lanes, and cars that looked for cyclists. I couldn't wait to pick up the one I'd seen online.

A quick test run around Berlin's biggest bike shop and I'd found my new best friend. A Tiffany-Blue fixie. I was riding her home from the store on an early summer day in my new city, feeling excited and free. It had been nearly a year since I'd been on a bike. Drunk on freedom, I was going too fast in a city I didn't know well.

A guy on his phone stepped out into the middle of the bike lane. I slammed my brakes on to miss him. Roadworks had thrown a sand patch up onto the bike path and my tires skidded out from underneath me. I hit the ground at speed, left knee first, and then left hand, palm grinding against the cement. I came to a halt by the side of the path. The guy came running over to help me. He was older, spoke no English, and I shooed him away, insisting I was fine.

I picked up my bike, straightened the wheel, walked to a nearby bench, and sat down. It was then that I saw I'd ripped open my pants and blood was leaking fast from a huge scrape across my knee. There was gravel in my palm. The pain started kicking in. I went into a pharmacy and the lady behind the counter was soon out, sitting me in a chair, dressing the wound, and gathering the medical supplies that I'd need.

I was furious. Not with the guy, but with myself. It was such an amateur move to race through a city you don't have a feel for. I felt like I'd ruined my Berlin adventure before it had even begun.

After a painful cross-city journey, I arrived back at the collective and hobbled up the stairs to the fifth floor. Showered, wounds re-dressed, I lay on the blow-up bed in my room seething with anger, waves of pain radiating from my knee and hand. I had this strong urge to call Gunnar. Which made me angrier for needing him, sadder because I couldn't call. So, I lay there feeling an overpowering sense of injustice. And after about an hour, I started crying.

Since New Year's, when I'd set up Berlin as the Promised Land, I hadn't shed a tear. It was the thing I'd needed to keep it together and get out of LA in one piece. It had made my now nine-month-long divorce seem like it had all been for something. The Berlin fantasy had done its job. It had gotten me here. But the enormity of what I'd gone through since August now came home to roost.

I lay in bed unable to move as the post-accident adrenaline wore off, realizing how badly I'd banged myself up. It was my back, shoulder, and a foot as well. Bawling my eyes out, I went back over everything that had happened since I'd said to Gunnar that I wanted a divorce. It had cost me everything I'd had to give, and anything left had been taken by work. Now I'd been robbed of my new start. Injustice was what I wanted to feel, but instead a sense of inevitability descended.

Martin had been right. An emotional crash had always been coming. I'd just needed a physical one to kick it off.

PHYSICALLY, EMOTIONALLY, AND LEGALLY SPEAKING, YOU'RE SCREWED

I woke up the next morning and enjoyed the first two seconds before my body reminded me of the day before. Wiggling my fingers and toes, I rolled onto my side and a shot of pain from my knee hit my brain. OK, body, I thought. Other side. Got it.

Slowly, I sat up in bed. Everything hurt. I stood up using the wall for balance and tested putting weight on my bad knee. It wasn't great. I could walk, but with a very severe limp.

Getting to the bathroom to pee took an age. Making coffee in the kitchen was an epic task. Adnan was alarmed to see the state I was in. He very kindly went out to get groceries. Then I remembered the crutches. In the small storeroom at the end of the hall, two crutches were leaning up against a wall. No one knew how they got there. I pulled them out and found they were not just in working order, but they were relatively new. It was a strange thing about the collective—pretty much anything you can think of was probably on a shelf or behind a door somewhere in the building.

After adjusting them, I was mobile. I looked down at my three-legged dog tattoo.

Was this a prophecy?

The phone rang. It was John.

"What happened?" he asked. "I can't shake this feeling that something happened to you yesterday. You were furious. I felt it."

I laughed. At least our psychic connection wasn't damaged in the accident.

"I had a bike accident. It's not good. Banged my knee up, having trouble walking."

"Dammit! The day I leave! Why didn't you call me?"

"There's nothing you could do," I said, wanting to sound brave, "and it was totally my fault. I'll be OK, I just need to rest now."

"If you need anything, please call me."

"John, focus on your work. I promise I'll let you know if something goes awry."

We talked a bit more before John had his first workshop. I was touched that he was so concerned. The pit of loneliness I'd been in the day before was abating. You have enough money to last a few months, I told myself. You just need to rest up.

Then I checked my emails. A new one had come in from Lily. Attached was a letter from Gunnar's counsel demanding this month's alimony and threatening legal action if it wasn't there in the next two days. Baffled, I wrote back asking her why I had to pay it since I didn't have a job anymore. It was still the middle of the night in LA, so I would have to wait another six hours to hear back.

Finally, I got a text from Lily after lunch and we got on the phone.

"Didn't you pay it this month?" Lily replied.

"No, Lily. I don't have a job."

"Karl, you still need to apply to have it altered. It's not automatic. We can apply now. But it's already too late this month. You'll have to pay it for April."

"But that's going to wipe me out. That's almost all my savings!"

"How soon can you get your work visas?"

"It's going to be months. There's a process. My savings were going to tide me over."

"Why didn't you apply from America?" Lily asked.

"Why the fuck didn't anyone at the firm apply to have my spousal changed after I got fired?!" I yelled.

"Karl, don't swear at me."

I took a breath. "OK, you need to get Gunnar to sign the escrow agreement. That's the only way I'm going to have any money."

"They're stalling. I can't compel them. It's a tactic. You're over a barrel and they know it. They won't sign, they'll choke you out. I've seen this before."

"Why didn't you mention that? I thought he had to do it in a certain time frame post-sale. I need that money! What can you do?" I demanded.

"You need to transfer the spousal support for April today. Then we need to take them to trial. They are saying no to everything and offering no counter. Honestly, I've never seen anything like this. Nearly ten months and no settlement when there are no kids is insane."

"What's a trial going to cost?" I asked.

"Twenty to twenty-five thousand," Lily said. "And that's just yours, you may have to pay his costs too. The judge will decide. But you have half a house locked up in escrow. They'll have to release it sometime, so you'll be able to afford it."

"So, I'm about to have my savings wiped out, I have no way to make any money, I have to go to trial because they won't budge, and I might have to pay all their costs for that too out of my half of the house that I have no idea when I'm going to get. Please give me some good news, Lily."

"Karl, you were the one who earned more. The law is on his side. There is no good news. Look out for spousal support adjustment documents that you'll have to sign, and the trial docs that I'll generate today. I have to go, I'm at court with another client. Bye."

I listened to the dial tone.

She was angry with me. I wanted to call her back and vent more. Instead, I opened my laptop and sent most of the last of my savings over to Gunnar. Looking at the seven hundred euros I had left, I started making survival plans. On the back of an envelope, I figured out how long I could make it stretch for. It wasn't long.

Lying back on my bed, I stared at the ceiling. Ludo's words came back to me: "This isn't happening to you, it's happening for you." I willed myself to believe it. But I couldn't.

I woke the next day in a rage and found the emails in my inbox as promised. Numbers, numbers, numbers. More legal mumbo jumbo. I'd spent $20,000 already with this firm and here's where I was? So I unloaded. I wrote back a searing email telling them exactly what I thought of their firm and appraising their work from the start. As I outlined incidents, I thought over and over again that I should have left them a long time ago.

Then I pressed send.

Six hours later, my phone rang.

"Hi, Lily."

"Karl, you are way out of line."

"I don't think I am. You've made a hash of my case. You haven't gotten one thing you promised done, and now I'm broke."

"You have no idea what I've done for you."

"Really? Enlighten me." Wow, I thought, I sound like a dick. But I couldn't stop.

"No other client has my private cell number. I gave that to you because I felt bad for you. No other client has talked my ear off for two hours on a Sunday morning. That's time away from my children."

I didn't know she had a family. I'd never asked.

"I spoke to the rest of the partners and we've decided that we've taken this case as far as it can go."

"What does that mean?" I asked.

"We're going to resign you as a client. I'm going to pack all your files up. We can send them to your next solicitor."

I was gobsmacked. "Whoa! Lily! How am I going to go to trial?"

"That's something that your next solicitor will need to figure out."

"But I don't have enough money left to hire another attorney…"

"Then you can represent yourself. That's an option under the law. I'll send you a link."

"They'll kill me in court. I won't stand a chance."

Lily took a moment. Her voice changed. "Look, I'll help you. I can tell you how to prep. I'll do it for free. But we can't handle this case anymore."

"OK," I said, my voice suddenly very small.

"I'm really sorry, Karl."

"OK."

"I hate this. I feel like we're breaking up or something. I always liked you, Karl. I wish we'd met under different circumstances."

"I'm going to go now," I said.

"I'm sorry."

"OK." And I hung up.

I went to the bathroom and vomited. Then I lay in my bed wide awake until dawn. It was the most afraid I can ever remember being in my life.

HI GUNNAR. IT'S ME.

The next morning, I woke and took stock. My body felt worse. On crutches, I made it to pee, then to the kitchen to make coffee. All that effort exhausted me. I replayed the last two days, reeling from how fast my fortunes had changed.

But also asking the question, what was my role in all this?

I should have left Lily's firm many times over. Why had I stayed? Pulling out the emotions diary, the book proceeded to read me.

You stayed because you wanted to be a victim. You loved telling your friends about your latest lawyer dramas. And you fed off it. But how many were real, how many were just the law, and how many were your fault? In every case, you beat them up for it. You are just like Gunnar in this way. Victim and perpetrator. And you used your lawyers like an emotional punching bag, just like Gunnar did to you. No wonder you two stayed together for so long.

There it was. The ugly truth. I was sleeping on an air mattress, in a former squat, in a foreign country with a few hundred euros left and no visas. I didn't even have enough cash to buy a ticket home or back to the States. My credit cards were maxed out. But it was all my doing. The warning bells had been ringing for ten months but I'd ignored them all.

I'd kept thinking the divorce would be wound up soon, so changing lawyers seemed pointless. Now I realized maybe the reason it had gone on for ten months was because I hadn't changed lawyers. Then again, maybe other lawyers would have gotten exactly the same result. They would have had to go up against the same laws. And they would have had to represent the same client, who didn't get his victory in two phone calls and so had chosen victimhood instead.

Worse than that, I had treated Lily very badly. I beat her up over calls and emails because I wanted a result that maybe no one could have achieved, while completely overlooking that she was a human being with a life. I'd never even inquired about her family or her life outside of the office. In ten months. Who had I become?

I hated myself.

Options. What options did I have now? I didn't know anyone with the amount of money I'd need to start a new trial. Finding a new lawyer in America while I was in Berlin was going to be a challenge. And how much longer would this go on for anyway?

I just had to face the facts.

I'd lost. For real this time.

The law wasn't written to help me in any way, and Gunnar and his attorney had played it masterfully. They hadn't done anything illegal. So maybe this was what I deserved, I thought. The full truth of why I'd gotten married and what I'd done in the last nine months in my divorce made me wonder if I was the bigger villain.

My mind went back to sitting with Joshua in his office the previous August: "Just give him the house." I wished I'd had a time machine.

So I rang Gunnar. We hadn't spoken since the night he sucker-punched me with that hard truth of me throwing money at him so he would love me. I hoped he hadn't blocked my number.

"Karl?" I could hear the surprise in his voice.

"Don't hang up, I need to talk to you."

"Sure, give me a second. I'm in a restaurant. I'll go outside."

I waited while he had a muffled conversation. Probably the new boyfriend.

"OK, I'm back," Gunnar said. "How are you?"

I could hear the LA traffic and city noises in the background. I felt homesick.

"I may as well tell you because you'll find out soon enough. Lily fired me."

"I heard."

I was angry that I hadn't even been able to give him the news. "So here's what I propose. The house is in escrow. You won't sign anything, and we both know why. So give me a number on how we split it. There's no more spousal support or lawyers' fees paid by me. We make this deal, then we never have anything to do with each other again. Do you understand?"

"Understood."

"And Gunnar, the number has to be something I can live with. Or I'll fight to the death. Because right now, I have nothing left. So I have nothing left to lose. Do you understand?"

"I understand."

"You've got twenty-four hours."

"Got it," he said. "Listen, all this aside, how are you?"

"Gunnar, we're so far beyond that. Twenty-four hours. Send me the offer in writing in an email. Goodbye."

MONEY, MONEY, ALWAYS THE STUPID MONEY

Less than twenty-four hours later, Gunnar wrote back. He wanted his half. But he also wanted all the spousal support he felt owed. It would leave me with less than five percent of our total.

All those years and all that hard work and this was how it was going to end? I thought about it though. It would be over. I could start again. There were no guarantees that this isn't what I'd end up paying over the next few years anyway. Maybe a lot more.

I grabbed the crutches. I had to get out of the house. Managing to make it to the park at the end of the road, I found a tree and sat on the grass underneath it. I watched all the young people on picnic blankets, jealous that they had so much time and all their choices ahead of them.

I started thinking about what it would look like, starting again with nothing. Or was it nothing? I'd asked for my freedom. Be careful what you wish for, I thought. This might be what freedom really looks like.

Money hadn't just been the end of my relationship, but also the best parts of myself. I'd sold off my conscience and all my waking hours for cash. I threw money at every problem. I tried to buy love with it. But I knew after a couple more months of living in the collective, I could learn how to live cheap and smart. I was constantly amazed by how people there could make anything out of practically nothing, find every shortcut, every work around, stretch pennies.

I felt calm. A real sense of calm. Like all was going to be right with the world. Losing everything felt like I was gaining everything.

The old rainbow I'd been chasing my whole life was well and truly a pile of ashes now. But maybe out of the ashes, a better one would rise.

For years, I'd had this fear that I was going to be on my deathbed, look back and think, "Oh shit, I did it all wrong." There was an even greater fear that it wouldn't be as an old man. Instead, I'd have this flash of understanding a second before I died in a car crash on the freeways in LA—that I'd spent my whole life postponing my life.

Bronnie Ware is an Australian former nurse who specialized in palliative care. Basically, she took care of people in the last twelve weeks of their lives. She wrote a book called *The Top Five Regrets of the Dying*[15]. No prizes for guessing what it's about.

She noted that many people didn't realize until right at the end that happiness is a choice, and that they wished they'd allowed themselves to be happier. Instead of making changes that would allow them to laugh and be silly, the fear of change and the familiarity of old patterns kept them stuck in a life that they pretended was going well. Ah, I thought, that sounded familiar.

People also suddenly realized that all the toys they'd amassed didn't amount to a hill of beans next to the personal connections they'd had (and potentially lost) in their lives. And at the end, people were impossible to track down again. I thought about Justin, my best friend from high school. Also gay. We'd been Facebook friends for years, but not set eyes on each other in over twenty. A couple of years before my divorce, I'd been in London—where he lived—on a business trip and we'd met for an afternoon coffee. Then we'd spent the next fourteen hours together. We parted early in the morning in tears. It was one of the most amazing days I've ever had.

Many people regretted having spent a lifetime not saying what they really thought in an effort to keep the peace. Ware noted that people settled for a mediocre existence instead of becoming who they could be. Many also fell into her care after developing conditions nurtured by the bitterness and resentment of biting their tongues.

Every single male patient she nursed said they wished they hadn't worked so hard. Every. Single. One. Gunnar often spoke about how I was never around and even when I was, I wasn't really there. Digging a little deeper, I asked myself where this manic need to work and amass wealth came from. The emotions diary offered the answer. I had a lifelong fantasy of going to a high school reunion, rich and famous, and showing them all. All those boys who'd made my life a misery.

My career had been propelled by the scared kid I was in high school.

And the top regret of the dying—number one with a bullet—was that people wished they had lived a life true to themselves, rather than others' expectations. This was the most common regret across both sexes. When they were coming to the end, people dismayed over the sheer number of dreams that they hadn't realized. Places they never visited, art they never made, careers they never pursued.

Other people's fears had fueled mine and created a script I'd followed because I was told it would make me happy. Get an education, get a job, and now that it's legal, get married. Buy a house, plan a retirement, make as much as you can. These fear-fueled directives made up all the stripes of my rainbow.

I'd been living someone else's life, waiting till I was rich enough to live mine. Now that I was broke, I could finally do what I wanted to do. The irony of it all made me laugh. It was time to make some changes. I'd haggle with Gunnar a little, but essentially, I'd decided to take the deal. The day after, I went up and down about it: anger, regrets, shame. But after all the studying I'd been doing of my emotions, these were clouds that passed.

Then the phone rang.

THIS IS HOW YOU HIRE A LAWYER

Scott Presman rang me out of the blue to check in. Scott and I both worked in advertising and had also been in a band together in LA. Something I had always admired about Scott is that he would never suffer at least one of the regrets of the dying. Scott always said exactly what he thought.

He's a huge fan of Berlin and wanted to know what life was like there. But also how the divorce was going, as he'd gone through one a couple of years before.

"So, basically Scott, I've done the math and I figure I can make what I'll have left stretch over…"

"Nope," Scott interrupted. "This is complete bullshit."

"I know, but maybe this is the lesson that I have to learn from the universe."

"Spare me the Cali-namaste crap. You're using my lawyer now. I'll lend you the money if you need me to."

Scott went on to tell me about his lawyer, Michael Nathan. It probably goes without saying that Scott isn't intimidated by many people, but Michael was one of them. Scott described him as six-foot-five, a powerlifter, always in a suit. "And he will save you from yourself. Do whatever he tells you to. I didn't, and it cost me more in the long run."

I had nothing to lose by having a conversation. Scott introduced us over email, we agreed on a time, and later that day I was on the phone with Michael Nathan.

"We can fix this, " Michael said calmly. "We set a court date and take them to trial over spousal support."

"Michael, we already did that and it didn't go so well for me."

"No, Karl. We take *them* to trial over spousal. He has a job, you don't. He should be sending you money every month.

A divorce is a two-way street. So forget signing over the escrow money. As far as I'm concerned, he owes you now."

Michael officially had my attention.

Our conversation was very business-like, peppered with questions like, "Why did you do that?" and "Why haven't you done this yet?"—all with a very let's-waste-no-time, full steam ahead attitude.

Michael didn't indulge the emotions of my divorce and cut me off if I started going down the rabbit hole of anything he couldn't use in a courtroom. He was scientific, only interested in hard facts that were going to help the case, getting evidence to prove it, and thinking three moves ahead.

Every bone in my body told me to say yes to Michael. Instead, I did what I should have done ten months ago in LA. I called every straight divorced guy I knew and got referrals. One of them even recommended his wife's lawyer: "I wish she'd been mine," he quipped. Now that I had no more shame about it, now that I knew there was a brotherhood to tap into, I had a list of several great lawyers in no time at all.

Had I still lived in LA, I would have taken time to visit their offices and looked them in the eye. Instead, I had a day of calls and I read all their Yelp reviews. Yes, even lawyers get reviewed on Yelp.

Many reviewers complained about not getting the results they wanted, but they could have had expectations beyond what the law would allow. I didn't know and I didn't care.

I was hunting for patterns.

Reading Lily's firm's reviews, several people complained about exactly the same style of work that I'd experienced. Lost documents, missed deadlines, do-overs, forgetting whole chunks of their defense. Oh well, I thought. I was doing it right the second time around. By the end of the business day, I was satisfied that Michael was the man. His attitude, his strategy, his confidence. People loved him on Yelp, and a pattern of professionalism and satisfaction was clear. So I called him back and did the most American thing I think I've ever done in my life. I paid for my second divorce attorney on a new credit card.

Swapping lawyers could not have been easier. Michael's office sent me a form to sign called a "Substitution of Attorney." It's essentially a standard letter to my previous firm saying he was now representing me and to send all my files over. He filed for a court date. The earliest he could get was in seven weeks, but I was to pay no more money to Gunnar. Not a cent.

I'd had so much fear about changing lawyers, and so much invested in being a victim, I couldn't believe how easy and fast it had been to find a good one, change firms, and sleep at night again.

THE BEST THINGS IN LIFE AREN'T THINGS

Michael and I got busy prepping an offense against Gunnar. Michael had already started sending letters to them, outlining our plan to take them to court over spousal support. He hoped to settle before, but I warned him. Gunnar never settles.

This time, though, was a very different experience than with Lily. For one, Michael was a completely different kind of lawyer. But equally important was that I went into round two with a totally different mindset. I didn't care what the final result was anymore, I'd already accepted the worst. No expectations.

This was the most profound of shifts because until this point, our whole divorce had been about winning and losing. I realized that this new mind state was just the evolution of a long line of events.

Berlin, nearly two years before, with Myriam's Law and swearing I was going to figure out who I was. Meeting John Hare. Trying for another year with Gunnar. Leaving Gunnar. The voice and the emotions diary. Making my divorce my crisis of identity. Writing the manifesto. Being set free from full-time advertising. Moving to Berlin. The collective.

Accepting that I was going to lose everything.

Over the next couple of months, I stopped watching TV and started reading. I went to museums, exhibitions, and openings so I could meet new people. I learned patience. I stopped wearing a fitness tracker because I decided that technology wasn't allowed access to anything below my skin. I studied German. I cooked my own food. I set budgets and stuck to them. I smelled flowers. I smiled at animals. I started growing plants. I rode my bike everywhere. I would only do three things in a day and always leave two nights a week for myself to have quiet time. I stopped talking about my divorce. I met new people and didn't tell them about that part of my life.

I began a massive reeducation on how to make money stretch. I don't want to make out here that I was destitute. If I had really had no money to eat, I could have borrowed a little from my family or friends. But I thought, I've come this far, how long can I last and what else can I learn?

I had noticed that there were people around Berlin who collected plastic bottles for a living. You get twenty-five cents per bottle at the recycling machines in the supermarkets. So one day I found and took sixteen water bottles to the supermarket, got the €4 refund, and used it to buy a sandwich, beer, and clementine from the corner shop. Then I went and sat in the park and had my lunch. In Germany, you can drink alcohol in a park in the middle of the day. Because civilization.

The sun was shining, people were around, I[1] had a free lunch. I felt like a king as I ate my little picnic. The flowers had come out on the trees in a blaze of red and pink, the sunshine tickled my skin, the bread was fresh and spongy, the beer was cold and delicious. I had a book that a friend had lent me.

I couldn't remember being this happy in years. It was all so simple. Old me would have breezed right by the park in an Uber on his way to that restaurant that he'd waited two months to get a reservation at.

My new friend Turlough texted. A bruiser of an Irishman with a fierce intellect, he'd been living in Berlin for almost ten years. Like me he sat in front of screens all day, so when he was out, he was out out. Also like me he was reading a book, but in another park. He rode over so we could read together. Instead we talked about books for six hours over a couple more beers. A whole part of my brain that hadn't been used in a long time was suddenly firing on all cylinders.

As I walked home, the sun still high in the sky at 8 p.m. in the European summer, I realized this was one of the greatest days I'd had in a long time. I liked this day, and I liked the person I was in it. So I had more of them. I started calling them "plastic lunch" days.

CHAPTER 13

"Listen Karl, life will give you everything you want, just not on your timetable."

— JOHN

MAY 2018

THE DISAPPEARANCE OF JOHN HARE

AND SO, LIFE WENT ON in Berlin. I spent my days writing this book. I began to prep all the documents I'd need for my work permits. I made new friends. I had days where I was happy and grateful that this was how it felt to be Karl that day. But I did very much feel like I was emotionally at a loose end.

Until John came back from his trip. Just knowing he was around made me feel anchored in a way I wish it didn't. I knew this was something I should have kept working on, but it was just more pleasurable to bask in his rays.

John was inquiring about my visas and preparations for my upcoming interview at the Ausländerbehörde, the much-fabled immigration authority. Every foreigner you meet in Berlin has an Ausländerbehörde story. They're never short, easy, or happy tales. So naturally, I was freaking out about it.

John insisted on making sure that I was in good shape for it. Despite my protests, he countered with, "Accidental Angel, mate. This is what I do." So, I happily accepted. And we got very busy over a few days gathering some of the trickier, must-be-in-German pieces of the documents puzzle.

"You know," I said to John one day, "I've always moved countries for a job. So the company has always given me a person to handle all this stuff. It's a lot harder when you have to organize it all."

John shot me a look. "But you're not, I'm helping you."

"And I'm very grateful. I don't how I would have figured it all out without you."

"I'm not your 'person' who helps you do these things."

I was alarmed as I realized I'd offended him. "John, I know that. You're my friend. I'm always worried that I'm taking advantage of you."

"I'm doing this because I want to, just so we're clear."

"Got it. Clear."

"Good. Let's get on with it then."

I was taken aback by his reaction. I guessed we were getting to know each other. John had a line, and I hadn't figured out where it was yet.

The line came a few days later. It was a Saturday and I was trying to print something. There were several copy shops around, and with no idea which was the best one to try, I dropped John a text. Wanting to make it quick and easy for him, I kept it brief.

Printing question. Any recommendations for a copy shop in the area?

I saw him read it, as the tick appeared next to it on the screen, and not answer. He was a lightning-fast responder when it came to local knowledge questions. After half an hour went by, I decided to head out and try my luck.

Eight hours later, I got a reply.

Karl. I didn't like the tone of your text. Felt as though I'm your Meat Siri. Hope you found a copy shop and that you had a productive day.

My first instinct was shock at how extremely he'd interpreted what I thought was a simple request. Then anger at "Meat Siri." It was intended as a slap and it had landed hard. Then came on a wave of desperation; John was my lifeline in Berlin and the idea that he had felt so wounded by me was too much to bear.

So I began my texted apologies. I explained how I'd wanted to make it easy for him hence the brevity of the text and that I was sorry it had been read the way it was.

Read. No response.

A few minutes later, I sent another apology.

Read. Again, no response.

Then, a third apology for making him feel like he was some kind of servant.

Finally, John responded, all happy that we had gotten that out of the way. We made some plans to get together the next day.

The next day, John cancelled our plans. Then the line went dead.

He barely returned texts.

We didn't see each other. I would walk past his front door in the collective on the way up to mine and wonder who he was with and what he was up to. But so be it. If John's pattern was to take up all the space in someone's life, then pull the rug out without warning and disappear, my only choice now was how I was going to feel about it.

I wish I could say that I used it to bolster myself and start building. However, John had been my only certainty. And now he wasn't.

Plus, there was no guaranteed future for me in Berlin. If Gunnar was awarded a high enough spousal support payment each month, I couldn't make enough money in Europe to service a US debt.

The enormity of what I'd given up in the States was just becoming apparent. I missed its familiarity. I was older, feeling it, and had been beaten up by the previous year. It had been thirteen years since I'd made the move to America and the one to Berlin had taken more out of me than I was expecting.

I was tired. Beyond tired. And the wall I'd been propping up that held back all the unresolved emotions started breaking. It was too heavy. So I let go of it, lay down, and let everything come. I thought I'd had the crash on the bike. I thought I'd already had the emotional crash too. But just like Martin had warned me in LA, this was the real one that had always been coming.

THE CRYING TREE

This is how Berlin was supposed to go. I was supposed to have my divorce wrapped, my house money, take a year off and become an artist. I'd write this book, but also—in my atelier that I'd rent with views over the city—put together a printing area where I was going to make posters like I'd always wanted to.

I was supposed to be at every underground art and literature event, speak fluent German in six months, and make my dent in the cultural world of Berlin.

Simply by having my feet on the ground, my sexual mojo was going to magically return, and I would eat my way through Berlin's infamous sex scene as a true adventurer.

I wanted to try everything, be everywhere, meet everyone. And for much of it I wanted John Hare to be by my side. My cock-eyed plan had been to build my own world and become a master of my aloneness, all while I became John's muse. It wasn't supposed to be straight away, but that John and I would end up together was inevitable. In retrospect, this was an insane person's plan. An insane person's expectation.

Berlin in early May 2018 was looking very different.

My days roughly fell into three parts. Firstly, I'd wake up in the collective and do exercises for my knee, then write this book for three hours. After that, I'd walk a short distance to the local park on my crutches. This would take a lot of the physical energy I had at the time. I'd collect and recycle bottles, grab lunch on the way, then cry for hours under the tree with the flame-red leaves, at the bottom of the grassy knoll where friends and lovers lay with each other on the greens. If I sat on the far side of the tree, no one could see me.

It may sound strange, but I sat there crying every day for weeks. I couldn't believe how much blocked-up shit had to come out of my system.

I cried for my marriage, for my husband, for everything that had gone wrong and how we'd treated each other.

I cried to mourn the death of the relationship, because the war had been so immediate and all-encompassing, I'd never had a chance to just say goodbye to what Gunnar and I had.

I cried for all the friends I'd left behind, for my loneliness, and for the distance I felt between me and everyone around me, who came from a different culture and spoke a different language.

I cried for all the money I'd made and let fall through my fingers, the coulda, woulda, shouldas of my screenwriting career, and all the time I'd lost going back into advertising.

I cried for my injuries, the injustice of my situation, the new life that I couldn't even move around in properly.

I cried for my parents, my family, the dog I gave away in Singapore fifteen years before, who'd died of a broken heart because I left her behind for a job in Japan.

I cried for my last four relationships, constantly choosing men who'd left me emotionally and financially bankrupt.

I cried because I had days where I still missed Gunnar.

I cried because I hated myself for missing him.

I cried for all the years, all the years, all the years of everything.

Then I'd get up, pick up my crutches and shuffle back to the fifth floor of our building and hang in the apartment because I didn't feel like doing anything else. Each day though, I felt the load getting lighter. Chipping away at this thing under the tree was helping. Despite the yearnings for any kind of companionship, I kept to myself.

What that time under the tree helped me see is that for my whole life I'd thought that I wasn't good enough, and so I'd chased rainbows and handed power and approval over to others. And that's where I had to start focusing.

At least the next part of my journey had a compass.

BERLIN WILL OFFER YOU MORE THAN YOU CAN IMAGINE

When I was finally down to only one crutch, I was getting around again on public transport, sitting in the disabled seats, walking very slowly with the old people up the stairs, discovering where the elevators were in the stations.

At first my speed frustrated me. Then I learned to like being in slow motion. The people were like fish, all swimming quickly past me. I remembered being like one of them, always in a rush doing something I thought was very important.

One day I was talking to a young American woman who worked in the store where I was buying some stationery supplies. She was an artist, with long black hair, a tiny fringe, and a tattoo over her eyebrow that said "Peace."

We got talking about Elizabeth Gilbert's book *Eat, Pray, Love*. Gilbert writes about every city having a mantra, the thing that you're supposed to do there. In New York, it's "Achieve." In LA, the mantra is "Succeed."

"Berlin doesn't have one," the woman told me, folding my receipt with ornately patterned black nails. "That's why I moved here."

At my confused look, she continued.

"Berlin literally asks you to do nothing. Take advantage of it. You can go into the nightclubs and come out two years later. You can look in the mirror for hours every day if you want. Run from yourself or confront yourself. Both are correct. When you slow down to Berlin's speed, it will offer you more than you can imagine."

Soon, I was off the crutches. Physically and metaphorically.

Berliners don't give a toss about your bank balance. Berliners are interested in who you are as a person—what you're reading, what you're thinking, what you're pursuing.

No one dresses to impress. My fancy designer clothes, which I was now a little ashamed of wearing, got ripped by the city every time I wore them. I caught jackets in subway car doors, snagged myself on random nails and hooks, put holes in T-shirts from… Actually, I don't know how most of them got there. People call this sort of semi-disheveled state "the Berlin

Style." I thought it was an affectation. But no, Berlin destroys everything that doesn't matter.

After a month, John texted. Replying felt like picking up smoking again but I texted him back. Slowly, we started hanging out again. His hair was longer. It suited him. He was very fond of a new rainbow kimono a fuckbuddy had given him, which he seemed wear and mention a lot. But one day at coffee, I had to ask what the whole copy shop thing had been about.

"I thought we were past that," he replied. "I had to draw a line."

"Yes, but you don't give a lot of clues about where that line is. One day you can't help someone enough. Literally the next day, you feel hurt because you think your help is being abused. From where I'm sitting, it's pretty confusing."

We had a weird conversation about tone. It seemed he wasn't interested in understanding my side of it.

Finally, I gave up. "So we're clear, if I ask you a question now it's because you're literally the last person I can. I'll exhaust all other options before I get to you."

"That was mean," John said.

"Wasn't that your point though?" I asked. "To not rely on you all the time? Wish granted."

"OK," John said, a little hurt.

"New deal," I offered. "We don't pull each other's strings and instead talk about stuff, OK?"

"Deal," John agreed.

We shook hands on it, a little too theatrically.

Yet still, every time I saw a text from John, I leapt at it. Even though my life was slowing down, when it came to John, my heart sped up.

JUNE 2018

STOP HIDING, START BUILDING

Flowers I'd planted started blooming in the window of my room that looked out into the courtyard. I'd sit here most days with a coffee watching the residents of the collective get their days going: asylum seekers, teachers, artists, musicians. We'd wave to each other. I liked my neighbors a lot.

I was riding my bike again as my knee healed. The divorce was in limbo till the middle of the month when the court case had been set. There was nothing to do but look for a place to live.

With John due to move in at the end of the month, I'd been apartment searching like mad, but with no luck. "You'll find something through a friend," said Taina, who had now also moved into their share house. "Those apartment sites are a waste of time."

Berlin had gone from somewhere with hundreds of landlords on the streets begging you to rent their apartments even five years before, to a place where now hundreds of people turned up to see every vacancy. It was one of the hottest cities on the planet when I moved there. If I was a landlord and had a choice of five different German couples with full-time jobs or a single foreigner with no visa yet and no money in the bank, well, I wouldn't have needed any think music.

Then, the day of my visa interview finally came around. The Ausländerbehörde looked like a gray filing cabinet, where hope was filed away to perish. Summoning courage, I walked in with all my documents checked three times over and three times again.

In the waiting room, surrounded by nervous people from all over the world, I read texts from friends wishing me well.

On the stroke of my appointment time, my number flashed on the board. OK, I thought, please let my interviewer not be here just because they couldn't get a prison guard job. Walking into the room, I rubbed my sweaty palms on the back of my pants.

To my great surprise, a short, thin, sparky lady spun around in her chair, beckoning me to sit with a chirpy, "Good Morning!" We exchanged pleasantries as I handed over my file. She flipped through it, nodding her head.

"Well, this all appears to be in order," she said sunnily. "We need to scan it and review it. Please wait outside for twenty minutes. When you see your number again, come back. We will have questions."

I thanked her and returned to the waiting room. I tried to read a book but all I did was look at the words printed on the page. As promised, twenty minutes later my number came up. Wipe hands, walk in.

"Mister Dunn, how long would you like your visa to be? Is two years fine?"

"Two is great," I said.

"Wonderful."

And with that, she stamped my passport, put a sticker in it and handed it back. "Welcome to Germany."

Thanking her profusely, I hustled downstairs before anyone realized that they'd made a profoundly grievous error and called a SWAT team. Then I walked quickly out into the sunshine and stood in the grassy block opposite the building. Ducks floated by on the river, quacking loudly as I stared at the visa in my passport just to make sure it was really there. After so much had been taken, finally something was given.

The first brick to build with.

EVOLUTION IS A MESSY BUSINESS

In the tough slog with my emotions that was those early months in Berlin, I looked again at that drink lid Catherine had sent me with the Charles Darwin quote: "It's not the strongest of the species who survive, nor the most intelligent, it's the ones that adapt most readily to change."

So, I picked up a copy of Yuval Noah Harari's *Sapiens: A Brief History of Humankind*[16]. In it, he outlines how 100,000 years ago, there were at least six different types of humans in existence. Now there's only us, Homo sapiens. Probably because I had been scribbling fashion designs during high-school science classes, I had always thought that these different humans had evolved from one type to another, rather than all six species taking part in a battle where only one version would dominate and survive.

Homo sapiens were smarter, faster, and more capable, and they gradually took the resources of the others, who then literally died away. But I'm sure they fought for their lives.

As parts of me became smarter, sharper, and more sentient, other parts were dying hard deaths. These were patterns and ways of being that I'd relied on my whole life, and they were going down swinging.

I felt uncomfortable in my skin every single day because underneath it, a battle was being fought.

"The only thing I can say about your whole situation is that I'm jealous," John said one day as I shared this emotional evolution idea with him.

"Jealous?"

"Yep. It's all ahead of you."

"I don't feel jealous of me," I replied.

"You will. You're about to discover it all. It's like when you meet someone who's never heard of your favorite TV show and you put them on to it."

"Wishing you'd never seen it so you could watch it all again for the first time?"

"Exactly," John said. "It's going to be a bit crunchy for a while, but so worth it. Buckle up, amigo!"

"But John, I feel like I've wasted so much time. On Gunnar, on my career. Like the last decade was just pissed up the wall."

"Think about it like this," John offered. "You are Future Karl, say two years from now. You're looking back at Today Karl. What would you tell him to do?"

I thought about it for a moment.

"Write your book," I answered.

"Great," John said. "I was hoping you were going to say that. Fits with your manifesto."

"I'm just worried about money, mate. I don't trust that I'll get the house money. Something's going to happen."

"Got any freelance yet?"

I shook my head. "Nope. Trying."

He leaned in. "Listen, Karl. Life will give you everything you want, just not on your timetable."

We went on to talk about my house-hunting, which had not been going well. In a week, John was moving into the room that I'd been living in for three months, which meant I was essentially going to be without a place. I woke up every day full of dread about it, relenting to the idea that I was probably going to end up living in a shared house with a bunch of twenty-somethings. That I'd be the dad they didn't want around.

Then John had an idea. Days after he was moving in, he would be heading to England for six weeks for another round of workshops that had just come up. The plan was that he'd move in, stay for a few days, head off, then I could keep staying in the room. Sounded perfect to me, except for one detail.

"I'll vacate your spot for you while you're there," I said.

"No, you can stay in my room," John replied.

I was pleased. Things had been going well between us and I was very keen to see if something physical might happen again. Nothing like that had occurred since that disastrous night when I first arrived.

"I'll set up in the living room. It's only a few days, I don't want to kick you out," John said.

"Great," I said, crestfallen. "I'll give you a hand with the moving then."

THE COURT IS NOW IN SESSION

The day before John moved in was my court case. My lawyer Michael had made an application for me to appear telephonically, which had been accepted. So I was at Turlough's house on his landline. I didn't want to leave anything to chance on the somewhat spotty cell phone signal in Berlin.

Even though I was now unemployed, Gunnar had been unwilling to modify any spousal support payments. He still wanted his money. That I wasn't making. Michael's tactic had been to have Gunnar pay me, since I was the one now without income. I would have just been happy to be off the hook.

Wiping my palms on my shorts, I sat on the phone in Turlough's home office, waiting to be connected into the courtroom. A court official came on the line, read out the procedure and then asked me to wait a few minutes longer. I sat up straighter in my chair.

Then, a moment later, I was connected to the courtroom. It was a phone call, yet my first thought was that I should have worn a suit. As the judge came into the room and I heard the people rise from their seats, even though no one could see me, I stood up too.

Then everyone sat and the session began as our case was heard. First, the judge confirmed that Gunnar and I were both present. I heard Gunnar's voice. He sounded like a strange memory.

The judge heard the opening arguments. From our side, I'd been let go from my job, was looking for work in a country where I had a track history, had my work visas, but—as of yet—no income. Michael went on to note that we had made many attempts to settle with no counter from Gunnar and that they had refused to sign the escrow documents, so I was essentially being put over a barrel. And that we were seeking spousal support in return. From Gunnar's side, they claimed that I was avoiding working, that I could have stayed in America, and that since I had made such a high income before that, I would again. Therefore the payments should continue.

The judge listened to all of it and came to his conclusion. He began by saying that his "eyes popped" when he saw how much spousal support I had been paying, and that a figure like that was something that would never have been awarded in his courtroom if he had heard the initial case.

On our application for spousal support to be paid to us, he noted that he would have considered it, had it not been for all the proceeds of the house sale sitting there waiting to be divided. He ordered instead that there would be no spousal support paid in either direction, pending a further settlement. And the escrow money was to be split between us within two weeks from that day.

With that, the gavel came down. After months of anguish and trepidation, the whole thing took less than twenty minutes.

I came out of Turlough's office in a daze, finding him on the sofa surrounded by his antiques, ice clinking in his whiskey glass as he devoured a book.

"That was fast. How did it go?" he asked.

"We need to go out tonight," I replied.

SURRENDER AT THE TV TOWER

I can tell you from personal experience that one of the worst things you can do with a raging hangover is move house. But the next day, I was carrying John's boxes and furniture up two flights of stairs from his old apartment into his new one. Everyone was excited. Adnan, Taina, and John had been dreaming of this day for almost half a year.

"Put one hand up, facing me," John said excitedly as he carried the last box in.

I put it up.

"And now the other one!"

I put up the other and he double high-fived me hard.

I watched the three of them talk excitedly about the traditions they wanted to start for the house, the ways they'd set it up, how they'd paint it, what would go where. I was so happy for them. But listening to their plans reinforced that I still didn't belong anywhere. The exertion and excitement of the day finally gave way to tiredness and we all went to our separate rooms.

I couldn't sleep. Being in the same house as John with all these unresolved emotions made sleep impossible. I hadn't even had a moment to process the complete lottery of the day before in court. I knew Gunnar wasn't going to settle though and it's anyone's guess what the next judge would say about the situation. I'd won this round at Vegas, but that's no guarantee for the next.

I got up, got dressed, and slipped out into the Berlin summer night air to walk. It's what I do when I don't know what to do. I tried to turn it into a walking meditation but couldn't still my mind.

Finally, I ended up on the steps of the Volksbühne, the people's theatre in Rosa-Luxemburg-Platz. Built before World War I, it survived both wars to become the jewel in the DDR's cultural crown. Sitting on the low, descending circular steps at its entrance, you have a clear view of the Fernsehturm, Berlin's famous TV tower. The tower dominates the skyline. Built at the height of the Cold War, the East Germans used it to spy on West Berlin. Its job was to watch. And watch it had. This tall, shining tower had observed a lot of history, the spherical viewing space at the top like a huge eye, reflecting back the lights of the city.

We sat there staring at each other.

It made me remember the times when I'd started to come to Berlin to freelance over ten years before, still a hustling screenwriter trying to sell a script in Hollywood. I'd walk the streets on nights just like this one, and talk to the tower, telling it my woes and fears.

"Hi, TV tower. It's me again. I'm back. And things aren't going so great. I won the court case but the divorce is all still up in the air. Who knows if I'll actually get the money. I'll believe it when I see it. Till then, I'm down to my last couple of hundred euros. I don't have anywhere to live in a few weeks, and no way to pay for it.

"I'm majorly screwing things up with John. I don't know what I'm going to do with my life. I think I missed the ad career I wanted. Even if I still wanted it. I don't feel lovable and don't know if I ever will again. Because I think something broke in me.

And I don't think it's fixable. Everything's a mess and everything hurts. Any suggestions?"

I looked at the tower. It didn't say anything.

It didn't do anything.

Maybe that was the answer.

I thought back to a few weeks before under the crying tree, where I'd let go of the steering wheel of my life. But letting go isn't doing nothing. Really, I was still sitting in the driver's seat, ready to grab it. I already had a few times.

Staring up at the TV tower, I took its unspoken advice. Do nothing.

So, I surrendered.

This was it. I would do whatever happened. I would stay here in Berlin or have to go back to America if the case didn't go my way. I would be with John, or I wouldn't. Either way, I would have a new life and it would start now at this moment of giving up any power or say.

Thanking the tower, I walked home, more tired with every step. There, I climbed the five flights of stairs, left a trail of clothes to the bed, and slept well into the afternoon.

ONE BEER AND AN APARTMENT PLEASE, BARMAN

"So how's the apartment hunt going?" asked Turlough as we were out one night at the Prinzknecht Bar in his neighborhood. It was the bar you find in every gay city. Big, decorated in the 90s, and—love it or hate it—you start or end a lot of nights there.

"Not great," I responded. "I've seen so many places, put in a ton of applications, and I'm not hearing a peep out of anyone. The whole thing is such a racket."

"In what way?" Turlough inquired, taking a sip of his beer.

"Well, now that I've given up on trying to find a place on the sites, I've moved onto the Facebook pages. People who have to break their lease are responsible for finding the new tenants, right?"

"Right."

"I went to see one place. Didn't love it, but it would be a place to start. They'll put me at the top of the list but only if I buy all their furniture when they leave. Two thousand euros for some second-hand, broke-ass IKEA crap."

"So, it's basically a bribe…" Turlough laughed darkly. "Desperate times."

"Correcto, friendo. And I, Turlough, am a desperate man. So I said yes. Was going to borrow some money from my folks but then the people rang later to say that another person had offered them more."

Turlough laughed.

"Right?" I said. "I'm looking for a WG now."

WG is short for Wohngemeinschaft. Basically a shared house. In the big, old-style apartments of Berlin—like those of the collective—the actual rooms themselves are enormous and there's usually no common area apart from the kitchen.

"I'm going to be the weird old guy with out-of-date 90s pop culture references, who tells them to clean the bathroom and turn the music down."

Turlough looked over my shoulder.

"You might be in luck," he said. "Some friends of mine are over there. They own a few apartments around Berlin. We can ask."

Like someone had just pointed out a hot dog to a starving man, I whipped around.

"Where? Where?" I asked.

"Follow me." And with that, Turlough led the way across the bar.

He introduced me to his friends, explained my situation, but the magic words that came out of his mouth were, "I vouch for him."

Here is a thing about Germany. Unlike LA where people will recommend someone they only met the day before, a personal reference in Germany is something that is given seldom and with great importance. If someone stakes you, they stake themselves.

Turlough's friends then told us that they had one coming up in Prenzlauer Berg, a former East German suburb that had been gentrified. It was a very nice area. Kind of famous for being where the ex-models and their club-promoter boyfriends had moved to have kids. Officially, it's the baby capital of Germany. There are more babies born in that zip code per capita than anywhere else in the country. Where punks had lived in squats fifteen years before, there were now yoga studios and kindergartens.

"I'll take it," I said.

"Would you like to see it first?" Turlough's friend asked.

"Yes," I replied, "but I'll take it."

A couple of days later, I had a tour. It was perfect. Back of the building, second top floor, a balcony overlooking the inner courtyard with a huge tree in full bloom. I shook the tree's branch in a handshake to say hello.

When I signed all the documents at my new landlords' office, they asked me more about why I'd decided to move to Berlin. And they were intrigued by the fact that I was moving with no furniture, just some clothes and art.

"When I moved here to Berlin in the nineties," my now-landlord shared, "all I had in my first place was a mattress and a television on a chair. Some of the best days of my life."

I hoped this apartment would be the start of some of mine.

CHAPTER 14

"We didn't win the right to marriage. We won their right to marriage. Which means we also won their right to divorce."

— KARL

WOULD YOU EVER GET MARRIED AGAIN?

SUMMER IN BERLIN IS SOMETHING to behold. I was discovering a whole different side of the city that was never apparent in all my winter work trips there. Berliners had often said to me—almost apologetically as we drank hot Glühwein in the snow and stamped our boots to keep warm—that Berlin was a completely different city from June to September.

Meeting Berlin in the summer is like suddenly finding out a friend you've known for years has an incredible singing voice, can dance tango, and juggle. And if you're looking for anyone you know in the summer, you'll find them at the beer gardens. Literally dozens open up all over the city. Throngs of people ride their bikes to them to meet friends, sit at long fold-out tables and benches, eat wurst or pizzas, soak up the rays, and enjoy the season.

Turlough and I were sitting in Café am Neuen See, the beer garden by the lake in the middle of Tiergarten, Berlin's Central Park. He was listening to me talk about the book. I'd just started to tell a few people about it, still feeling like I was an imposter, but also wanting to soundboard ideas I was playing with.

"So where do you come down on it all at the end?" asked Turlough.

"How do you mean?"

"Marriage. What's your take on it then?"

"Jury is still out on that one… Literally." I laughed at my own unintentional joke.

"Let me put it like this. Would you ever get married again?"

My beer stopped halfway to my mouth.

I had no answer.

I'd made my list of why I'd gotten married to Gunnar. Never again would I do it for those reasons. But the idea of ever doing it again made me think, hang on, what is marriage? I'd never even questioned or thought about where it came from originally.

I obsessed over these questions for a few days till I made my way to the bookstore. It was only now, in the middle of my divorce, that I started doing the research and asking the questions that I wished I had before I got married. I started studying the history of this thing I had jumped into blind and feetfirst.

Get out your library card. Marriage is about to get read.

SO WHAT IS THIS MARRIAGE THING, EXACTLY?

Before I get into this question, a couple of things.

I'm not a lawyer. I was a guy who was in the middle of a divorce and trying to make sense of it all in the research that I conducted to the best of my ability. None of what follows in this chapter is legal advice. And the facts when I wrote this may not be the same whenever, or wherever, you are reading this.

Also, this chapter may read more like an essay in the middle of a story. This, however, is where I was at in the journey. Anyone who's been through a divorce knows that you have a lot of questions that no one seems to have any answers for—at least not any that make any sense to you.

I draw my own conclusions here, and I'm sure a divorce attorney might well counter some of my opinions. By the end of my research, while I would say I had some answers, I had even more questions—ones you might want to ask about the whole institution too.

The question I started with was, "How did marriage become what we know it as today?"

What I found was that before marriage had its own industry, magazines, and same-sex couples lobbying for our right to have one, it had been many different things that weren't a man and a woman falling in love and staying together till the end of time.

Marriage as a custom dates as far back as civilization. It existed in some form in every society and religion. It was a functional tool of survival to provide a safe environment in which to breed, protect bloodlines, ensure continuance, and award property rights and wealth.

As towns and then cities developed, power went to the most established families. Marriage was viewed as nothing more than a contract between families to grow their mutual influence and wealth.

I was aware that in the Bible many people had married their cousins, but I was surprised to discover an estimated 80% of marriages throughout history were between first and second cousins[17].

I also was aware that polygamous marriages were practiced historically in the Mormon church and some other religious groups, and are still legal today in some West African nations[18]. But I also discovered ghost weddings, once practiced in central and northern China to appease the dead in the afterlife.

The list goes on and on, but the basic point is that marriage has been many things in many cultures in many periods of history.

The most surprising thing I discovered was that it was by no means a sacred act at the beginning of Western culture. From the ancient Athenians to the thirteenth century, marriage had zero religious significance. Most people got married at home in plain clothes, by literally signing contracts.

It was only in 1215 that the Catholic Church finally said that all marriages had to be publicly posted with the local parish to cut down on the number of invalid marriages[19]—in other words, to stop people marrying multiple times. It was only from this point on that marriage was canonized as a sacrament, a holy act in the eyes of God.

And in America in 1639, the government finally got involved. Massachusetts was the first state in America to begin issuing marriage licenses[20]. By the nineteenth century, all American states were doing the same.

"Love marriages" as a concept only started in the first Industrial Revolution. With money and income no longer tied to the ownership of land protected by tactical marriages, people were free to follow a new idea—that unions could be with people they found mentally and physically attractive, not simply whoever owned the plot on the other side of the hill.

At the same time, democracy—with its central tenants of individualism and liberty—was growing in prominence and fueling new ideas of personal determination as American historian Stephanie Coontz writes in her 2016 essay, "The Radical Idea of Marrying for Love."[21]

Romantic love had its watershed moment in the Victorian era, when the ideas of courtship and wooing were created. And when a teenage Queen Victoria walked down the aisle in a white gown with a train, a fashion trend was set that still exists to this day. Had the internet been around in 1840, that white wedding dress would have crashed it.

It goes without saying, but it must be said, that women have had the short end of the stick since the beginning of marriage, because they were always the property in a marriage contract. So in the 1970s, equality became the new ground being broken in the world of marriage, with the idea that men and women had equal obligations in a union. Gender-based roles gave way to the flexible division of labor and income.

And here, finally, is where we LGBTQ+ folks come in.

From Stonewall onward, we're all pretty familiar with the recent history of the movement as it pertains to marriage. First decriminalization, then de facto recognition of same-sex couples, then registered domestic partnerships, then civil unions, then finally same-sex marriage.

But where same-sex couples differ in our pursuit of happiness is that we are always fighting to get what every heterosexual has had for free. When marriage equality finally passed, it was like a minor miracle occurred. I never thought it would happen in my lifetime.

I loved saying, "My husband." Every time, it felt like an act of love.

But also, an act of protest.

And that right there, is the big *but*.

For the last couple of thousand years, marriage was something that we didn't even think about because we were battling societies that made us illegal, jailed us, and—in many cases—put us to death. Societies that classified us as deviants, mentally disturbed, and usually some kind of scourge according to their holy books. Today in many, many societies, we are still fighting these battles.

Which made me ask the question: Considering marriage was something invented by societies who have been less than kind to us for most of human history, why did we want to copy them? Especially when they might just snatch it away again as politics shift.

I think the answer is that LGBTQ+ people share the same problem all minorities do when we fight for change against a larger, oppressive section of society—when something is put behind barbed wire, our focus and energy is all directed at the barbed wire. Not what's behind it.

Same-sex marriage, though, isn't the only wind of change in the landscape of matrimony.

Andrew Cherlin wrote an article for *The Atlantic* called "Marriage Has Become a Trophy."[22] In it, Cherlin notes that when the Pew Research Center asked Americans in 1978 whether marriage was an outdated institution, 11% of the country said yes. By 2010, it was 39%.

Are we as a community trying to play catch-up? To have what we've been denied, even as heterosexual society is rethinking marriage in growing numbers? In 2013, Pew conducted a survey of the American LGBTQ+ community. Only 46% said that the legal parts were an important reason to get married, versus 71% who said "companionship" and a whopping 89% who said "love."

However, companionship and love are not by-products of a marriage. Apart from tax breaks, Gunnar's and my legal status didn't change at all from being registered domestic partners to husbands. The law would have treated us exactly the same as if we'd been married.

So, a simple question from Turlough about whether I'd ever get married again had spawned a solid couple of weeks of research, which landed me in a place I wish I'd been before I walked down the aisle.

I'm not anti-marriage. I'm not pro-marriage. I am pro-choice. Someone's personal, informed choice. I wish I'd taken the time before my wedding to get to know what marriage was for me in every context: historically, legally, religiously, and spiritually. And for me alone. Not for society, the cause, or the chorus.

Then I wish I'd asked these same questions of Gunnar. In retrospect, we'd both made massive assumptions on the other's behalf.

The barbed wire around same-sex marriage is gone, and may it stay that way forever. But my hope is that we replace it with questions we ask ourselves before we blindly take up what's on the other side.

Here is what I will say in defense of marriage. I learned things about relationships and commitment that I only learned because I was married—about not letting things slide, about not compiling a list of grievances. Instead, since I was planning to be with my ex-husband forever, it forced my behaviors to change. To try and solve things. To be in partnership. To not give up because I was already planning the end.

Obviously, it didn't work out. And perhaps I might have learned these lessons in another way. But being married changed forever how I think about relationships and how to love someone.

I hope Gunnar got that out of it too.

DIVORCE NEEDS A DIVORCE

To say I'd become a little research-obsessed was an understatement. After taking a couple of days off to mull over everything I'd read on marriage, I dove back in. This time into divorce. After all, when we were granted the right to marriage, part of that contract is supposed to be the right to a fair divorce.

Here is something no one tells you when you sign a marriage license. You are signing over the ownership of your marriage to the state. If it ends, you are giving the government all the power and all the say in how it dissolves. It's their marriage now, so it's their rules. And if you don't sign the marriage license, your marriage isn't officially recognized.

So when you get married, there are actually three of you. You, your spouse, and the government.

Even though *Obergefell vs Hodges* levelled the playing field by making same-sex marriages legally recognized in every state in America, there are still grave problems for divorcing same-sex couples.

For instance, establishing the length of a relationship. Let's say you're a gay couple who started living together in 2005. Then, in 2011, you were finally legally able to register as domestic partners. Then you got married in 2013 once that was legal. Then you decide to get a divorce in 2017.

Legally, how old is this relationship? For same-sex couples, this is a huge gray area in the law.

Technically, domestic partnerships supersede any marriage. So, in our example, that's six years from 2011 to 2017. But in some states, you're considered domestic partners if you've been cohabiting for two years, which would now make the start of this relationship 2007. But in the case of same-sex relationships, those laws are being retroactively applied.

So this relationship that was legally six years old, overnight becomes ten. Despite the fact that for the first four of those years, this same-sex couple had none of the legal rights afforded to heterosexual married couples back when they first moved in together.

This makes a huge difference in divorce settlements, because alimony has to be paid for half the time that you've been officially recognized as a couple by your state. And if you've been married for over ten years in California, in many cases spousal support has to be paid for the rest of the lives of the divorcing couple.

On one hand, we should be recognized as equal to every heterosexual relationship. On the other, courts that represent a government and legal system that didn't recognize us at all for a long time, are now retroactively applying the social values of today.

In other words, because society now feels good about the fact that they feel good about us, it seems like some states are stretching those self-congratulatory feelings back to a time when we had no legal standing or comeback.

When we had no right to visit our partners in hospitals, no right to claim ownership of any property when one passed away, no right to any kind of tax breaks, health care, or social standing that heterosexuals take for granted. But now some same-sex couples are battling over it in their divorces like we did enjoy all those things.

Plus there's the aspect of gender in divorce. Marriage is an area where gender and gender roles are one of the most hotly contested issues.

In 1969, Ronald Reagan—who was then the governor of California and himself a divorcé—signed the Family Law Act, introducing the idea of "irreconcilable differences," or as it's commonly referred to, a "no-fault" divorce. Many states followed suit.

Prior to that, divorce was a difficult and arduous process, where one party had to prove "fault" by showing that the other had physically abused them or committed adultery. At the time, women were severely disadvantaged here; how do you get proof of an affair if you have no personal income and can't hire an investigator? So this change to divorce law, for this reason, I'm all for. In fact, there's a whole canon of feminist literature around divorce as a way for women to reclaim equality in their lives.

However, in most American states, today's divorce laws were written to take into account the battle of the sexes as it stood at end of the 1980s. While advancements have been made, particularly for fathers, the notion of needing to "protect women" in a divorce remains in place. The way this is expressed in nonsexist legal language is "the one who earns more" and "the one who earns less," which—for all the wrong reasons—almost always means "the man" and "the woman," respectively. Women typically earn less, are not given the same opportunities, and it's still expected that they will leave their careers to raise children. Please may this all change in our lifetime.

But, and I mean no disrespect to any divorcing heterosexuals, this has nothing to do with me. Or any other gay couple.

Of course I want to fight for the rights of women every chance I have. However, my ex-husband is from Mars and so am I. My marriage was gendered, but in a very different way. I wanted marriage equality with the heterosexual couple getting married next to me. But I wanted divorce equality with the man across the table that I was getting divorced from.

In California, "the one who earns more" may be compelled to pay over a chunk of their salary in alimony to level out the income between them and their ex-to-be (even if there are no children). They may also have to pay all of their spouse's legal bills, plus their own, and still be expected to cover all the community costs as well. Meanwhile, the "one who earns less" is faced with the moral dilemma of having the laws—that weren't written with them in mind—completely in their favor. The power in a same-sex divorce is one-sided and based on your pay scale.

And as a man who was divorcing a man, this law seemed like a punishment. So I have to ask, what was the crime? Or maybe the bigger question to ask is, "Will ending a same-sex marriage become the spanner in the works of current divorce law?"

I'll wrap this up with a story told to me by a friend. His lesbian sister, who lives in New York, got married to her wife. His sister was the biological mother of their child, and also the one who earned more. She went back to work while her wife became the child-rearer and homemaker. The relationship didn't work out, things got ugly, and she found herself several times in a divorce court. And every time, she felt she was treated by the system like the villain. Her wife, not being their child's biological mother, was treated as lesser than because in custody cases DNA trumps everything.

One day she'd had enough, and stood up, railing at the judge. She told him that she was sick of being treated like a deadbeat dad trying to avoid his responsibilities. She told the judge, "I am our child's mother, and you had better start talking to me like I am our child's mother." Then she pointed to her wife and said, "She is also our child's mother, and you had better start talking to her like she is our child's mother."

The judge I'm sure was no idiot but all they had in front of them is the law that's been written. They can see that these laws, and the acknowledged and unacknowledged intent of them, don't fit this case. But again, it's all they have.

We didn't win the right to marriage. We won *their* right to marriage. Which means we also won *their* right to divorce, and what they think a fair one is—or, since the government owns every marriage, what the government thinks is fair.

For heterosexuals.

THE RIGHT TO A GAY DIVORCE

Back in Berlin, between my laptop, the library, and the bookstore, I'd been spending a lot of time reading up. I knew where I stood on marriage. But divorce was a hot mess. Even though what we have doesn't work well, I didn't know what the answer was. There had to be a better way, and as so often in our history, when the rules aren't written for us, we've had to make our own.

So I started casting around my network. Did anyone know of a same-sex couple who had split up or divorced and done it well?

This was how I was introduced to Dylan, a friend of a friend in Australia. He had been a registered domestic partner with a man in Sydney. They had been together for eight years, RDPs for six of those. While they never married, because they split up before gay marriage was legalized in Australia (the country that gave us *Priscilla, Queen of the Desert* was very late to the game here), the dissolution of an RDP falls under the same laws as any divorcing married couple.

Dylan told me that at the start of their relationship when they moved in together, they sat down and looked at their finances. Dylan made less than his partner, so they split all costs 60/40. They bought a house, cars, holidays, and even paid household bills in this way. When their relationship was over, the dissolution was easy. Everything was an uncontested 60/40 split. All they had to do was have the paperwork ratified by a lawyer. Even these costs were 60/40.

The law in Australia is that everything should be split 50/50. I asked Dylan if he'd ever had any regrets about not pushing for that. It is the law after all. He replied that other people had asked him that as well, almost amazed that he could do it but wasn't going to. For him, it was immoral to "make a profit off the end of my relationship." Instead he described the arrangement he had with his ex-partner as "totally and utterly fair." Ironically, that's also the intent of the law.

In America, community property states like California consider both spouses as equal owners of all marital property, so a 50/50 split is the rule. And in these no-fault divorce states, there are substantial limits on evidence that can be taken into account about the end of the marriage. Infidelity, lies, broken agreements, addiction, etc.—which can be the whole reason for the divorce—aren't admissible and have little bearing on the ultimate decision on property.

However, an at-fault divorce state—where you can introduce a lot of mitigating factors for the judge's consideration—isn't necessarily better for gay men. Let's take, for example, infidelity. If it's a monogamous gay marriage, it's simple. But if it's an open marriage, like the majority of marriages between gay men that I've encountered, that's murkier. You might be allowed one-offs, but no regulars. Or regulars, but no boyfriends. Or there could be an "only when the other is out of town" rule. Now you not only have to prove that these rules existed and were broken, but you also have to present them to a probably heterosexual, probably male judge, who probably hasn't lived in a community that has had to make up their own rules because society's weren't written for them. However, he's going to pass judgment on your life and marriage.

Divorce lawyers will tell you that the number two reason gay divorces get ugly, after money, is the dog. For many same-sex couples, the pets are like the kids. Yet, by law, animals are actually classed as property. Whoever's name is on the document owns the dog. The other partner can't get visitation rights to the animal, just like they can't get visitation rights to the coffee table.

I don't like either option: being divorced by laws that weren't written for us, or being judged by someone who's never walked in our shoes.

I DON'T WANT A PRENUPTIAL, I WANT A PRE-EQUITABLE

So how could we do all this better? Not just for same-sex couples, but for everyone?

The only people who truly know what is going on in a relationship are the ones who are in it. No one else is allowed a say in how it starts, or how it runs, but every man and his dog has a say in how it ends—if you don't prepare.

We've all seen enough Hollywood films to know about prenups. They have historically been couched in terms of female predatory behavior or male domination, but thankfully these days you see more storylines where a prenup is about a woman understanding and protecting her worth. Either way, prenups have this dirty image because they are about planning for the end. This is something no one wants to think about when they are in the throes of love. Myself included, way back.

But now I think that prenups are about preserving the love that you have.

The start of a relationship, when two people are still in love, is the perfect time to talk about how the end of things might be. The reason being that if it didn't work out, you want to honor the love you had while you're still feeling it so strongly. In the same way that a couple will happily talk about wills, power of attorney, funeral arrangements, and pulling the plug on life support, preparing our marriages for the common probability of their ending is an act of love. You both get to choose how. No one else.

But I would say that there is an improvement on even this. I call it a pre-equitable, or a pre-eq, if you like. Taking inspiration from Dylan, a pre-eq wouldn't just be a financial agreement but also an operating one.

Let's say a couple are on the same income, and one wants to take a year off to try a new career, go back and study, or take a sabbatical while the other supports them. Should the existing agreement stand, or should it be adjusted and by how much?

It's up to them. No one else.

A pre-eq wouldn't be set in stone. You could revisit it at each change of the relationship to ensure its equitable distribution across both partners.

Of all the divorcing couples—gay, lesbian, and straight—that I met or read about in the course of writing this book, not one of them said that their divorce was totally fair, that they didn't fight about it at all, and that they are still great friends.

Except Dylan and his ex.

The only two who didn't use the law to do it.

GET YOUR HANDS OUT OF MY POCKETS

In the weeks after the spousal support hearing, the court had mandated that the payments stop, but also that the escrow money be divided within two weeks. That time had passed.

My first thought was that Gunnar and his counsel were dragging their feet. When I emailed Michael though, he had received a copy of the signed paper and confirmed it had been sent to the escrow company. It was now their job to divide the amount they were holding.

Yet after another week, this still hadn't happened.

When I got the escrow people on the phone, the reason they gave was, "We couldn't find the paper."

"I see," I said, as calmly as I could. "Have you asked for a replacement?"

"No."

"OK, so literally the only thing between me and my half of the escrow is a piece of paper that you've lost and haven't asked for it to be replaced. Was anyone ever going to?"

"It usually relies on someone like yourself to call and let us know."

The rage I'd felt for every pen pusher who'd been through my personal business rose up and I thought I was going to yell at him. Then I remembered the woman I'd unloaded on at the concert in LA. I stopped myself.

"Have you ever been divorced?" I asked.

"No," the guy replied.

"I'm pleased to hear it. Truly. But I'm in the middle of one. And I've had to deal with a dozen or more people like yourself, with jobs I don't understand, who are somehow crucial to this process, and who all charge astonishing fees that I have to pay. And I am just someone on their production line. Every time I turn around, someone has their hands in my pockets, and no interest in who I am beyond a name on a page and a fee that they charge.

But I am down to my last fifty euros. If I don't get that money soon, I might not be eating. So I'm going to call my lawyer, he'll send the paper again in less than half an hour and then you're going to solve this for me today. Can I rely on you?"

Silence. Then, "I give you my word," he said.

"Thank you, mate. I appreciate it."

That night, I was out with my friends having drinks and mentally counting coins. It was either that or sit at home and fret. And it was two-for-one night at Prinzknecht. Then an alert came through my phone from my bank. I opened up my account and put my thumb on the pad to ID myself. I looked at the number. Holding my breath, I closed the app then opened it again. The money was all there.

Suddenly, my legs started giving way underneath me. I had to sit down, fumbling for a chair. Turlough came over.

"Are you OK?" he asked, surprised by my wet face as I turned to him.

"Yeah. I got the house money. It just hit my account."

He pulled me up and gave me a hug.

"Let me buy you a beer," I said.

CHAPTER 15

"Your crisis of identity, Karl, is to have one."
— Turlough

I THOUGHT MY BEST WOULD BE BETTER THAN THIS

Taina and I were sitting at the breakfast table in the kitchen, reading things we'd written the night before. It was a little tradition we'd started. She was very encouraging of me writing poetry. I felt like an imposter, her being a famous poet in her home country, and me being some unemployed ad guy.

Taina though was slowly but surely making me a better writer, introducing me to themes and formats to flex my wordsmithing. I treasure those days in that kitchen built out of wood scraps and cabinets rescued from the street. Everything wobbled a bit. We'd sit on mismatched chairs, reading things to each other over the tiny table, our voices and breath animating the steam coming off our teacups.

"Where did this come from?" Taina asked about a new poem of mine about untrustable feelings.

"You know, Taina, one of the weirdest things about this whole divorce is that every time something happens, it never feels how I think it's going to. I mean, I'm off the hook for spousal temporarily, and I got half the house money, so I'm not over a barrel. I should be elated. But I'm so down every day. I don't get it."

"Firstly, you could cut yourself a break," Taina said. "You got here, what, four months ago? You were a mess when you landed. Then the bike accident, then all the dramas with the last lawyers, then the new lawyer, then the court appearance. Now you've got visas, cash, and an apartment of your own starting in October. It's been a whirlwind. You're doing great, mate."

"I just thought I'd be further along than this, inside," I said, tapping my solar plexus. "I've done all this emotional work but still feel like I have no handle on myself. Like with John. It's what we talked about; I'm projecting onto him, and it's the same thing I did to Gunnar. And Jochen, Robert, and Leonard. Everyone I've ever dated. And even Lily. I see the pattern, I see myself do it and I can't turn it off. It's not even about them. It's the thing they got stuck on in me that's broken. And that's my responsibility, not theirs."

"Well, I'll say this—you've developed a high self-awareness," noted Taina. "Which means you're on your way, even if it doesn't feel like it."

"I don't mind being imperfect," I said, smiling, "just as long as most of me is perfect."

We giggled. At least I was getting my sense of humor back again.

PATIENCE AND PERFECTION

When am I going to be perfect? That was the question that I'd been dogged by most of my life. I was in the process of letting it go. But it was really sticky.

Trying to feel perfect was a big driver for why I got married and why I'd worked so hard in my career. Both were wrapped up in the idea that I had to arrive at happiness. That there was an end point. That one day, after all this work, I would put my head up and say, "Hey, I made it." From then on, life was meant to be one long stretch of contentment. I would unlock the secret to happiness, stick the car on cruise control, and spark up the grill for the barbeque that was going to be the rest of my life.

Perfection is not a helpful idea. Letting it go was made easier by a few things. First, the bottle cap lid and the Charles Darwin quote. If we were always adapting, then perfection by its very nature is impossible. Everything is evolving and always will.

For years in LA before my divorce, I had been seeing a therapist. Perfection was something that had come up often in our sessions. One day, my doctor asked me a shocking question.

"Karl, have you ever seen a dead body?"

"Uh, no."

He nodded. "You know what strikes you, when you see one for the first time?"

I shook my head.

"They're perfect. Still, calm, and at peace. No internal struggle. They're kind of beautiful."

"So I have to wait till I'm dead to feel peaceful?"

"That's one way," my therapist mused. "Or else accept that you are imperfect in an imperfect world. The two cancel each other out."

The head was definitely faster than the heart on this one.

Years later in Berlin, I read a book by Mark Manson called *The Subtle Art of Not Giving A F*ck*[23]. Mark's point is basically that you can't give a fuck about everything. You only have a limited number of fucks to give in this life. And you have to give a fuck about something. So choose the things that are actually really important to you, and give the few fucks that you have to those. I was still at the stage of working out what was important to me.

At the end of his book though, Mark writes about how he realized the place of perfection he was striving for was a complete illusion. He'd never be perfect. "And why would you want to be?" he wrote. "It takes all the fun out of life."

Like me, he'd been treating it as a destination. I'd embarked on this journey as an explorer and astronaut, still thinking that I'd reach a promised land and begin life anew.

That land though, does not exist. There is no Planet Happy. I finally grasped that the destination was me. Imperfect and always evolving.

Which meant my old foe—patience—would become kind of irrelevant. Because if there was no end point, I wouldn't be sitting in the backseat of the car asking, "Are we there yet?" Instead, I'd be sitting in the driver's seat with my hands off the wheel, surrendering to the road as it unfolded and taking in the view.

Being imperfect is perfection itself.

Now if I could just do that, I thought.

JULY 2018

THE GAY WAY BACK MACHINE

Now that I had breathing room financially, I decided to start living a little. One part of my European dream was being close to friends there and visiting them. I had a list, and the first person on it was Jorge, my illustrator friend in Madrid. He suggested I come for Madrid Pride, so I found myself in his spare room in the heat of a Spanish summer, thinking about how I'd love to line up a bunch of sexy Spanish men and knock them down. Trouble was, my mojo was still all over the place, my dick unpredictable. I was a frustrated ball of desire that was having a punch-up with performance anxieties. My dick and I were best friends some days, fighting others, and not speaking for extended periods.

I was expecting way too much of myself too soon. Despite knowing that, sex was on my mind constantly, so I pushed myself too hard, too soon. A year of celibacy was something I was giving some serious consideration to.

It felt good to be out of Berlin and breathing different air. Jorge was working, so I spent the days writing this book and some therapeutic poetry, walking the streets, going to galleries, and eating my body weight in amazing tapas. Oh, my word, the tapas. There's always a new one you haven't tried. Tapas is cheeky like that.

Jorge and I, who are similarly aged, were getting dressed on the morning of Gay Pride and were about to leave the apartment. However, our mutual "Do we have to?" vibe was palpable.

"Jorge, why are we doing this?" I asked.

"I don't know. Because we're good gays?"

"We should represent," I commiserated. "But do you actually enjoy these?"

"Do I feel proud?" Jorge asked.

Laughing, I said, "I guess, yes."

"I mean, we're so Catholic here and had to hide for so long that it's good to have this thing, and it's out in the open and loud and in daylight. But for me…" Jorge trailed off and shrugged.

"Kinda over them?" I offered.

"Yep."

"Me too."

We looked at each other for a moment.

"OK, let's go," we both said.

On the upside, Gay Pride was loud and packed, which means it was very visible. On the downside, it was loud and packed, which means it was very young. I had to admit it to myself, I was just feeling too old for this kind of thing.

I'd gone to my first Gay and Lesbian Mardi Gras in Sydney in 1988 when I was sixteen and still in high school. My first gay rights rally was at seventeen, just after I'd come out. I had my first boyfriend at university, and my second job after graduation was working for the AIDS Council of New South Wales, a chapter of the Department of Health. If you had asked me then how things would be in twenty-odd years, I would have told you that homophobia would be over.

Yet, as much as things change, we're still fighting for things I thought we'd already have. And personally, I was still fighting for things that I thought I would have sorted out already.

I'd dated older men my entire life, but now I'd caught up to them. Young guys were calling me Daddy these days. But, as I looked at the men in the crowd, it was like I had no radar. I didn't know what I wanted or where I fitted in. I wasn't the young man I was when I met Gunnar, and I didn't feel like being anyone's dad. Maybe I should date someone my own age for a change. Yet there were so many sexual boxes I felt I hadn't ticked in my 'dating older guys' days. In all other areas of my life, I was finding room for patience. But in my sex life, I was angry and busted up, trying to make up for lost time. I just couldn't decide with what.

Realizing I wasn't at all present, I put these sex issues away. I wasn't going to solve them that moment on that glittered and unicorned street as the rainbow flags waved all around me. The fact that I was even there, on a street in Madrid with an old friend, with baby gays who would hopefully never know the extent of prejudice I grew up with, was something to celebrate. We bought drinks and got into the swing of the day.

In the days after, I started thinking about my life as a gay man to date. I was looking forward to seeing Justin, my best friend in high school, again. In school, we were both so scared of ourselves and everyone else, that we never told each other we were gay until after graduation. We'd reconnected in London a few years before, but now Justin was living in Madrid.

When we got together, we talked more about the young men we were, and the lives we'd lived. Beyond being friends, we were touchstones for each other, back to a time when we were newly born gays, deeply uncertain of our place in the world. What our conversations revealed to me was that that young, scared kid was still alive, living on his own in a room in my head with a door that was never opened. But it was open now.

So, I spent a lot of my time in Madrid with a sixteen-year-old Past Karl, who was afraid of his present and the future.

When I'd started walking down this path of using my divorce as my crisis of identity, I never dreamed of some of the places it would lead. I'd dug through a lot of emotions over the last year with Myriam's Law, the emotions diary, tuning into the voice, and sitting with emotions instead of acting on them.

I guessed that inside, I'd reached a layer where I was breaking through into some really old stuff.

So, Past Karl and I hung out in Madrid and I got to know him. Or rather, I didn't block him out. I started catching mental smells of my school uniform, snatches of atmosphere from the late eighties and memories of the summer where I reinvented myself for the start of university. Past Karl had grand dreams of the man he was going to be. But looking back there, I could see now it was just another new guise I'd invented for validation, just like I'd been doing my whole life till then. For my whole life until my divorce, actually.

But Past Karl was a tough time to go back to. So many friends and colleagues had died from AIDS-related causes back then. There was a time in Sydney where I was going to two funerals a month. The obituaries in the *Sydney Star Observer* sometimes ran for six double pages. I hadn't bargained on everything that Past Karl would bring with him. After a few days, I decided to leave him be for a while. We'd shaken hands, but Past Karl was too much for me to deal with where I was then. Still, I left the door of his room open so he'd know I wasn't ignoring him.

Divorce-wise, Michael and I were no closer to getting a long-term settlement. Despite Michael reminding them that technically they should be paying me, we were in a stalemate again. So we proactively filed for a court date. Michael cautioned me that there would be no guarantees. Back to Vegas we went.

We'd been granted a court appearance for a pretrial hearing on September 13, 2018.

Writing some poetry on one of my last days in Madrid, a line popped out: *I am the captain of my ship, not the master of the sea.* These felt like good words to ride back to Berlin on.

I had noticed that I was thinking a lot less about Gunnar these days. Or about any of the mistakes I'd made in the past with men. That had been a shift, and it was good to note. There would be flare-ups for sure, but my days had changed flavor.

In a couple of weeks, it was going to be a year since I'd asked for a divorce. I'd never be perfect, but I was becoming a better captain, which meant the seas were easier to traverse.

THERE IS A WARRANT OUT

How are the workshops in the UK going? I texted John as I sat at the dinner table of Turlough's house.

Got a lot of feedback from the actors, making me rethink the story. But actually, I'm back in my hometown. Family stuff.

How's that going? I asked.

Making peace with my parents, reconnecting with mentors, trying to figure some stuff out. Gotta go now, but can't wait to hear about your news when I'm back, you are missed, John texted.

Miss you too, mate, I texted back.

Turlough placed a bowl of Irish stew in front of me.

"Wow, this looks amazing, mate," I said. "Turlough," I exhaled loudly, "I'm shitting myself about John coming home."

"Tell me," Turlough said matter-of-factly as he laid a linen napkin on his lap. I did love this about Turlough. He's the most gregarious and fun person to be around, but his serious analytical mode was only ever a gear shift away.

"I'm trying to be his friend," I continued, "but it's hard. I just feel that we're supposed to be together. But I know I'm not ready. So I should just be cool about it, enjoy the time in between now and when we get together. But I'm not. I'm obsessed with him."

"You don't sound like a friend," said Turlough. "You sound like a groupie."

I let that sink in for a second. "I do, don't I?"

"Yep, and it's understandable. You believe he saved you, so you're having a rescue romance. It's a version of hero worship."

"You're right. He's like a spiritual Yoda for me. But it's more than that. There was that text that he sent me, and our psychic connection, even how we met."

"Tell me about that text again," Turlough said, "from that Christmas trip."

"He wrote something like, 'And for the record, if we ever find ourselves in the same city again and we're both amping on our lives, maybe we could try dating and see if we're an even better team than we already know.'"

"'Something like'? Hmm. Sounds like it's engraved on your frontal cortex."

I shrugged in agreement.

"Does he have warrant to say that?" Turlough asked.

"Warrant? What do you mean? Like, 'Wanted: Dead or Alive'?"

"No, Karl. Warrant. It's permission, but also something that needs to be earned."

"He's earned it," I said quickly.

"Has he though? You called him Yoda. So, you're Luke, right? That means your relationship is this."

Turlough held his hands up like they were levels on a mixing desk, one hand way higher than the other.

"It's teacher and student," he said, moving his hands slightly to emphasize the difference in stature. "You mentioned that Accidental Angel thing of his. He's used to this kind of relationship. He's good at it."

Turlough then brought his hands to the middle.

"He's floated dating possibly in the future. You're presuming it's this," he said, equalizing the position of his hands, fingers touching, "but do you think he can do this?"

Everything I had observed about John so far didn't give me a no. But not a yes either.

"I don't know," I said.

"It's important," Turlough said, leaning in. "Because if he can't, he doesn't have warrant to text what he did. That's what I mean about warrant. It's something you have to earn. Otherwise you're offering something you can't deliver."

Turlough looked at me as I thought about his words.

"I don't doubt that you two have a deep connection. It's clear," he continued, "but what it's supposed to be isn't clear. I'm going to say something else. From what you've described to me of Gunnar and your other relationships, you become a fan of your partners. A groupie. You're expressing your identity through the man you're with, instead of the man you are. And that is the whole point. Your crisis of identity, Karl, is to have one."

"Jesus, Turlough!" I said, the verbal slap stinging.

"I know this is heavy, but I've been giving it some thought. Am I right? It's just my opinion, you can say anything."

"OK. Can I have some damn ice cream now please?"

We laughed a little as Turlough cleared the table.

"But seriously, thanks," I said, catching his arm. He smiled as he carried the plates off to the kitchen and got dessert ready. I felt tired. The path was going uphill again.

I GET OUT OF JAIL

A few of my friends and I were out at a club in Berlin on a Friday night. It was a Bear night, and a huge chunk of the local Bear guys filled the space, everyone drinking and dancing.

It was my round, so I went to the bar. As I waited, a big leather Bear guy came and stood next to me to order. He was my height, probably half my weight again, bearded, imposing, oozing dominance. My spidey-sense was tingling. In the years that I'd lived in San Francisco, the leather scene was something that I had wanted to try out. I had a friend who'd been involved with it after suppressing the interest most of his life, and he'd found an almost spiritual awakening in it. There were several masters he'd met and had times with.

I was jealous of my friend. He looked the part and sent out the right vibes. Unlike me, who had long hair at the time that I refused to cut, was taller than most of these masters, and—to be honest—felt like a lot of them were just doing another version of drag. I never found a leather master who I clicked with and who was prepared to give it a go with me. I was angry that I'd never had the chance. Yet scared of it too.

Back at the bar, I turned to the leather guy next to me. He looked my way.

"Hi," I said.

"Hello," he replied. "Having fun?"

"Yeah, out with some friends. You?"

"Also."

We smiled at each other. Then we leaned in and kissed. He was a good kisser. He stood up straight, grabbed me, and pulled me in. I loved it. His smell mixed with his worn leathers was intoxicating.

"Do you want to come back to my place?"

"Yes," I replied.

"I should warn you, I have a dungeon. Is that OK for you?"

"Yes, but I've never done this before. Is that OK for you?"

"Definitely," he said, grinning.

The voice said, "Let's go."

"Let's go," I said to him.

He wasn't lying. He really did have a dungeon. The walls of this dungeon also had photos of him and some of his slaves in full gear. He gave me a safe word and told me to use it if I wasn't comfortable with something. And then he made me take my clothes off and we got into it.

It was an amazing experience. There's something wonderful about finally being able to try something you've longed for, then give yourself to it completely. He enjoyed himself a lot too. I don't think you often get the chance to give someone their first BDSM session.

As I went home in the taxi, I knew it would also be the last time. I can only speak of my own experience, but after that one excellent night, I realized that my quest for BDSM was from a time when I was working like hell, in charge of huge ad accounts and staff, a sexless time in my marriage, and feeling like I somehow needed to be punished for all of it. There was also an element of wanting to use BDSM as a shocking way to get inside my emotions and delve into my inner world. But a lot had changed since then. Emotionally, I'd covered a lot of this ground since walking the divorce path. Instead of needing to be handcuffed in a basement to give up control, I'd learned to do that a different way.

I was happy though. I'd had the courage to go with instinct into something that scared me and fully give myself to it. I'd taken the time to understand what it was that had driven me there, and that was I was a different man now.

The writer in me couldn't help but notice the symbolic irony of it; I'd gone into a dungeon only to walk out of a mental jail.

AUGUST 2018

ARE WE FRIENDING?

Karl, are you up?

Hey, John. I am. What's up?

Can you Skype? I need to talk to someone.

A couple of minutes later, John's image popped onto the screen, I could see he was lying in bed.

"What's up, mate? You OK?" I asked.

And with that, John burst into tears.

"John, what happened?"

"Everything did," he sobbed.

John then proceeded to tell me a long story and I just let him run, nodding occasionally. I knew he'd had a difficult relationship with his family, grew up queer in a small UK town, and had had a tough time trying to find his people. I knew also that this trip had been about facing off with all of that to get some peace.

John told me about conversations with his parents, his siblings—the ones he liked and the ones he hated, tracking down old mentors of his, gathering a kind of tribal wisdom from them, and talking with the pagan tribes he used to commune with.

Somehow, all of it had culminated in an epiphany for him where he realized what it was he was supposed to be doing with his life. I could hear in his words that something had been lifted that had been pulling him down for a long time.

I felt nothing but the love of friendship for him. I wished I'd been there to give him a hug. When I looked at him on the screen, I could see the hurt kid that he worked so hard to hide all the time—Past John, the one he was always protecting. And these confusing feelings I'd been having for him somehow evaporated. In this one Skype call, John made more sense to me than he ever had.

"Mate, you're back in a few days. How about I come get you from the airport?"

"You don't have to do that," John said, wiping his eyes with the back of his hand.

"I know, that's why I'm going to," I responded.

"Thanks, Karl. And thanks for listening. I really needed to say all this."

"Mate, I'm glad I was here. I'll see you in a couple of days."

WE ARE BEGINNING OUR DESCENT

"Hi, tower. Me again."

It was 3 a.m. two days later and I'd been walking the streets of Berlin for hours, finally ending up on the Volksbühne steps again. After the call, my feelings about John had wandered all over the place. I looked up at the TV tower, lights flickering in the clear summer night.

"You know, one of the most frustrating things about this whole process is that I can feel something so strongly one day, then the next day be back to doubting myself all over again. Which brings me here to these steps to annoy you. Again. I can't figure out if I have a friendship love for John, if I'm falling in love with him, if I'm a groupie, if I've changed totally, or if I haven't changed at all."

I watched a bunch of drunk kids walk loudly past.

"Anyway, I'm scared. I'm scared that I'm going to go to the airport and I'm going to know I'm in love with him, because I don't even know if he's able to do that with me. And that I'm going to wreck our friendship and be heartbroken. And I just can't go through all that after this year I've had."

A homeless guy walked past, toothlessly mumbling for change. I gave him a couple of euros.

"Busy night," I said to the tower. "Do you know what today is? It's my anniversary. It's a year to the day since I asked for a divorce. Crazy, huh? I can't believe it. And it's just over two years since I met John here in Berlin. So, my whole mess, what do you think?"

The tower stared back.

"You're right. What you think doesn't matter. It's what I think. Well, I guess all will be revealed tomorrow. One part of me that I know hasn't changed, for sure, is that I still talk to you."

THE EPIPHANY

The next night, I wiped my hands on my shorts as I waited at the arrivals gate. I felt excited, nervous, and full of dread. Somehow it was more intense than any of the court visits that I'd had to make. I watched people coming through the gate. They scanned the room and when they saw their loved ones, they exploded in smiles and embraced.

What was I going to feel when I saw John? Would all the old emotions come rampaging back? Would I cry? Would he? Would it be the lovers reunited at the airport in the final scene? Or just one lover?

Why did I say I'd come?

Then finally John rolled through with his red suitcase. Wearing a flouncy orange hippie top that he made look good, a pair of anarchist cargo pants with tattoo prints, and bright-blue trainers. Despite the state of my stomach and heart, I smiled. The outfit was classic John.

Wordlessly, he walked up to me.

He'd combed his beard.

He smiled, and I smiled back.

"Fancy a cuddle?" I asked.

"Go on, then," he replied.

We hugged and breathed each other in. A nice, long hug. And I waited for my heart to speak.

"Friends," it said.

Loud and clear. The voice. The heart. The head. In my relief, I noticed that this was a new sensation. This feeling of all three parts woven together, speaking as one.

Then John and I started giggling.

"Welcome home, Mr. Hare."

"Nice to be back, Mr. Dunn."

I grabbed his bag, and we rolled to the taxi stand, John regaling me with stories of Britain, and I caught him up on the news from Berlin. As we stood on the curbside, I kept looking at him.

Yep, friend. Definitely friend.

But on the way home, as we chatted in the backseat, this incredible feeling of sadness came over me. I couldn't shake it. Yet another moment in this journey that didn't feel the way I thought it should.

I mean, this was it. I'd gone through so much and that moment, right then, felt like what it had all been building up to. Old me would have fallen hard for this guy. And instead, it was as I hoped it would be.

Yet, I was sad.

We arrived back at the collective and climbed the stairs to the fifth floor where Taina and Adnan were waiting at the door. There were hugs all round as they welcomed John home and we settled into the living room, where we'd laid out a dinner that the three of us had prepared. Sitting on the floor around a makeshift cardboard box table lit by candles, we ate and listened to each other tell stories. The four of us basked in the glow of friendship, where fate had made all our paths cross in this big, old apartment in a ramshackle building in Berlin.

We'd been having a heatwave all summer. But that night, the rain fell and cooled the whole city down. Washed it clean, like a fresh slate, ready to be written on again. Taina caught me in the kitchen as I was clearing plates, looking at the raindrops as they hit the windows with their stained glass made from taped-on cellophane.

"Are you OK?" she asked, well aware of how nervous I'd been. "How did it go when you picked him up?"

"It was great. We're friends. I know it now."

"Honey! Yay!" said Taina, hugging me. "But you seem sad somehow."

"I know. I can't figure it out. Maybe it's that the thought of being in love with him was so strong, I'm mourning the death of it…? No, that doesn't feel like it. I don't know."

"Nothing ever feels like you think it will, huh?"

"Say that again. Anyway, it's a good day. We all have reason to celebrate. I'll bring another bottle in."

Later that night, with the dishes washed and everyone in their rooms, I settled down into the living room where I was sleeping. I drifted off, no closer to figuring out what this weird sadness was all about. But I woke the next morning, haunted by the same lingering sense. Without thinking, I was up at the table, emotions diary out. And I started writing.

What the hell is this sadness all about? I should be thrilled.
I waited.
I'm waiting, I wrote.
Then the answer came.
You're sad because you said goodbye.
Nothing else came.
Goodbye to what? I wrote back.
You said goodbye to the man you've been for forty-six years.
I looked at the page, stunned.

Then it all made sense. That's what this feeling was. A farewell. I'd said goodbye to the man I'd been right up to the moment I hugged John at the airport.

The one who was the fat, gay kid in high school.

The one who couldn't appreciate his achievements.

The one who worked so hard and didn't think he deserved any reward for it.

The one who ran from country to country only to get there and find himself waiting.

The one who dated the men that he thought he deserved.

The one who treated other people so poorly because he was so busted up inside.

The one who hid in designer houses and clothes like they were fortresses and armor.

The one who walked around with his begging cup in bars.

The one who never thought he'd ever measure up to the straight men around him.

The one who thought he'd be broken forever.

The one who dated men he hoped would make it all go away.

The one who thought he would just never, ever be good enough.

Everything I'd been though, not just in my marriage or my divorce, but in my life… I finally got it. The man I met at the airport was me. The man I'm falling in love with is me.

The great romance of my life is with me.

I didn't need anyone else anymore. I didn't need that job running the world in advertising. I didn't need that next level of income. I didn't need that fancier title. I didn't need an Oscar.

Because I finally, finally, finally knew in my deepest self that I was enough.

I was free.

I leaned back in my chair and exhaled. Everything made sense. My entire past was suddenly clear. Every version I'd ever been of myself walked into that room and touched me on the shoulder. I could feel them all. And I had only love for them and their part in this journey.

Because right at that moment, I had touched God. I felt a huge arm around my shoulder that belonged to the universe.

Time was gone. My past and present and future were all one thing that flowed through me. The entire world looked different. I had never felt a calm like it.

I walked out into the hallway of the apartment in tears. Taina came out from the kitchen, John came out of his room. I cried so hard I could barely get any words out. All I could manage was, "I finally got it. I finally got it."

They ushered me back into the living room and we sat on my blow-up mattress as I told them about the revelation. And I started to try and explain it—the past, the present, the future, all the old mes turning up. Like I'd held the hand of the universe.

Choking out the words, I was suddenly transported back to when I was seventeen, sitting in my friend Justin's bedroom, coming out to my friends. This felt like coming out all over again. As I explained it all to Taina and John, it felt like I shed a skin from the inside.

"I didn't go to the airport to meet you, John. It was to meet me. Oh my God, John, it's like I can actually see you, *you*, for the first time. No projections."

Taina had her hand on my back. "You actually feel like you're made of different stuff. I'm so happy for you."

John and Taina smiled at each other.

"Congratulations. You made it," John said. "Taina and I have both been through our version of this."

"You've been so close, we knew you'd get here. You wanted it and you were willing," Taina said.

"Just a matter of time," agreed John.

After I calmed down and the talk of my revelation ebbed, when all had been said that could be said, there was a silence in the room between all of us.

"So what do I do now? What do I do with this?" I asked them.

"Enjoy the next few days," said Taina. "Just let the epiphanies happen."

SUDDENLY, IT ALL MADE SENSE

After a hot shower, with fresh clothes on, I walked out onto the streets of Berlin and the whole city had a freshness, a sparkle of possibilities. It felt like physics had been changed, like the stars had been rearranged in the sky, like the whole planet was something new to explore and discover for the first time because every rule had been tossed away.

I was absolutely famished. So I sat in my favorite café, having my favorite pastry, marveling at how everything tasted better.

Ordering another coffee, I watched the world go by, thinking back over my life as the next layers of dots connected and things in the past all started to make sense. Every question mark was knocked away.

That thing that I had been hunting for my whole life, that feeling of wholeness, had been buried inside me all along. When I'd started down this path, using my divorce as my crisis of identity, I never thought this was where it was going to lead.

But now it all made sense. When I was in the middle of it, I'd felt so incredibly lost. Now it was clear, like a map that I could finally see and trace back my journey on.

If I hadn't had that fight with Gunnar in Europe two years ago, I would never have come to Berlin and met John. Or had that conversation with Myriam.

When Brian and I had dinner that night, if he hadn't said what he did, I wouldn't have asked for a divorce at that moment, and maybe never.

If Gunnar hadn't served a summons on me, I would have given him the house and the journey inside would never have started. And if he hadn't acted with such anger toward me, it wouldn't have sent me into the emotional downward spiral I went on.

Which means I never would have started keeping a video diary.

Which means I would never have shown it to Brian and had him say, "You know, you should write a book about this."

Or kept an emotions diary.

If my client hadn't left the agency, I would never have been able to get to Berlin.

And if my first place in Berlin hadn't fallen through, I never would have ended up in the collective, broke, and received a reeducation about life, money, and what's really important.

My bike accident was the grinding halt that I'd needed to let all my emotions catch up and drain out, and it had forced me to learn to walk again with more intention.

If I hadn't been in such a legal bind, and backed into corner where I thought I was going to lose everything, I would never have learned how to accept the idea that losing everything might be what I needed.

And then Scott wouldn't have needed to put me in touch with Michael Nathan, who rode in like a white knight and saved the day.

John cutting me off made me sit through all the emotions that I was drowning in. So I'd finally realized that it wasn't about him, just a broken part of myself that I attached to all the men in my life.

And if I hadn't gone to pick John up at the airport, I don't know when I would have had the epiphany.

Without all these moments, and the dozens of other guides, friends, and family who supported and imparted wisdom along the way, I would never have emerged on the other side knowing with every fiber of my being that I was all I would ever need.

And I would never have written this book. Because all of this would never have happened. I would probably have been in New York, in another new job, dating another version of the same men I'd dated before, living the high life, and wondering why I still wasn't happy.

Thinking about Gunnar, I smiled. The people you hate the most are the ones you have the most to learn from. I wasn't even angry at him now. Instead, I just had a true empathy and prayed that something like this had happen to him too. I hoped he was walking the path.

Smaller epiphanies pinged over the next few days. The most important being that my divorce was actually irrelevant. It just happened to be the incident that set me on the path of questioning the life I'd built, rejecting it all, and throwing myself out to sea. It could just as easily have been an illness, the death of someone close to me, or bankruptcy. I was just a human seeking meaning, who—after a long journey—had found it in themselves, the place where it resides for everyone.

THE END?

When I was in my twenties in Sydney, I had dated a man called Dale who was a producer of musicals. Broadway was a gay gene that I had missed out on completely; I had zero interest in the history, divas, and stories of the musical stage.

Determined that he was going to find a musical I liked, he took me to many productions in Sydney, where I'd do my best not to look at my watch.

Then one day I was hanging out at his house when he returned from the post office. He ripped open a large, padded envelope and pulled out a VHS, smiling to himself.

"You know Sondheim, right?" Dale asked.

"I think I've heard the name," I replied.

Dale closed his eyes and patiently exhaled.

"OK," he continued. "Stephen Sondheim wrote a musical called *Into the Woods*."

He waited for a moment of recognition from me that never came.

"The London office is staging it right now. They're in rehearsals and want my opinion on the progress," he said. "I think you're going to like this one."

Dale inserted the VHS, pressed play, and settled next to me on the couch.

"Please, don't look at your watch."

Into the Woods is a story woven together from the fairy tales we all grew up on: Little Red Riding Hood, Cinderella, Jack and the Beanstalk, and Rapunzel. The first act is a clever mashup of all these characters and their narratives. By the time the first act closes, it's a satisfying happily-ever-after ending for all of them.

I turned to Dale and shrugged.

"Just wait," he said.

Act two begins and proceeds to swiftly unravel everyone and everything. The fairy-tale endings of act one fall to pieces under the weight of real-world problems—unresolved jealousies and unfulfilled desires that these new lives aren't answering.

I was gripped.

By the time the curtains fell, all the characters had made hard decisions, given up all their fairy-tale ideals, and become honest versions of themselves.

Back in Berlin in August 2018, what I hadn't realized post-revelation is that I was living with two fairy tales myself. Two more rainbows.

The first was that John and I were going to be friends for a while, grow closer, eventually wanting our hearts to be with no one but each other. We'd move in, and our house would be a meeting place of his artistic world and whatever world it was that I was in the process of building for myself.

The second fairy tale would be revealed to me very soon under the crushing weight of the real world.

CHAPTER 16

*"You need to get cool with normal...
You need to live a boring life."*

— JOHN

LEAVING THE TEMPLE

I MOVED OUT OF THE COLLECTIVE. It was time. John, Taina, and Adnan had a life they were setting up together and I was welcome, but felt in the way. Also, I felt I'd learned everything I could at the collective.

A friend had offered to put me up as there were still a few weeks to go before my apartment in Prenzlauer Berg was free. The day I moved out, I felt very much like a young monk leaving the temple and setting out on my own path. It was a poignant day. John, Taina, and Adnan had done so much for me. The collective had been such a reeducation. I would be forever grateful to the people in that building and all that they had taught me.

John looked different now. He was off the pedestal I'd put him on and we were meeting more like equals. We made an agreement with each other to share our worlds. He told me that normally he'd have kept his sexual life fenced off from someone he liked. It was large, varied, and intimidating for a lot of people. But he wanted me to know all of him. I was ready for it now. I wanted to know him more, not as a teacher but as a friend, although he was much more than that to me. Now that we weren't sharing a living space anymore, it would be a lot easier.

Before I left the house though, I pulled him into the living room.

"John, before I go, there's something I want to say. I have never met anyone like you. The hundreds of hours of time you've put into helping me over the last two years… I don't even know how to thank you for it all. You have changed my life."

"Aww, nah, it's all good. More a group effort," he replied.

"Mate, listen. We're not boyfriends, maybe one day, but we're much more than friends. And I love you. I have a deep and profound love for you. And I just wanted to say it, so you would know."

Paralyzed by a compliment as the British often are, John said nothing, and we just hugged instead.

And then I was off into my own life.

John started to introduce me socially to sex mates of his, interesting men he had long histories with. I liked getting to know them and was surprised by how unjealous I was, considering weeks before I'd been desperately trying to play catch-up to John and cannibalize his experiences.

The high of the epiphany still echoed in my life, and in those couple of weeks afterward the calm of my new self-knowledge radiated out.

Then I got a phone call. One of my oldest friends, one of the first men I ever dated and still a great friend of my family, was ill. Rafael called to tell me that he had cancer, that he was going in for tests, and that they didn't know much yet. He lived in Queensland, way north of my home in Sydney.

I cried on and off for two days. Rafael was a bedrock. A touchstone to the life I lived in Sydney before I'd left twenty-two years before. Whenever my life had gone to the dogs, Rafael was always the first person on a plane to come and see me. So, I booked a flight to Queensland for straight after my birthday, which was in a few days.

My forty-seventh birthday was a wonderful day. I woke up to a phone full of well wishes from friends and family. I giggled, thinking about the conversation I'd had with my brother Tony the year before, getting back a whole year in my head because I'd been counting my age wrong.

It had been a year well spent.

That night, twenty people I knew in Berlin came to a local queer bar in Kottbusser Tor, drank, ate, and met each other. It was great to see all these wonderful people, who'd contributed to my journey, all in one place. It felt like a good life was actually possible. I still had lingering fears about the pretrial hearing in early September. I didn't know how it would turn out. I might not be able to afford to stay in Berlin, so who knew where my forty-eighth birthday would be. But right then, life was good.

The next day I was at John's place. We had been talking about "gathering the crew" post-revelation. John told me about how once he'd found his truth, he set out to find like-minded souls, living and dead. We'd discussed writers, painters, and musicians till the wee small hours of the morning. We were falling asleep in the living room when he gently shook me awake.

"You can crash with me if you like."

And with that we ended up under the covers in his room. A hug turned into a kiss, which turned into hours of exploring of each other's bodies. In all the time that we'd known each other, this was the first proper meeting of equals, the first time we ever really had sex. And it was wonderful. We moved energy around each other's bodies with our hands, with fingers, with lips for hours. I was glad it had taken this long for us to finally have this moment together.

I woke up, kissed John goodbye, and went back to my friend's house to grab my bag before boarding the plane to Queensland.

BACK TO THE PAST

Twenty-six hours later, I landed in Brisbane. The smell of hot, salty air blew through the doors of the airport before I'd even stepped outside. It smelled like home.

It was fantastic to see Rafael again. But the cancer had taken its toll. He was thinner, and so was his hair, but he was smiling. We hadn't seen each other since my wedding over three years before. There was a lot of catching up to do.

His sister lived in a community on the top of a hill in a town outside Brisbane. Semi-rural, the next-door neighbors kept cows in their paddock and you'd hear them thudding around when you swam in the pebble encrusted pool. The eucalyptus trees hummed in the heat of the day, and the frogs belched an orchestra at night.

Most days, I drove Rafael to the hospital in town for chemo. He'd had the operation to remove the cancer before I'd arrived, so I became his driver, confidant, and hospital buddy for his chemo sessions.

Being back in Australia was strange for a few reasons. After all this time in Berlin, where I didn't understand most of what was going on around me, I suddenly understood everything. Every nuance, every accent, every word spoken and written. In one way it was wonderful to be completely understood by everyone around you on every level. In another way, it was overwhelming. I'd gone through so much in such a short time, I didn't even know how to put it into words. So when people would ask me, "What have you been up to?" I didn't even know how to begin to answer. Strangely, the question annoyed me.

Hitting the emotions diary, the answer soon came as to why. It was Past Karl.

Every time I went home to Oz, Past Karl was waiting. I could feel him with me everywhere, the hurt and scared kid that couldn't wait to leave the country, go overseas, and be successful and fabulous and show everyone. I'd spent so much of my life on the run from this guy that being confronted with him in Australia always made me want to leave again within a week.

This is where the internal work was going. In a way, it didn't surprise me. I knew I'd only put him on hold when I shook hands with him in Spain. And despite the epiphany, where I'd said goodbye to so much, Past Karl and I still had things to sort out. Inner-child work is deep and old. Now I felt ready though, and spending my days in hospital waiting rooms meant I had a lot of time on my hands.

John and I often talked about it when I was away.

"I'm not surprised all this came up for you," John said one time on a call. "I mean, you're living in Australia, in someone else's house, on the top of a mountain, with no way to get around. Must feel like being a teenager again."

"Bingo! That's exactly it," I agreed emphatically.

"You told me about that guy Dan Savage, who does those videos. What are they called?" John asked.

"*It Gets Better.*"

"Right. Well, you can do that for yourself. In your next meditation, why don't you travel back to Past Karl and tell him that everything is going to be OK. Revisit really painful episodes, appear to him, talk to him, and give him a hug. You can be your own angel."

So that's what a lot of my time was spent doing in Australia. I'd take Rafael in for his treatment, then find a quiet space down on the miles of beach that stretch up the coast and do my own.

When I started to travel back to painful times in pure meditations, I wasn't trying to relive or change them, I just wanted to be with myself as I was back then. Amazingly, I could see young me so clearly. And it felt wonderful to just say, "Hi, Karl. This is Future Karl, come back to say it all works out. Takes a while, but you'll get there."

More than anything, I'd empathize with the young, hurt, and confused boy I was then. Whether I actually went back or whether it was all in my head, it didn't matter. It was working. Every day I felt lighter.

Something was healing that had been a long-forgotten open wound.

Rafael also was responding well to treatment and the doctors were very happy with his progress, though of course the inevitable happened and some of his hair started falling out. But he rocked a pretty mean bald head, channeling full Telly Savalas, Kojak-style—who, for younger readers, was the Vin Diesel of his day.

John and I also talked about the last night before I left and how much we had enjoyed each other. There were jealousies and emotions on both sides because of the distance between us, but now we could talk about them and, even better, laugh about them. We felt like two adults who were carefully navigating something together. I liked this version of us. I really liked this version of me.

Yet there was something else I couldn't deny. I wanted to impress John, whether it was with stories of sexual escapades in Queensland when I went to Byron Bay for a few days or quickly reporting in with new spiritual revelations. A part of me still wanted his approval. This felt like old me. It was like I had a foot in my past behaviors and a foot in my new ones. Head is faster than the heart. I worried it would cause a problem down the track, but for now all I could do was note it.

One day, I was telling Rafael about some of the meditations I was doing as he smiled and listened in the passenger seat. Rafael had been a meditator for a long time.

"You're always so busy, Karl," Rafael noted.

"What does that mean?" I asked.

"The goal of meditation is ultimately to do nothing. To just be."

"Well, that's what I'm trying to do. Get rid of the things that are in the way so that I can just be."

"That's my point." Rafael smiled. "If you could just be, these other things would take care of themselves."

I was angry. Not just because there was part of me that knew he was right, but because I was enlightened now, dammit! For Rafael to question my enlightenment riled me.

As I stayed silent and watched the road ahead with the Queensland bush rolling by, it occurred to me that I wasn't sure of myself at all. Even though I knew so much more about what made me tick, I still wanted John's, Rafael's, and the world's approval.

The clouds parted and I could see how much higher the mountain was.

LET'S GO TO COURT. AGAIN.

For weeks while I was back in Australia, Michael and I had been prepping over email and calls for the pretrial hearing. Gunnar and his counsel had refused all efforts to make a settlement. So September 13th had finally arrived.

"Today is for a judge to decide if your case is worth the trial court's time. But there are no guarantees," Michael had cautioned me. "You never know what a judge will decide. Their case though is built on an idea that just isn't how the law works. They can't make claims against you for income you don't make, based on income you used to. But today we will probably just argue in front of the judge, he'll see that no resolution is possible, and we'll be given a date for a trial."

"Do your best, mate," I said to him. "It's going to go however it goes."

I wasn't surprised by how little attachment I had to the outcome that day. All I expected was a pantomime, followed by a trial date. The sooner, the better. I just wanted the decision, any decision, so I could figure out my next steps. Brian had even checked in from LA to offer his place again if I had to go back to service some crazy alimony.

Michael had gotten me the right to appear telephonically, but due to the time zones, it was 11 p.m. on the top of the hill in Queensland. I rang in at the appointed time, talked to the court clerk, and was put on hold. Then I was put through.

By some amazing stroke of fate, the judge was the same one that had presided over our spousal support adjustment a few months earlier.

After some preliminary housekeeping talk about orders and pretrial documents, the judge interrupted to ask, "So, what's going on? Why can't we get this case settled?"

Michael filled the judge in on the attempts we had made to settle and that there had been no progress. Gunnar's counsel maintained that I still had a stellar career ahead of me at a high earning capacity. It was established again that the house had sold, there was a small amount in escrow yet to be agreed on how to split it, and that I had no income and Gunnar did.

I didn't expect much to happen, just that we would simply set a trial date when the judge realized we were still at an impasse. I certainly wasn't holding out for some hellish takedown against Gunnar and his counsel, but what happened next was almost Zen.

"I have very good family law lawyers in front of me," the judge said suddenly, "but sometimes—and not these lawyers—family law lawyers feed off of drama and people's unhappiness, and they encourage it sometimes, and then what happens is the parties end up spending money that they don't have. And then they get to a result where they have spent more than it's worth to fight, and at the end of the day, everyone looks at each other and goes, 'Well, that wasn't too much fun.'"

He continued, "I never met anyone who said they enjoyed their divorce proceeding. I'm waiting. I am still waiting… so I feel comfortable saying this. It looks like a draw to me, under the circumstances… and I just think the case should settle today."

Michael concurred. Gunnar and his counsel were silent.

"Why don't you guys go outside and chat? And we'll figure this out… and we will see if we can't get this knocked out today," the judge concluded.

Michael thanked him. I thought I heard muffled and heated discussion between Gunnar and his counsel. Then, after a moment, she spoke.

"Thank you, Your Honor."

And then down came the gavel.

It was all so fast and calm, I wasn't sure what had happened. Next thing, the phone line clicked, and I was back with the court clerk again.

"Thank you, Mr. Dunn."

"That's it?" I asked.

"Yes. That's it."

Moments later I was on the phone with Michael, who spoke in hushed, excited tones. "I'm walking with them now. We're going to go to a room and hash this out. I'll call you in a few moments. I know it's late there, but I need you to stay up."

"I'm going to make some coffee, mate," I replied. "Let's get this done."

After nearly eighteen months, my divorce case had been closed in less than fifteen minutes. My mind couldn't make it real.

Soon, Michael patched me into a conversation that he, myself, Gunnar, and Gunnar's counsel would have over the next few hours.

Gunnar wanted a single buyout of spousal support. Michael had to remind him that wasn't what the judge just ordered. The amount dropped and dropped, till finally he let it go. Then we got down into way too much detail about the value of things. To be honest, it got embarrassing. Two grown men talking through lawyers about how much a picture cost to get framed, or the resale value of a dining table.

I was surprised by my level of disgust that we were so close to this being done and we were stalling over the price of a vase. At some point, our lawyers' hourly rates must have been more than whatever amounts we were arguing over. It was like someone had put superglue on the last fifty feet of the marathon track before the finish line.

But after four hours of talking, drafting, emailing, and signing, the agreement was in place and was taken back up to the judge to be signed. Michael bid me farewell on the call and said that we would be talking more in the next few days.

"I never expected that outcome today, Karl. You hope, but it actually happened."

"I can't believe it either. So what happens now?"

Michael explained I had a couple of pieces of paper to send Gunnar then the state had to ratify it. Which would take a couple of months. Then we'd be officially divorced. Since Gunnar lodged the case, the ratification would be sent to his counsel and then they'd send it to us. And a final caution from Michael. "No bragging about this on social media. I've had clients write things like, 'We crushed them!' on Facebook, which angers the other party so much that they re-up the challenge."

"You have my word," I said.

It was 4:30 a.m. in Queensland. The sun was just starting to tint the top of the hills purple. I went out on the back porch and looked over the scenery.

It was over.

The divorce was actually, finally over.

I posted the sunrise on Instagram.

THE LAST WORD

A few days were spent gathering bits of paperwork from banks, lawyers, escrow people, financial controllers, and the entire orchestra of humans it takes to unwind a life together.

After a week, Gunnar and I exchanged emails, sending necessary documents to each other.

No comment was made on either side about the hearing. It was very formal.

Found the old statements. Attached them below with the 401K doc. Unless there's anything you need from me, I think that's it. The 401K guy, the lawyers, the accountant, and our financial planners all know what to do and have what they need – Karl.

A couple of moments later, Gunnar replied.

All done then. Be well – G.

I closed my inbox.

Wait, was that it?

Surely that couldn't be it, I thought.

But it was. Unless something radical happened—and the voice told me it wasn't going to—that would be the last time we spoke.

No… That was not how it was meant to go.

For over a year, I'd been rehearsing my final speech to Gunnar. I'd been planning on channeling full Meryl Streep. My words would devastate him, make him sorry for what he'd done, and also show him that I'd evolved to a higher plane of consciousness—because I was going to be levitating by the end of my scene. I wanted to see in his eyes that he knew I'd won on some level more valuable than money. I'd been clinging on to this idea of having the last word.

Instead, I realized that there'd be no final talk. And I unwound.

Rage filled me in a way I hadn't felt since my kickboxing days.

All done? Be well? Are you kidding me? I thought darkly. I wanted an apology. And I was never going to get one. I would happily have apologized too; I'd also done terrible things. But to think that there was no remorse or revisiting on his side turned my mind the darkest red.

So I sat down with the emotions diary, almost pushing my pen through the paper as the answer came. This was when it presented the second fairy tale that I'd been clinging to. And I watched this rainbow and its pot of gold go up in smoke too.

You thought your epiphany was a superpower. It wasn't. It was a lesson. One you still need to learn how to live.

I leaned back in my chair and looked at the ceiling. When I'd had the epiphany, the feeling was so strong, clear, and absolute. Now it was a whisper. What I'd felt was the rush of finding the answer. But living it was another whole thing. I was still trying to impress John. I was trying to prove my spiritual prowess to Rafael. I wanted a mea culpa from Gunnar. If I was truly living with the knowledge that I was enough, then none of these other things would have mattered.

My divorce was finally over. I was in the clear and was free to do anything that I wanted. I should have been popping champagne corks. Instead, now that Rafael had finished his chemo and was staying with a friend on the Gold Coast, I just wanted to go home. Friends and family were supposed to be the most important thing in the world to me now, yet I didn't even visit mine in Sydney. I don't know what I was thinking.

Instead, I sat on the plane back to Berlin, looking out the window, sliding into a depression again.

Nothing feels like it's supposed to.

OCTOBER 2018

MAKE FRIENDS WITH NORMAL

I'd been back in Berlin for a week. With my temporary place no longer available and still a week before I was moving into my own apartment, John suggested I come back and stay with them at the collective. I couldn't wait. I wanted to be in the nest again. My possessions from America had arrived and were in the corner of the room: a few boxes I'd put in the back of a Prius in LA many months before.

John had been away on a work trip, had arrived back that same day, and the two of us were out at a bar that night. Once again, John was patiently listening to me complain about my emotional state. About how everything I'd hoped for had come to pass, but that I was paralyzed by the enormity of the abyss of freedom in front of me. Mostly though, I was seething over never having had that last talk with Gunnar.

"I had the epiphany," I almost yelled, thumping the table. "I shouldn't give a toss about this now. But really, that's the ending? 'Be well'?! Well then, Gunnar, why didn't you do anything in the last year that actually helped me be well, you—"

"OK," John said, interrupting. "I have two things to say about this. One, this is the problem with revelations. You have them, then it's, 'We now return to your regularly scheduled programming'. It's a crash back to Earth."

"Why didn't you warn me about it?"

"And deny you the privilege of discovery? I don't think so." John finished his drink. "And two, you need to make friends with normal."

John went on to explain that I would have some mild PTSD going on. "You went to war on two fronts. One, with Gunnar and the legal system. And two, with the old you that you were trying to grow out of. One of them is over now. Although it's never really over; Gunnar will never be gone from your life. He'll just get smaller, less significant. Imagine what you'd say about him in a year."

"OK, I see that. But 'make friends with normal'?" I asked, grilling him.

"Slow down, I was coming to that. So now you need to learn how to live a life that isn't about lawyers and money and courts and not having a roof over your head. That's been your twenty-four-seven for about eighteen months, running from one disaster to the next like your life depended on it. Now you need to get cool with normal. Going to the gym. Paying your phone bill. Running out of toilet paper. You need to live a boring life. It's not an easy adjustment."

Then I admitted to John that after everything I'd been through, none of it felt in the end like it was a victory.

"It's just so…" I hunted for the word. "…pointless. In the end, it just got divided down the middle. I can't find any meaning in it. I don't feel good about it. I just feel empty. And really, really tired."

John smiled. "You have emotionally evolved more than anyone I've ever seen in such a short space of time, without going into a monastery or something. So cut yourself a break there. And on a personal note, it's been beautiful to watch."

"Why, thank you," I demurred darkly. "Hey, but really. Thanks for sitting in the front row for the whole performance. Same again?" I asked as I picked our glasses up.

"Wait," John said, getting up, turning my body to his. "Face me. There's something I want to say."

I put down the glasses. John looked me in the eye.

"I love you, Karl Dunn."

"I love you too, John Hare."

We hugged for a long time as the other patrons walked around us.

TEAR DOWN OLD STATUES

The next morning, John and I lay in bed as the sun beamed past the morning glories in the window box, the sounds of the kindergarten next door coming to life. The night before had been passionate, but also honest and open. Things were said on both sides. Private things, vulnerable things.

"I really enjoyed last night, mate," I said.

"Me too," said John, readjusting in my arms.

"Thank you for hearing those things I said, and trusting me with yours."

He nodded. "And the sex."

I rolled my eyes.

"I know, it's pretty wild."

"It's also the only sex that I'm having," I said. "Not out of choice, but you know… that's what's going on."

John rolled over and looked at me. "I don't know why you're telling yourself that. That's just not true."

"Really?"

"Well, there were those two guys in Australia, that mate of yours on the west side, and you've mentioned a couple of others besides."

As I listened, I realized he was right.

"I think you're so used to telling yourself this undesirability story, it's become a monument. But life changes, and you have to force the stories to catch up. Don't erect statues to old scripts, pull them down instead."

"Gosh, you're smart, John."

"Not really, just seen some stuff. You might want to give that some thought though, see where else you've got a statue that needs to be torn down."

We kissed. We got up. And John and I went about our days.

That night we climbed into his bed. Things started up. But then something was different. Like a switch was flicked. He was all there, then he wasn't. John wound it down and we went to sleep.

The next morning, when John woke, he was furious.

"I have an appointment. I'll be back," he said, getting dressed.

"Everything OK?" I asked.

"It's fine," he said. Then he was out of the bedroom and I heard the front door close hard behind him.

When he came back about two hours later, John exploded into the apartment. He found me in the kitchen, and he let fly.

"You need to stop thinking that my bedroom is your default place to stay in this house! You're a guest and guests sleep in the living room! I need my space. I need a door to close."

It was like getting hit by a freight train.

"What happened, John?"

"Nothing happened. I've been away on a trip. I need time to myself."

"I'll go you one better then," I said. "I'll move out. Clearly me being here right now is not a good idea. I'll find a hotel. I can be gone in half an hour."

His tone changed fast. "You don't have to do that."

"Feels like I do."

"I just need my space."

The voice told me to get up and go. But I didn't want to believe that any of this was happening. We'd just gotten so close. Closer than we'd ever been. I hoped it was a passing flare-up.

So I moved into the living room, left the house, and walked the city. I was so angry with myself. I'd opened up a part of me and let someone kick it hard. Waves of emotion surged and all I could think to do was keep walking. After pointing the finger of blame at John, I started to think about how I'd gotten here. I knew what he was like—an amazing mentor, who'd become a friend. But he was also emotionally unpredictable, could turn on a dime, pull the rug out from under you, and tell you it was your fault. He'd done it to me a couple of times. I'd seen him do it to other people too. And we'd just gone to a really vulnerable place. I should have expected him to kick hard.

What I didn't realize till much later was that John wasn't trying to prove a point to me, but to himself.

I texted Turlough and he told me I could move in straight away. I went back to the apartment and packed my clothes. I'd have to come back for my boxes later.

John came out of his room and walked into the lounge. "Are you going?"

"To Turlough's. I'm going to stay there till I can move into my apartment."

"OK," said John. "Yeah, maybe that's better."

There was a knock at the door.

John smiled and opened it. One of his regulars, who I'd met, walked in.

"You two know each other, right?" John asked.

The guy waved. "Hi, how you going?"

"We're going to… you know…" John said.

"OK," I replied.

And with that John and his friend disappeared down the hallway and into his bedroom.

I took my things downstairs, pushed the spare keys into the mailbox, and caught a taxi to Turlough's.

A week later, I had the keys to my new apartment and I was back at the collective to gather my belongings. John helped me and Turlough carry all the boxes to Turlough's car. The mood felt very much like a breakup to me. Neither of us mentioned what happened. I didn't even know if John thought something had happened.

I could barely look at him. More than anything else in the world, I just wanted to be in my apartment. Something that was mine. A place to start from where I wouldn't have to ask a favor, tiptoe around, or need to leave fast.

As the last box went in the back of Turlough's car, Turlough jumped in the driver's seat.

"Well, thanks for letting me stay all that time. And helping me get set up here in Germany," I said to John.

"Pleasure, mate. Can't wait to see your place."

I nodded, not wanting to say yes or no.

Then we hugged. For some reason, he giggled. Maybe that was the apology.

On the drive to the new apartment, if I could have gotten out of the car and pushed to make us go faster, I would have. My impatience to be in there and close the door was hot and desperate. Turlough got a parking spot right outside the front door.

We started carrying all the boxes inside to the foyer, only to discover that the elevator wasn't working.

"What floor is the apartment on?" asked Turlough.

"The fifth," I replied, looking at the staircase.

"Right…" Turlough trailed off. We started lifting the first few boxes up the stairs to my front door. My hands were shaking as I inserted my key. Then it wouldn't turn.

"Hang on a second, mate," I said, jiggling it every which way in the lock. I tried every other key on the ring. The door remained quietly and determinedly locked.

"This *is* your apartment, right?" Turlough asked.

That's when I realized I didn't know for sure. Here is an interesting thing about German apartment blocks. The apartments have no numbers. At the front door on the street there are buttons with people's names. When someone buzzes you in, they have to give you an elaborate set of instructions to follow, because there are no door numbers to mark your way. The Germans hate it, but they haven't changed it.

I had been to see this apartment only once, months ago. So much had happened. I tried my key in a half-dozen doors with no luck. As I messaged my landlords feverishly, Turlough noted that they were away on vacation.

I looked at my things spread out over the hallway, thought of the other boxes in the foyer. Where would I put them? And where would I sleep tonight? Feeling hot tears starting to well, I willed them down and just started knocking on doors.

A neighbor answered, and by luck, he knew my landlords. He led me to my apartment door. I put in the key, and it swung open.

"Here it is, Turlough!"

"Mm-hmm."

Twenty minutes later, my boxes were safely inside with a blow-up mattress, coffee maker, and a starter set of IKEA plates and bowls from Turlough. With well wishes, he then went on his way.

And I was alone in my place.

My place.

Mine.

A place to live. A work visa. A divorce done. I had everything I needed.

Gunnar and I had bought a total interior look in about two weeks for the trophy house. All the things we thought we were supposed to have. This time, I wanted to take my time. My style idea was, "if I love it." It didn't have to match. It didn't have to go with anything.

In the meantime, without wi-fi, chairs, and a table, I spent the rest of the month riding my bike to the library and working there. And fobbing off John's texts—which I'd answer minimally, if at all.

THE END OF THE STATUE ERA

One thing John had said that I was thinking a lot about was the statues idea. Any time that I noticed a firmly held belief I had about myself, I'd give it a second examination. I'd stand at the foot of a statue that had existed for years or maybe even decades and scrutinize it. I started reading back through my diaries and writings that I'd been keeping since the start of the divorce to see if I could find any commonalities.

My undesirability myth was a statue I'd erected, as big as any I'd ever seen in real life. As I read over my top five reasons for getting married, the worst reason of all was built at the feet of this monument—that I was lucky if I could find someone interested in me.

So, in a meditation, I imagined the statue and what it might look like. I knew straight away. Me, in a corner, with that look I get on my face when I feel out of my depth and think everyone is out of my league. In my mind, this self-defeated version of me was a Goliath-sized metal monument to everything I hated about myself, standing in the small green space outside the Volksbühne. And I was David at its base.

Then, in the meditation, Future Karl appeared and stood next to me. He smiled as he handed me a giant harpoon gun with a rope attached. Taking the harpoon, I aimed it squarely at my statue's metal chest and fired. The harpoon sailed along, humming through the air before embedding in its solar plexus, a sonorous thud echoing over the rooftops of Rosa-Luxemburg-Platz.

Taking the rope, I started to pull. Future Karl joined in too. Then hundreds of Karls from over the years started running up and grabbing the slack. Another harpoon fired from a different part of the Karl crowd and hit the statue. Then another. All of us worked together to crack the statue's feet off its foundations. Then a teenage Karl gave one final, small push on one of the statue's metallic heels.

The sound of concrete, rebar, and metal breaking went up like the crescendo of an industrial orchestra and the Karls ran to get out of the way of the statue, which fell face-first onto the ground and its own shadow.

A thunderous roar of joy went up from all the Karls, who then climbed it, jumped up and down on it, and took selfies.

I came out of the meditation laughing.

CHAPTER 17

"Know where your line is… and that you let it be known."

— Jordan

NOVEMBER 2018

LEARNING TO LIVE IN PEACETIME

John had been right about another thing too. I did need to make friends with normal.

So, as all the leaves started yellowing and falling off the trees, I enrolled in a two-month immersion course at a language school. It was great to have somewhere to be first thing in the morning. Classes till lunch. Homework all afternoon. But I struggled.

I'd always had a talent with languages, picking up a decent amount in every country where I'd lived. I'd never spoken another one fluently though. It had been a life goal.

My classmates and I had all done placement tests, written and oral, and been sorted into levels and classes. From the first lesson though, I could see that I was behind. The only place where I was ahead of my class was age. One of our first in-class exercises was to do a "Hello. My name is…" to tell the class our name, but also where we came from and how old we were.

When I told the class I was "siebenundvierzig," an audible laugh went up from one of the students, a young girl from Norway.

"Forty-seven! Oh my God! My dad's forty-seven!" she exclaimed. Seeing the look on my face, she started backpedaling. "What I mean is, you're cool, but my dad's not cool at all."

I wanted to tell her that the forty-seven virus affects people differently. The symptoms change depending on the severity of the condition.

As it turned out, I could have been the father of most of my class—the majority of whom were from Europe and already spoke at least two languages.

I had walked into this course with a massive expectation that I was going to work hard but sail through it, and probably speak functional German by the end. Instead, I was one of the slowest students, suffered imposter syndrome daily, and—by the time we hit the six-week mark—my brain was full. Nothing else would go in. Every day I'd walk in determined and leave mortified. I had no patience with myself.

When I asked the emotions diary, it gave me the answer I already knew: *You're in too much of a hurry to be perfect in a new life. Slow down. Enjoy being crap and getting better. Not focusing on why you aren't the best.*

Yeah, yeah, yeah. Fine.

Instead of celebrating the fact that I was giving myself the gift of knowledge and investing in my future, I made it a battle that I was losing every day. With a grand meditation one morning, I found the answer.

I had no idea how to live in peacetime.

Gunnar and I had gone to war straight away. I'd been running for my life from lawyers and my job. I'd couch surfed for almost six months straight. I'd nearly lost it all. I was so used to having massive obstacles in the way that if they weren't there, I'd invent them. I didn't know how else to be.

But it's no way to live. So I was going to have to change it.

I started being kinder to myself on the language school front. And while I'd love to say that I hadn't thought about John much, I had. Every day. Huge chunks of every day. Then, right on cue, as was so often our way, just as I decided it was time to for us to talk, the text arrived from John that I'd been expecting.

OK, Karl. What is going on? Why are you so distant?

Gunnar and I had never had that last talk. And if that's what John and I were going to have, then regardless of the outcome, that would be a good thing. So we met at a café a couple of days later. It had been a month since I'd seen him. I sat at the table opposite him. We didn't hug hello.

"Do you want to start or shall I?" I opened.

"Well, I just don't understand why you've been so distant. It seems obvious to me that you just don't need us anymore."

"No, I'm not in contact because you kicked me out of your bedroom—"

"I was back from a trip and just needed my space," John interrupted.

"OK, this isn't going to work if you're just going to interrupt all the time. I'll speak first, get to the end, then it'll be my turn to listen. Deal?"

John nodded. He put his cup of coffee down, folded his hands, and waited.

"OK. So it's not what you did," I said. "It's how you did it. Coming in, yelling, tossing me out, then insisting I stay in the living room so I can have a front-row seat to watch you hook up with your fuckbuddies? That's psychotic. You wounded me, I think on purpose, because you were feeling vulnerable. That's why I haven't been in contact. Your turn."

"Well, I needed my space. And you have been a lot of work. You're exhausting. So I just needed you away. And when my friend came over… I mean, you could have joined in."

"I didn't want to join in!"

"I'm speaking now." John continued when I acknowledged it was his turn. "And it is my place. You know my life, you know how I live, yet you chose to stay. I didn't make you. Your turn."

"You're right, it was my choice. But we had just gotten so close, mate," I said, then paused and took a breath. I leaned in and looked him in the eye. "Here's what I think about you, John. You want connection. You want to feel close to someone. But you're not good at being vulnerable. You panic, then kick hard to show someone how little they mean to you. It's your safety mechanism. But we'll never get any closer if this is how you stay."

John got a look on his face I hadn't seen before. "You don't know me at all," he said stiffly, leaning back in his chair.

"I disagree. I think we've gotten to know each other very well. And I agree with you, I have been a lot of work. If you were finished with me now, I would totally understand. So, is this our last conversation?"

I was surprised to see that John was surprised at my suggestion.

"I hope not," John replied.

"Then how do we do this differently? I'll start. I don't want us to have a physical side at all right now. We just work on being friends. If that goes OK, then maybe down the track you and I can talk about being more than that."

"OK," John agreed, "but I think we should also have more fights. If we aren't happy with something going on, we get it out in the open and talk it through."

"Agreed. But that means we also both have to listen," I finished.

I extended my hand. We shook.

"You know," John went on, "I probably could have phrased all that stuff that day better than I did."

"Is that an apology?" I asked.

"There was a lot going on," John mitigated. "It's just how it came out."

We talked more, but I never heard the words "I'm sorry." That was the one thing I realized I'd come there looking for.

As we walked back to the collective to see Taina, I was already cursing myself for not laying that out. We had both made that situation together, but I still felt an apology was in order. And if I didn't get one, how could I be his friend? But I didn't say that. Instead, right at the moment we had agreed to have more fights, I chickened out of the first one because I thought we'd just built a bridge and I'd be burning it down.

It was a huge mistake. I had planted the seed of a grudge, and I knew already I was going to water it.

Then suddenly, John turned to me as we walked up the street. "Listen, I know things have been rough, but I really truly feel that we are going to end up together."

"OK," I said, shocked by his sudden announcement, "but that can't be the script. Or else we'll never get there."

I had put out the flame of John and I as a couple, yet with John's words the flame popped up again, small but inextinguishable.

I wished he'd never said it. The chorus was already making plans.

DECEMBER 2018

WHERE'S YOUR LINE?

I'd heard about a place in Berlin that was a center for gay, bi, trans, and queer men to come together to work on their spirituality. The mission statement of the place is a great one: they are there to help GBT men work on intimacy, with themselves and others, that has nothing to do with sex. This was the medicine I had been looking for.

When gay men gather as a group, it's most often a meeting of a sexual nature. The bars, the clubs, the parades, the bath houses. We seek each other out for the potential of physical connection, but then leave just as quickly. It was an experience that had always left me feeling emptier afterward but I'd never found an alternative, until now.

The spiritual life of gay men is often a vacuum. We are a minority group not born to our own kind. Straight people have gay kids. So I didn't grow up in a house with gay parents, a gay brother, gay music, gay thought, gay history, gay leaders. I didn't have a gay grandparent to bounce me on his knee and tell me how things used to be with the straight people in his day. We don't have a land we can point back to and say this is where we are from. Because we are everywhere. And yet we have to fight for our right to even exist.

If there was a gay soul in me, I hadn't had the tools or space to find it.

So I checked out the center online and liked the sound of their courses. One that really caught my interest was the Cuddle Puddle.

After the fallout from John, my dick wasn't working again. I'd finally accepted that I had to put sex on a shelf for a while. But I craved intimacy. Nervously, I went to my first Puddle and was happy to find it was conducted in English with several other first-timers among the forty or so men there.

The evening was in two halves. In the first, you found your own space and started a solo meditation. The topic that night was your hand—a meditation about your hand's ability to either help or harm other people. When the leader of the night, Jordan, asked us to think about our friends, and I imagined all the folks who'd helped me on my journey, I felt a love and gratitude that I would unquestioningly offer back. Jordan asked us to focus that feeling into the hand we had stretched out in front of us. I felt the energy in my heart travel down into my palm, radiating from my wrist down to the tips of my fingers.

Then Jordan flipped it. He asked us to take that same energy and direct it back to ourselves. Without instruction, I took my hand and put it into the center of my chest and felt that energy flow back into myself. What surprised me was how alien this felt. How this energy I would offer to anyone I loved, I would never think to give to myself. Right at that moment, something about the epiphany rekindled. That feeling I'd had, that I was enough, returned. In the attempts to live in peacetime and all the drama with John, I thought I'd lost it. But there it was, waiting for me to remember it.

That alone would have been enough to take from this night.

Then we partnered up. We took turns putting our hand on our partner's body. One was the giver, the other the receiver. Then we swapped halfway through. The instructions were very explicit that this wasn't sexual. The idea was that the one being touched lets the toucher know without words what they were comfortable with or not.

"Know where your line is," Jordan said. "Focus on that line. And communicate it. It's OK for the line to change, it probably will. Just be sure *you* know where it is and that you let it be known."

The line. For my entire life, I don't think I'd ever exactly understood where mine was. I'd never consciously defined it in this way. I knew when things felt bad, but only because someone had overstepped my line. But I'd had to wait for them, not define it for myself.

This felt like a small revelation on its own.

I thought about the concept of the line a lot. I liked the simplicity and the truth of it. I meditated on it most mornings, and several times in the day I would focus good energy into my hand and lay it on my chest as I walked around or sat in class. An endless loop of creating and receiving.

A LIFE WITHOUT GRACE

I woke up one morning crying. Sitting up in bed, shocked by my waking state, I sat with the emotion and listened. Then the realization came.

I would never be a father.

Gunnar had wanted to adopt. We'd decided not to. And thank God. That morning though, I understood it was because I hadn't wanted to adopt with him. Then, without even knowing that having children was a possibility I'd been holding on to for myself, I watched it leave me that morning.

I was forty-seven and didn't know where my life was going to be in a year, or two, or five. By then, I'd really be too old to start a family.

There's a little girl I've always imagined raising for my entire adult life. Her name is Grace. Grace Dunn. I've never been able to describe how she looks—her physical appearance often changed depending on the country I was living in—but I knew how Grace felt.

She was fierce. I'd wanted to raise her to be unafraid of all the things that society told her she should be. Growing up LGBTQ+ and outside of mainstream society in a community of people who'd always had to write their own rules, I'd wanted to pass that gift onto her. There's what society says, then there's what you say.

Even though she would probably not have been my blood, I'd hoped she'd inherit my father's brain, intellect, and compassion, and my mother's heart, intuition, and likability. And if there are any good bits of me, then those too.

I'd wanted to hold Grace's hand as I walked her to school, then listen to her day when she got home. I'd hoped I'd be able to be the friend that she wanted, and the dad that she needed.

I'd also wanted her to have the fiercest collection of mothers that any girl has ever known. Women I admired, who I had befriended over the years: artists, writers, businesswomen, healers, chefs, teachers. I'd wanted Grace to nurture her female power and know that it could do things no man was capable of.

I would make peace with the teenage years, where she'd hate me more than anyone else, and then welcome her back slowly as she became a young woman—which is when I probably would have taken the baseball bat out of the trunk of my car, kept there in case anyone had bullied her or broken her heart.

I'd wanted Grace to do whatever it was in this life that she felt called to do. And do it magically.

But there was never going to be a Grace Dunn. So I said goodbye to her and cried for a little girl that I would never meet.

I think I would have been a good dad.

In the days after though, I realized that there was a child I could raise.

Me.

Past Karl was still there. Still the broken, terrified, mask-wearing teenage Karl with the big secret. He was the one who needed a parent. What I couldn't do for Grace, I would do for him.

Very, very gently, I took down her statue and laid it to rest.

BACK TO THE PUDDLE, THEN TO THE OCEAN

A few weeks later, after drowning in more German lessons in my days, I was so happy to return to the Cuddle Puddle one night and see what I might learn next.

A big, tall German guy and I paired up for the exchange of touching. Physically, it doesn't often happen that I meet someone taller than me. Stronger, yes, but somehow my height always balances that out. This guy was a big, strong dude, almost clumsily unaware of his strength. Following the natural rhythm of our exchange, we soon were in a full hug on the mat. All lines were being respected. He then made the next natural move and pulled me in. It was sudden, and overwhelmingly strong.

And the fear leapt up out of me from somewhere deep.

For a split second, I was seventeen again and having my first encounters with men older than me. All those scary feelings came flooding back. Not knowing how much to give of myself, I felt out of my depth a lot at that age but never wanted to show it. I let a lot of older men do things with me that I didn't enjoy, because I thought I was supposed to. I had no line and didn't know that I was even allowed one. Past Karl never really got over it. I was never sexually abused, but I was lost, uncomfortable, and unsure.

It took till I was in my mid-twenties before I began to understand what I liked, what I didn't, and how to tell people. But the damage had been done. No one's fault. Just the early days of being a gay kid with no one who'd been through it to sit you down.

I promised Past Karl that I was going to come back to him and be that elder for him.

A few days later, I prepared for a meditation on that feeling that had come up in the Puddle. I lit some candles, turned off the lights, and tuned into the feelings that had come out from somewhere deep.

It didn't take long before I was sitting next to my teenage self in my old bedroom. I put an arm around Past Karl and told him that he'd done nothing wrong and made no mistakes. And that everything worked out for him in the future. He put his head on my shoulder, exhaled, then wrapped both arms around me. I held him, stroking his hair. In my nostrils, I could even smell the very eighties aftershave I wore, Bryan Ferry's *Bête Noire* album gently playing in my eardrums.

I'm not sure how long we sat there together, but after a while, it felt like it was time for me to go. I didn't want to leave him there alone. So I took Past Karl by the hand and somehow, we were at my grandparents' place on the water on the south side of Sydney.

My grandfather had taught me and my brother how to fish in his little runabout dinghy called "Tiki Two." Taking Past Karl by the hand, we walked down the back garden to where Pop was pushing the boat out. I got to hug Pop again, a nice long hug, and asked him to watch over this young me.

Pop smiled, and he and Past Karl jumped into the boat and set out to catch some fish. I waved goodbye to them both. Everything felt right. So I opened my eyes, wiping away some happy tears.

Something very old felt like it was starting to heal.

YOU DON'T NEED OTHER PEOPLE TO HAVE SEX, IT'S ALREADY IN YOU

As the language school wrapped up around the end of the month, I had lunch with a friend called Carina. We had met at an art gallery earlier in the summer. She was standing outside in a stunning dress, her personal style echoing the greatness of Germany past. There was something 1930s about her, and yet she was a totally modern woman. I have to know her, I thought.

Since then we had met up many times to talk about life.

I was telling her about John. That my mojo was all screwed up again and that I didn't know when it would come back, let alone whether I'd ever have that kind of sexual high again like I'd had with him.

Carina made an astute observation: "You couldn't have felt that if it wasn't in you. He didn't put it there. John tapped into something you already had."

As soon as she said it, I saw that I'd been outsourcing the approval of my sexual self to others. Like so many other things in my life. Something clicked inside and I felt myself turn a corner.

We discussed New Year's Eve plans. Carina had a family get-together but also, she was planning to make her lists.

"What lists?" I asked. "Like resolutions?"

"I've given up on those," she laughed. "No, at the end of every year, I make two lists. All the things that make me happy, and all the things that don't. On the 'don't' list, I go through them one by one. If I can't fix them or change them, I get rid of them. A little life housekeeping."

After lunch, I went home and made two lists. The "Things That Make Me Happy" list was surprisingly long. A nice moment to acknowledge and celebrate. The "Things That Don't" was shorter.

John appeared on both.

Could I fix how I felt? Could I change it? No choice really, I'd have to find out. Even though I had already gotten rid of everything and everyone where I had to be my old, pre-divorce self, John was the one person I would still twist into an unhealthy shape to be around.

There was nothing more present on my mind as I watched the fireworks in the park with Turlough and Erik—his partner—on New Year's Eve, sharing a hug and freezing in the snow as we said goodbye to 2018.

CHAPTER 18

"If you meet Buddha on the path to enlightenment, cut his head off."

— JOHN

JANUARY 2019

GOODBYE JOHN

IN THE FIRST WEEK OF January, the lists were resolved. John and I had a fight via text. It was over him cancelling to meet two days in a row. Of course, the fight wasn't really about cancelled meetings. It was about the incident in October, and me never laying out that I wanted an apology.

John suggested we meet to talk, and then take a break for a while.

I wanted to go straight to a break. That was my line. I sent John an email, explaining that after the incident in October, if we were really friends, he would have said sorry. I couldn't accept that he wouldn't, especially since he'd always want an apology from me when he'd felt even marginally slighted by things I'd done.

I acknowledged that I had been a big, hot mess for most of the time that we'd known each other. And that even though I knew he was a damaged soul too, I adored him.

A week later, John emailed me back to wish me well with the rest of my life. He thanked me for walking with him on the path for a while. It didn't surprise me at all. In the time I'd spent with John, he'd told me several stories of people in his life he'd gotten close to and cut off. Relationships, creative partners, friends. After I'd heard a few of these, the voice told me that one day I'd be a story he'd tell someone else.

How could I be angry at John for doing exactly what I knew he would do?

That same day, he blocked me on almost every app and site we were connected on. So I did the same on the few that he'd missed. Then I deleted our three-year chat history, all emails, everything. Amazingly, there wasn't a single photo of the two of us together.

I was really sad about it. But mostly, I was intensely relieved.

At that moment, looking at the John-shaped hole in the universe, I realized something.

That huge space of freedom I'd been clearing, which had seemed for so long like a gaping chasm that I stood on the edge of and stared into with complete fear, had changed in my mind.

It wasn't a burden but a gift. One that I'd fought hard for. Something that was mine and mine alone.

So I set out to build a kingdom.

And every year, I follow Carina's advice and make two lists.

CUT THE HEAD OFF BUDDHA

Months before the end, John had read an earlier version of this book. Back then, it was an actual guidebook. A "how-to" called *The Gay Man's Guide To Divorce*.

"I come off as a bit of a guru in this book of yours," John said, holding a thick printout of A4 sheets in his hand.

"Well, that is a dynamic between us, let's not pretend," I said.

I thought he'd have been pleased. Instead, his face was perplexed and thoughtful.

"Do you know the Buddhist saying, 'If you meet Buddha on the path to enlightenment, cut his head off'?" asked John.

"Um, no. I've never heard that. Sounds a little violent to be Buddhist."

"In any case," John continued, "it means that you didn't meet Buddha. You met another human being struggling along the path. That's why you have to cut his head off and keep walking. Buddha isn't someone else. Buddha isn't the path. Buddha is in you. But you only find him as you walk."

Back when I was still with Gunnar and giving it another shot after Vienna, John had gone through a massive depression. We talked about it over text. Then I sent him a bracelet. I'd bought it years before when I'd split up with a previous long-term partner. It was the first thing I'd owned in my new life. It was heavy silver, an antique Scandinavian design that was a pattern of chunky links. It had given me strength on days I didn't have it. But I hadn't worn it in years. I'd been waiting to give it to someone. So I mailed it to John the next day.

Two weeks later, John sent me a photo of the bracelet around his wrist. It fit perfectly. He told me that when his friends saw it, it looked so natural on him that they wondered if he'd always worn it and they hadn't noticed. He never took it off.

Months after John and I ended things, we walked past each other in a bar. Neither of us acknowledged the other. He wasn't wearing the bracelet anymore. He used to tell me that when he wore it, it felt like I was holding his hand.

John and I had never held hands. Not once.

I guess in some way I'd been a Buddha for him too.

So we cut each other's heads off and kept walking.

THE REST OF THE YEAR

2019 continued to be a year of growth. I thought about a John a lot. Then I'd realize I hadn't thought about him in days. Then it was a week. Then it wasn't much at all. He never completely went away, but like Gunnar, his size changed.

As for Gunnar, I never did hear from him ever again. No surprises there. But through the grapevine, I heard news that the animals had all died of old age. I lit a little candle for both of the dogs. And for Frannie, I said a prayer of thanks for all the love she'd shown me in my darkest period. I know I'm going to Heaven, because Frannie will already be running the place and I'll be on the guest list. She'll yell at me a bit for being away. Then I'll lie down on a cloud so she can jump on my chest and we'll clean each other's faces.

When I finally landed my first freelance job in February, it was for a huge online clothing retailer. And the project? Weddings! All the clothes everyone in the wedding party could possibly need. I laughed and laughed when I read the email.

Sure, I thought. Why not?

It's too perfect.

I had a minor panic attack walking into the building on the first day of work. But the moment the brief was in my hand, a whole part of my brain fired up again. Within an hour we were discussing first ideas. But I keep the manifesto I wrote for myself close, and only work on things that I feel good about.

My friend circle also grew. I started learning German again after giving up for a while, and I turned my apartment into a proper home. Many great things happened in 2019. But of all of them, there were a few that really stood out.

Uli, me, and a bunch of our friends went to a concert to see one of our favorite bands. We'd staked out our place in the standing area when two songs in, a loud, drunk, very high group of twenty-somethings planted themselves alongside us. They talked through the songs, fell against us as they tried to dance, and generally had no interest in anyone else around them. All of us were getting riled. Then, I walked calmly into the middle of their circle.

"Hi, everybody," I began, stopping all conversation between them. "I want you to know that I want nothing more than for all of you to have a great time tonight. But my friends and I, we're here for the music. We can't have a good time if you guys are going to talk all night. So do you think you could talk just in between the songs?"

The leader of this little gang looked me in the eye and put out his hand.

"Absolutely. Sorry, man," he said as we shook. He then schooled up all his friends as I returned to my group.

"Wow, Karl," said Uli. "That was different to the last time we went to see a band."

But the young kids were young kids. They couldn't keep quiet. So finally, the leader came to me and said, "Sorry, we're too trashed, we're going to go and stand somewhere else."

"Thank you," I said, "I appreciate that."

In early summer, I met a German trans man by the name of Peter at a spiritual conference. We got chatting about life, including my divorce and the lingering effect it'd had on my sexual performance.

Whereas the people I'd shared this with before had commiserated, Peter took the complete opposite stance.

"Listen up," he began, "you are a tall, handsome, desirable, intelligent man and for you to walk around acting like you are anything less is, quite frankly, obnoxious."

"Oh," was about all I could manage in return.

"You have no idea what I have had to do to be in this body I'm in now. You got yours for free, and it's a great one, an incredible biological gift. But you need to own it and love it. Where do you live? I'm coming over tomorrow and we are going to fix this."

Good to his word, Peter arrived the next day, and after some tea, he said it was time to get started.

"Go into the bedroom, take your clothes off, and I'm going to as well. And then we're going to have a meditation."

Not long after, we lay naked side by side.

"Close your eyes. Take some deep breaths. And let's talk about your penis."

The meditation began with him asking if my penis and I ever hung out together. When I didn't understand, he gently explained how the two of us should have a place we go.

"Now build it," Peter continued. "What would this wonderful place look like, that's just for you and him?"

In my mind, an image of a big, modern, log-and-glass cabin-style temple in the woods came sharply into focus. I could see the exterior of it, the forests around, the warm and cozy interiors, and the bed in the middle of the room.

"Now, lie down there on the bed with him. And he can be huge, by the way. Make him as big as a person, because you're going to have a talk now."

So, even though it felt weird, I imagined a life-size version of my penis and I lying together in bed.

"What's his name?" Peter asked.

"I don't know, I never gave him one."

"So give him one. First thing that comes to mind."

I giggled. "I've got it," I said.

When I told Peter his name, he wasn't sure.

"You really want to call him that?" Peter asked.

"It's my penis," I replied.

"Fair enough," Peter said. He then instigated a talk between us.

I began. Speaking out loud, I said to my penis that I was frustrated with him, that I wished he'd work when I wanted him to, that I felt like he'd let me down a lot.

Peter then asked, "What do you think he would say about you? Does he like you? Does he have any reason to?"

That really hit home. I accessed some kind of sexual memory bank and went back through it. In truth, I'd been angry at him for years. I'd had an on-again, off-again rash for almost a decade before I finally gave up and got a medical circumcision three years previously. I blamed him because I thought he'd cheated me out of my birthright.

But then, in that moment, I realized it was psychosomatic. My undesirability myth. I'd been angry about my sex life for so long that the rash had been his reaction to being hated.

I burst into tears, so ashamed at how I'd bullied him for most of my life.

"So how are things going to be different now?" Peter asked.

I spoke to my penis again and told him I'd take much better care of him, chat with him, check in with him and see what he needed. That we'd hang out in the log cabin whenever he wanted. That we'd be friends.

By the time Peter and I were done, my whole body felt connected in a way it hadn't since I was a teenager.

"And for God's sake, buy yourself a big full-length mirror. So he can see himself and you can tell him how handsome he is."

One day when I was doing the full-length mirror moment and thinking how much I actually liked what I saw, my mind went back eighteen months to the Karl that had done the brutal self-analysis in the bathroom mirror of the trophy house. I felt him shrink at the memory.

"Sorry, mate. We don't ever have to go back there again."

Tim sent me an email. Tim was the friend that had been Gunnar's and my partner in crime in San Francisco—the third in our unconsummated throuple and the first person I'd lost in the divorce.

I was suspicious. I thought maybe he was fishing for news for Gunnar. But soon we were on the phone and everything came out from both sides.

When we'd exchanged texts way back at the start of the divorce, Tim had been angry with me. Not because he'd sided with Gunnar, but because I'd left him. I disappeared to LA to freelance, the divorce started, and I'd never called him to talk about what was going on. He felt, quite rightly, like he'd been dumped. All because I presumed he'd be on Gunnar's side.

Tim had missed me. And I'd missed him too.

I apologized profusely. All I could say was that I was a different man back then.

The next time I was in San Francisco, we arranged to meet at our favorite restaurant. When we saw each other, we practically ran toward one another and hugged hard and long. It was good to have a good friend back.

And then there was the final notable moment. The smallest one that turned out to be the biggest of all.

My friend Ahmad and I were sitting in a beer garden on a warm night in the late summer of 2019. We were catching up on news. I'd been freelancing, writing my book, doing a lot of exploring my inner world, and travelling to see friends around Europe. I was also excited about seeing my family, who were all coming to Germany in a week.

"You know, mate, life's going well," I told him. "Berlin's been good to me. Though I have to say, I wouldn't mind meeting someone. Maybe someone from another city. Nothing serious. My sex life is good, but something a little more meaningful would be nice."

Ahmad smiled. "Well, I have a small confession. That friend I said was going to come and meet us for a drink, I thought maybe the two of you could be interesting together. He's from Munich, and he's in town for a week. Don't worry, I didn't say anything to him."

Ahmad and I play this game in summer. If one of us sees a handsome man, we point above his head and talk at great romantic length about the tree behind the guy in question. Berlin is a very green city, so this game works everywhere for six months a year.

A strapping guy walked into the beer garden.

"Ahem! Ahmad, see that tree? Strong trunk, sturdy branches..."

Ahmad glanced over at the tree. "That's the friend I was telling you about."

Moments later, Tobias and I were shaking hands. He had a fantastic energy, but more interestingly, he had left his very successful career just the week before. We got talking and Tobias was going through a version of what I had. He'd built a life according to what everyone said you were supposed to do, then found he wasn't happy. So he'd left it to start questing. He was walking the path.

We all arranged to meet the next night. But I didn't google Tobias. I didn't find him on Facebook. I didn't wonder what we going to call the puppy.

Instead, a group of us met up at a bar and Tobias and I picked up our conversation.

Then at one moment, I laid out my cards.

"Tobias, I just want to say that I was very struck by you when we met yesterday. I think you're very handsome. I mean, you're gorgeous. But more than that, I admire what you're doing, leaving behind a life that doesn't fit."

Tobias stared at me for a moment before replying, "Do you think we could rewind to the part of the conversation before you said any of that, and just pick it up from there?"

"Sure," I said.

And that's what we did.

I went home that night, not wondering what was wrong with me. Not replaying parts of the conversation to decipher if I'd said something wrong. I woke up the next day and carried on with the life I was building in Berlin.

I'd always thought this book would end with a great Hollywood moment.

The epiphany.

Or John and I dating.

Or Gunnar getting back in touch to apologize.

Instead, it was a tiny moment, one that could almost have gone by unnoticed. A man I liked said, "No, thanks," and my world didn't change one bit. In that moment, the final piece clicked into place. Without even noticing how or when it had happened, I'd learned the lesson of the epiphany.

John had been so right when he'd said to me that time was the one ingredient you can't fake. The journey that had started in Berlin three years before with me looking at my reflection in a store window, that had taken me from Berlin to San Francisco to LA and back again, learning from all the guides I'd met along the way, that had involved giving up so much to get way more in return, had finally reached where it was heading.

I was happy.

Just with perfectly imperfect me.

I'd fallen in love with myself. And maybe that's something I'd share one day with someone who felt the same way about themselves.

And maybe not.

It didn't matter.

Because for the first time I didn't just know, but truly felt, that I was enough.

I didn't need a rainbow.

I was the pot of gold.

ACKNOWLEDGMENTS

I F IT TAKES A VILLAGE to raise a kid, it takes half a dozen to write and publish a book. A big heartfelt thank you to all these people whose support and advice made this book happen.

To my parents and brother–Robert, Denise, and Tony Dunn–whose unconditional love saw me through the worst period of my life. And who've been champions and cheerleaders of this book in its six-year gestation.

To my West Coast friends Brian Meiler, Mike Tien, Mike Mauro, Guy Sandin, Gabe Zichermann, Jason Schragger, Dennis Grant, Tom Jarman, John Kritch, Jacques Martinet, Caroline Wachsmuth, Gary Baker, and Windy Chien; thank you for your friendship always and for being pillars and guides in that nosedive of a final year in LA. Not to mention the years before and after.

To my European friends Uli Lützenkirchen, Jamie Kilbane, Jorge Liquete, Jonas Vail, Roald VanWyk, Vincent Fichard, and Marco Mienert; your support over the years has meant the world to me. Every time I was ready to throw my laptop out the nearest window, you encouraged me to keep going.

To the beta readers, your notes made this book a better one by far; Miya Bastefjord, Diana Prince, Bryce Edwards, Q

Caylor, Brian Mangin, Ryan Bubion, Alexandra Lier, Johannes Jost, Angela Heather, Marty Horenburg, and Gene Ho.

And to Ross Cali and Stephen Ayers in Australia, thank you to both of you for our friendships that are two decades and counting.

To the friends who fell away over the years, I am grateful for when we were together. Maybe our paths will cross again.

Every writer stands on the shoulders of giants, drawing inspiration from those who've sat at the keyboard before them. A huge thank you to all the ones I referenced, but in particular to three:

To Elizabeth Gilbert: *Eat, Pray, Love* gave me the courage to set out on my own journey and your TED talk saw me through all my mad, bad, sad days.

To Mark Manson: thank you for the article that pushed me off the end of the diving board, for *The Subtle Art Of Not Giving A F*ck* for helping me to make sense of those insane couple of years, and for agreeing to be in this thing if it ever gets turned into a TV show.

And to Malcolm Gladwell: you have no idea how those fifteen minutes you gave me in a café in Brentwood all those years ago changed my life.

And finally to my beautiful Erik… for simply being you.

FOOTNOTES

1. Manson, Mark, "Every Successful Relationship Is Successful For The Same Exact Reasons," January 13, 2017, *Quartz*. Retrieved 23 July 2023. https://qz.com/884448/every-successful-relationship-is-successful-for-the-same-exact-reasons

2. Gladwell, Malcolm, *Blink: The Power of Thinking without Thinking*. New York: Little, Brown and Co., 2005.

3. Lin, "Banksy Said His Invisibility Is A Superpower," August 8, 2022, *Medium*. Retrieved 23 July 2023. https://medium.com/lin-writes/banksy-said-invisibility-is-a-superpower-10a044f2cfcf.

4. Ariely, Dan, *The Honest Truth About Dishonesty: How We Lie To Everyone—Especially Ourselves*, New York: Harper, 2012.

5. Vedantam, Shankar, "Liar, Liar, Liar," March 2017, Hidden Brain Podcast, NPR (transcription). Retrieved 23 July 2023. https://hiddenbrain.org/podcast/liar-liar-liar/

6. Walsch, Neale Donald, *Conversations With God – An Uncommon Dialogue*, Hodder & Stoughton, 1997.

7. Gilbert, Elizabeth, *Eat, Pray, Love: One Woman's Search for Everything Across Italy, India and Indonesia*, Penguin, 2006.

8. Hanh, Thich Nhat, *The Miracle of Mindfulness: The Classic Guide to Meditation*, Rider, 2008.

9. Headspace, "Remember The Blue Sky," April 6, 2020. Voiceover: Andy Puddicombe. Retrieved 23 July 2023. https://www.youtube.com/watch?v=56c1uL_O8Jk

10. Osho, *Joy: The Happiness That Comes from Within*, Griffin, 2008.

11. YouGov, June 3-5, 2015. Retrieved October 9, 2023. https://d3nkl3psvxxpe9.cloudfront.net/documents/tabs_OPI_exes_20150608.pdf

12. The Parents Promise, *HR Initiative*, 2023. Retrieved October 9, 2023, https://theparentspromise.org.uk/hr-initiative

13. Plutchik, Robert, *Emotions and Life: Perspectives from Psychology, Biology, and Evolution*, American Psychological Association, 2003.

14. Downs, Alan, *The Velvet Rage: Overcoming the Pain of Growing Up Gay in a Straight Man's World*, De Capo Lifelong Books, 2012.

15. Ware, Bronnie, *The Top Five Regrets Of The Dying*, Hay House, 2019.

16. Harari, Yuval Noah, *Sapiens: A Brief History of Humankind*, Harper, 2015.

17. Fox, Robin, *Kinship and Marriage: An Anthropological Perspective*, Cambridge University Press, 1983.

18. *Civil codes of Sahelian and West African countries, customary law and religious practices*, Sahel and West Africa Club Secretariat (SWAC/OECD), 2019. Retrieved 23 July 2023. https://www.oecd.org/swac/maps/77-polygamy-remains%20common-West-Africa.pdf

19. Twelfth Ecumenical Council: Lateran IV 1215, *The Canons of the Fourth Lateran Council, 1215*, Fordham University, The Internet History Sourcebooks Project. Retrieved 23 July 2023. https://sourcebooks.fordham.edu/basis/lateran4.asp

20. Funaro, Patty, J., *Legislative Guide to Marriage Law*, University of Iowa, 1991. *https://www.legis.iowa.gov/DOCS/Central/Guides/marriage.pdf*

21. Coontz, Stephanie, "The Radical Idea of Marrying For Love," The Sun Magazine, The Sun Publishing Company Inc., 2016. Retrieved 23 July 2023. https://www.thesunmagazine.org/issues/489/the-radical-idea-of-marrying-for-love

22. Cherlin, Andrew, "Marriage Has Become A Trophy," *The Atlantic*, 2018. Retrieved July 25,2023. https://www.theatlantic.com/family/archive/2018/03/incredible-everlasting-institution-marriage/555320/,

23. Manson, Mark, *The Subtle Art Of Not Giving A F*ck*, Harper, 2016.

Hi there, Karl here. I hope you enjoyed
How To Burn A Rainbow.

Did you know reader reviews are very important to an indie author's success? They validate our work and help others find our stories. Reviews also support our ability to sell books, appear on podcasts, and book talks and workshops.

If you enjoyed How To Burn A Rainbow,
please leave a review filled with stars.

And don't forget your free gift of the prequel
HOW TO CHASE A RAINBOW!
Click here to tell me where to send it.
https://bit.ly/HTCAR

You can always find me, my work, and future books at:
https://www.karldunn.com

Thanks again and go well,

Karl

Printed in the USA
CPSIA information can be obtained
at www.ICGtesting.com
CBHW030413100524
8110CB00004B/22

9 798990 604407